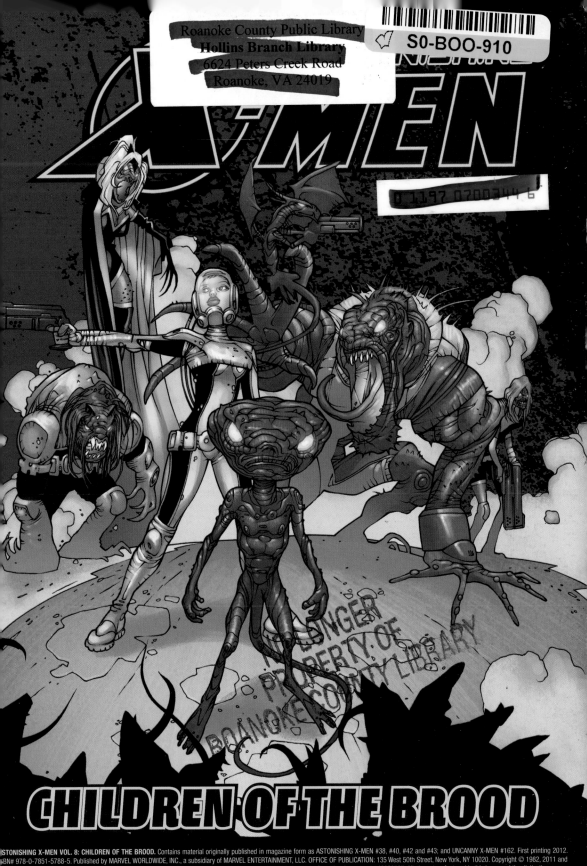

CHILDREN OF THE BROOD

ASTONISHING X-MEN VOL. 8: CHILDREN OF THE BROOD. Contains material originally published in magazine form as ASTONISHING X-MEN #38, #40, #42 and #43; and UNCANNY X-MEN #162. First printing 2012. ISBN# 978-0-7851-5788-5. Published by MARVEL WORLDWIDE, INC., a subsidiary of MARVEL ENTERTAINMENT, LLC. OFFICE OF PUBLICATION: 135 West 50th Street, New York, NY 10020. Copyright © 1982, 2011 and 2012 Marvel Characters, Inc. All rights reserved. $16.99 per copy in the U.S. and $18.99 in Canada (GST #R127032852); Canadian Agreement #40668537. All characters featured in this issue and the distinctive names and likenesses thereof, and all related indicia are trademarks of Marvel Characters, Inc. No similarity between any of the names, characters, persons, and/or institutions in this magazine with those of any living or dead person or institution is intended, and any such similarity which may exist is purely coincidental. Printed in the U.S.A. ALAN FINE, EVP - Office of the President, Marvel Worldwide, Inc. and EVP & CMO Marvel Characters B.V.; DAN BUCKLEY, Publisher & President - Print, Animation & Digital Divisions; JOE QUESADA, Chief Creative Officer; TOM BREVOORT, SVP of Publishing; DAVID BOGART, SVP of Operations & Procurement, Publishing; RUWAN JAYATILLEKE, SVP & Associate Publisher, Publishing; C.B. CEBULSKI, SVP of Creator & Content Development; DAVID GABRIEL, SVP of Publishing Sales & Circulation; MICHAEL PASCIULLO, SVP of Brand Planning & Communications; JIM O'KEEFE, VP of Operations & Logistics; DAN CARR, Executive Director of Publishing Technology; SUSAN CRESPI, Editorial Operations Manager; ALEX MORALES, Publishing Operations Manager; STAN LEE, Chairman Emeritus. For information regarding advertising in Marvel Comics or on Marvel.com, please contact Niza Disla, Director of Marvel Partnerships, at ndisla@marvel.com. For Marvel subscription inquiries, please call 800-217-9158. Manufactured between 6/20/2012 and 7/23/2012 by R.R. DONNELLEY INC., SALEM, VA, USA.

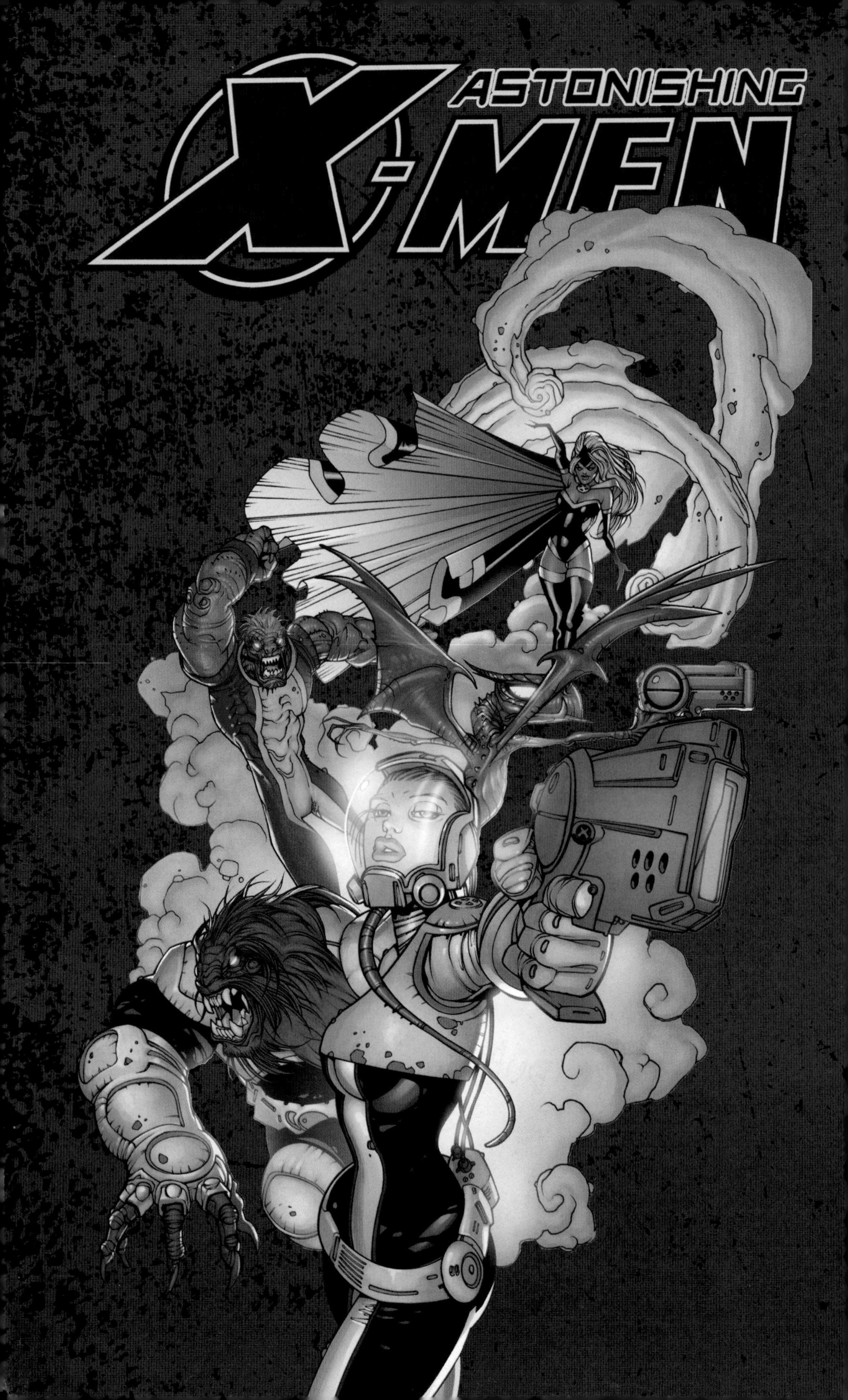
ASTONISHING
X-MEN

CHILDREN OF THE BROOD

Issues #38, #40 & #42
Writer: **Christos Gage**
Penciler: **Juan Bobillo**
Inker: **Marcelo Sosa**
Colorist: **Chris Sotomayor**
Cover Art: **Salvador Larroca with Frank D'Armata & Guru-eFX**

Issue #43
Writer: **James Asmus**
Penciler: **David Yardin**
Inker: **Norman Lee**
Colorist: **Rachelle Rosenberg**
Digital Plane Art: **Gabriel Hernandez Walta**
Cover Art: **Arthur Adams with Jim Charalampidis**

Letterer: **VC's Joe Caramagna**
Associate Editor: **Daniel Ketchum**
Editor: **Nick Lowe**

UNCANNY X-MEN #162

Writer: **Chris Claremont**
Penciler: **Dave Cockrum**
Inker: **Bob Wiacek**
Colorist: **Glynis Wein**
Letterer: **Tom Orzechowski**
Editor: **Louise Jones**

COLLECTION EDITOR: JENNIFER GRÜNWALD • ASSISTANT EDITORS: ALEX STARBUCK & NELSON RIBEIRO
EDITOR, SPECIAL PROJECTS: MARK D. BEAZLEY • SENIOR EDITOR, SPECIAL PROJECTS: JEFF YOUNGQUIST • SENIOR VICE PRESIDENT OF SALES: DAVID GABRIEL
SVP OF BRAND PLANNING & COMMUNICATIONS: MICHAEL PASCIULLO • BOOK DESIGN: JEFF POWELL

EDITOR IN CHIEF: AXEL ALONSO • CHIEF CREATIVE OFFICER: JOE QUESADA • PUBLISHER: DAN BUCKLEY • EXECUTIVE PRODUCER: ALAN FINE

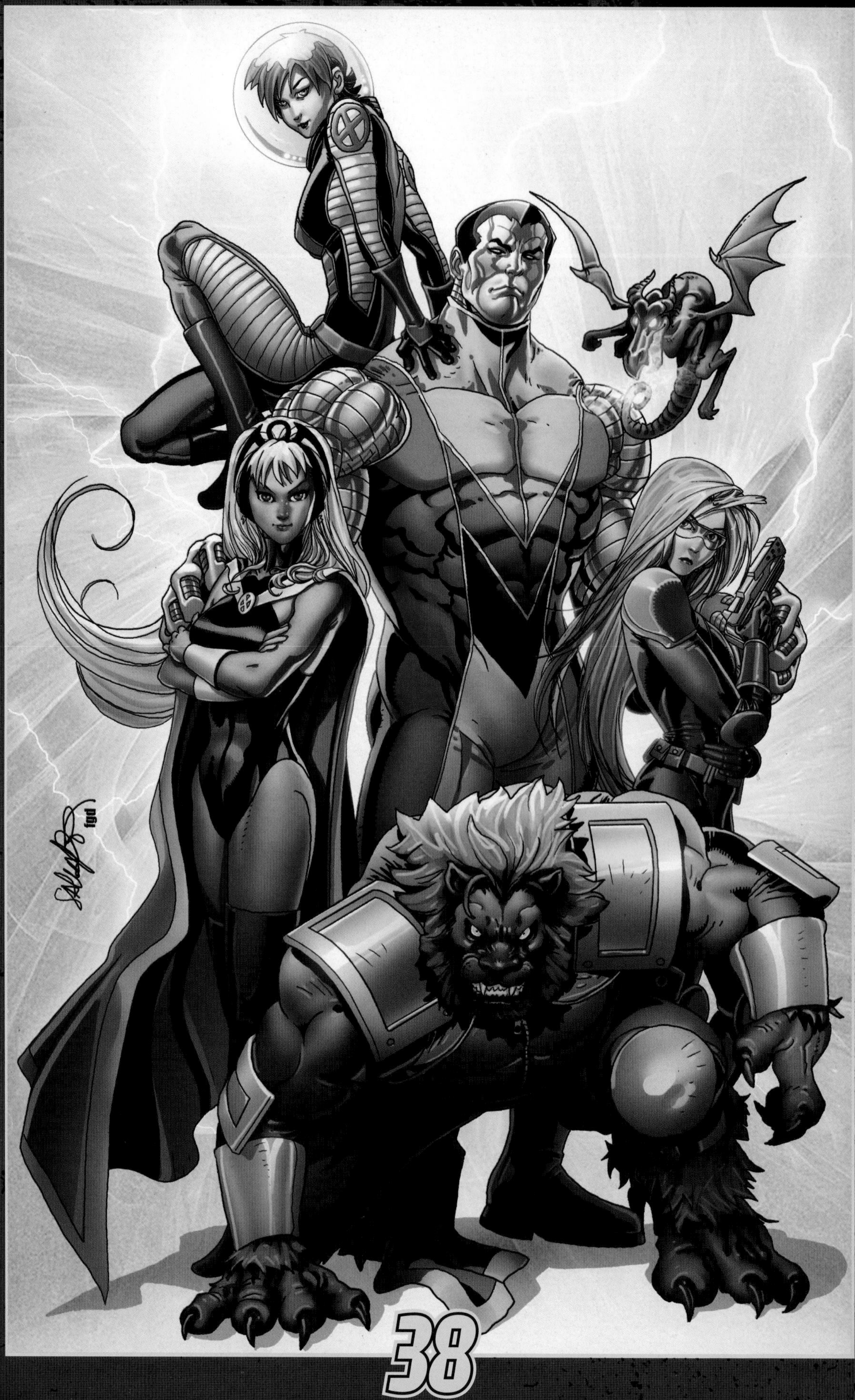
38

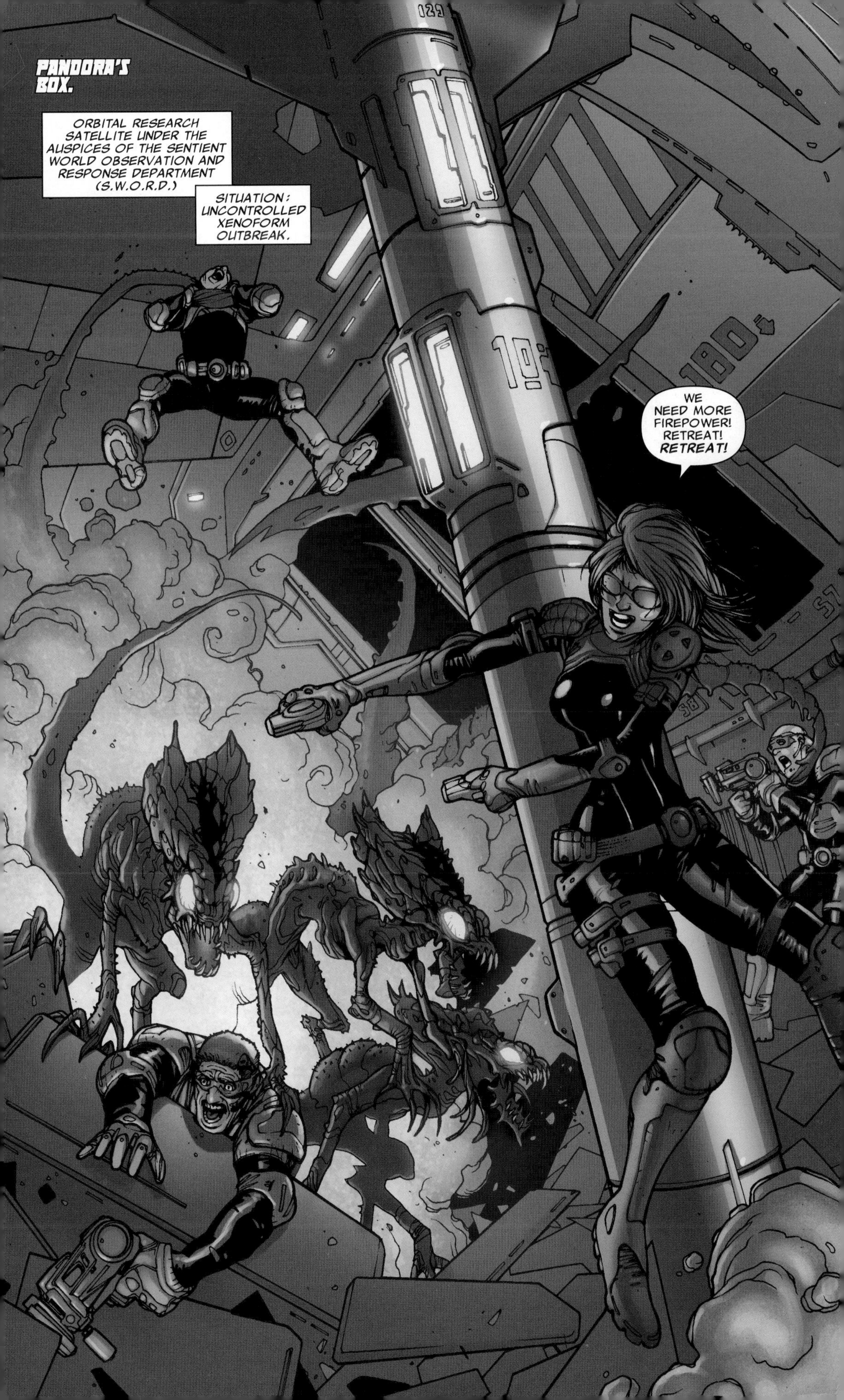
PANDORA'S BOX.
ORBITAL RESEARCH SATELLITE UNDER THE AUSPICES OF THE SENTIENT WORLD OBSERVATION AND RESPONSE DEPARTMENT (S.W.O.R.D.)
SITUATION: UNCONTROLLED XENOFORM OUTBREAK.
WE NEED MORE FIREPOWER! RETREAT! RETREAT!

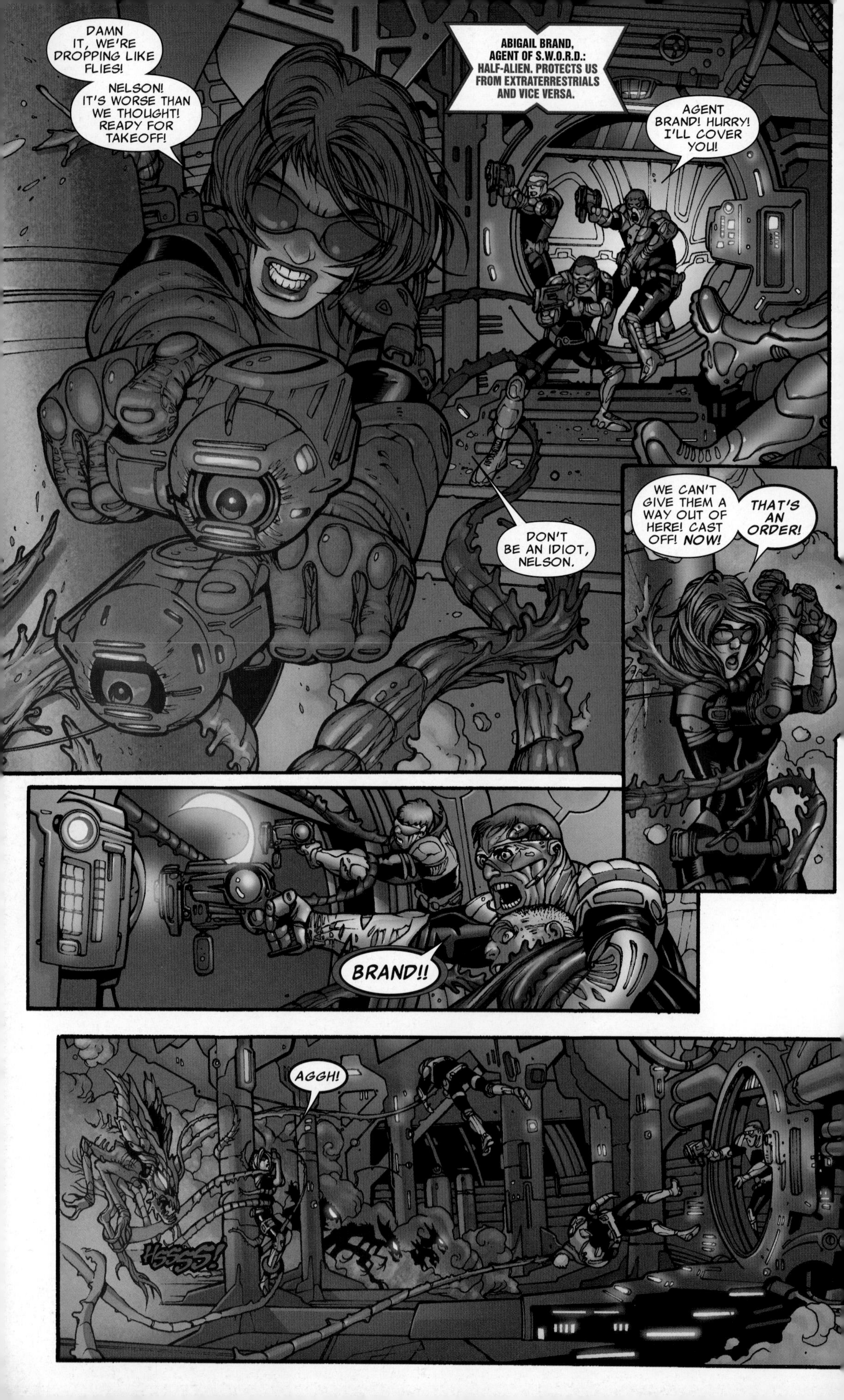
ABIGAIL BRAND, AGENT OF S.W.O.R.D.: HALF-ALIEN. PROTECTS US FROM EXTRATERRESTRIALS AND VICE VERSA.
DAMN IT, WE'RE DROPPING LIKE FLIES!
NELSON! IT'S WORSE THAN WE THOUGHT! READY FOR TAKEOFF!
AGENT BRAND! HURRY! I'LL COVER YOU!
DON'T BE AN IDIOT, NELSON.
WE CAN'T GIVE THEM A WAY OUT OF HERE! CAST OFF! NOW!
THAT'S AN ORDER!
BRAND!!
AGGH!
HSSSS!

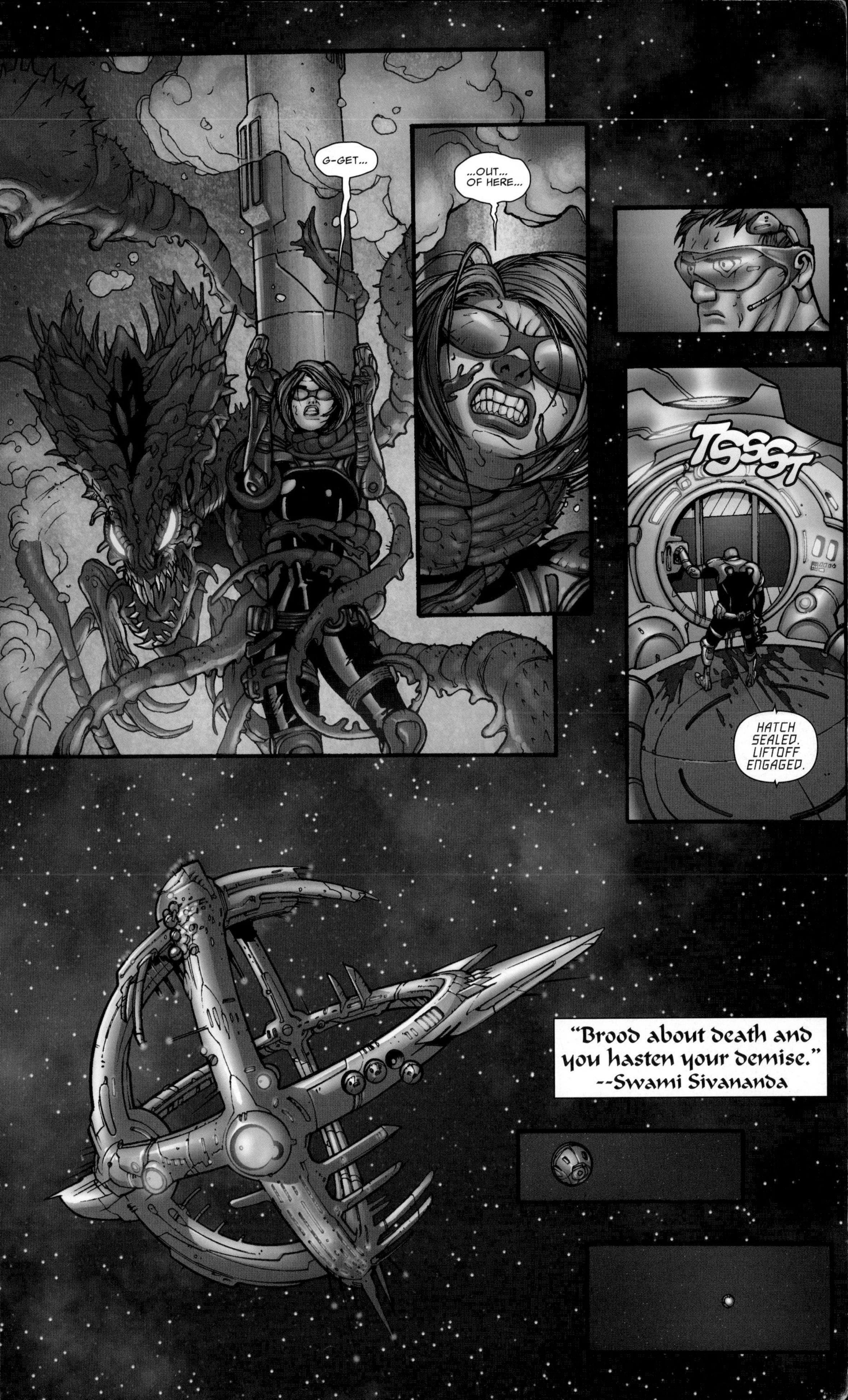
G-GET...
...OUT... OF HERE...
TSSST
HATCH SEALED. LIFTOFF ENGAGED.
"Brood about death and you hasten your demise."
--Swami Sivananda

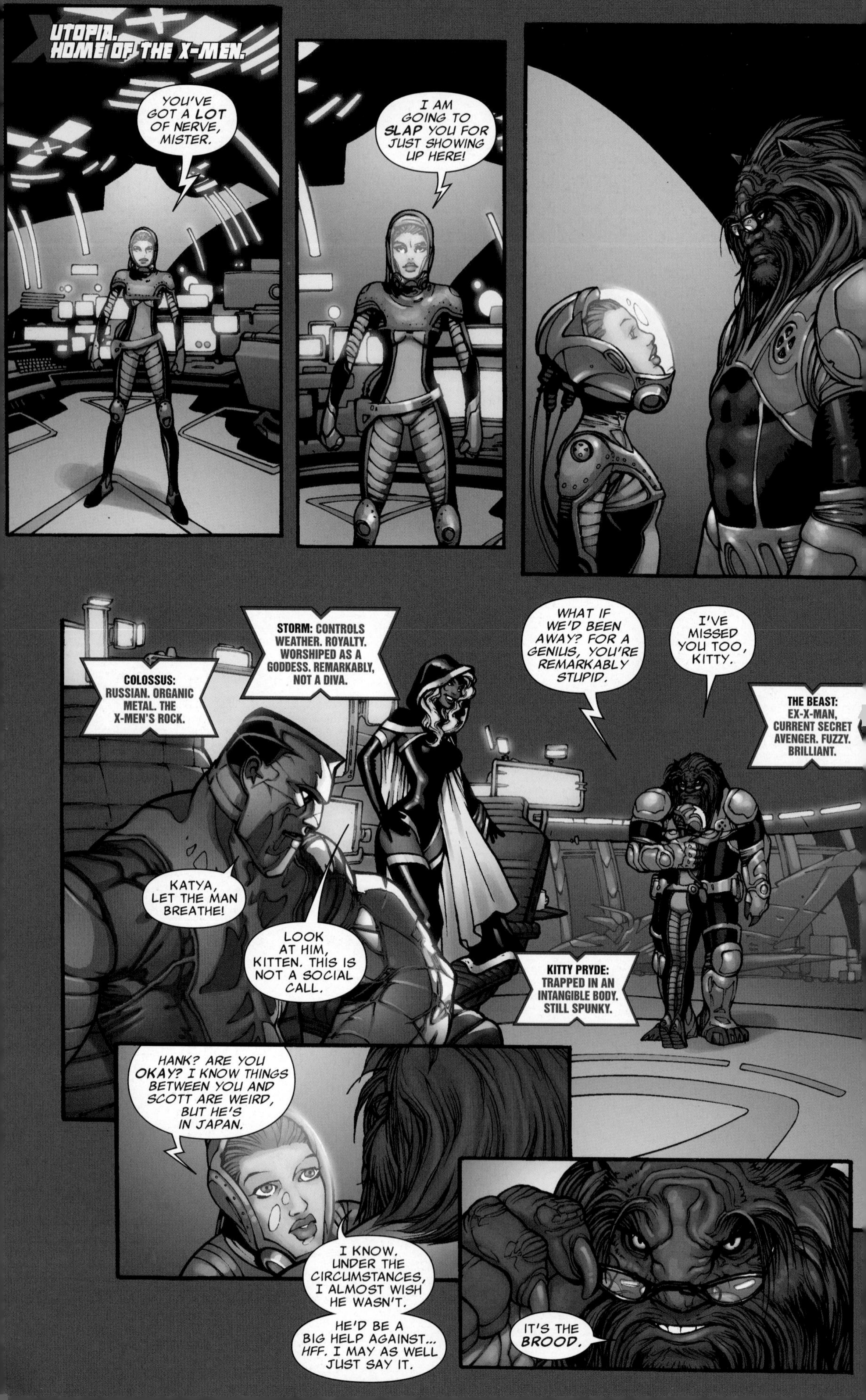
UTOPIA. HOME OF THE X-MEN.
YOU'VE GOT A LOT OF NERVE, MISTER.
I AM GOING TO SLAP YOU FOR JUST SHOWING UP HERE!
COLOSSUS: RUSSIAN. ORGANIC METAL. THE X-MEN'S ROCK.
STORM: CONTROLS WEATHER. ROYALTY. WORSHIPED AS A GODDESS. REMARKABLY, NOT A DIVA.
WHAT IF WE'D BEEN AWAY? FOR A GENIUS, YOU'RE REMARKABLY STUPID.
I'VE MISSED YOU TOO, KITTY.
THE BEAST: EX-X-MAN, CURRENT SECRET AVENGER. FUZZY. BRILLIANT.
KATYA, LET THE MAN BREATHE!
LOOK AT HIM, KITTEN. THIS IS NOT A SOCIAL CALL.
KITTY PRYDE: TRAPPED IN AN INTANGIBLE BODY. STILL SPUNKY.
HANK? ARE YOU OKAY? I KNOW THINGS BETWEEN YOU AND SCOTT ARE WEIRD, BUT HE'S IN JAPAN.
I KNOW. UNDER THE CIRCUMSTANCES, I ALMOST WISH HE WASN'T.
HE'D BE A BIG HELP AGAINST... HFF. I MAY AS WELL JUST SAY IT.
IT'S THE BROOD.

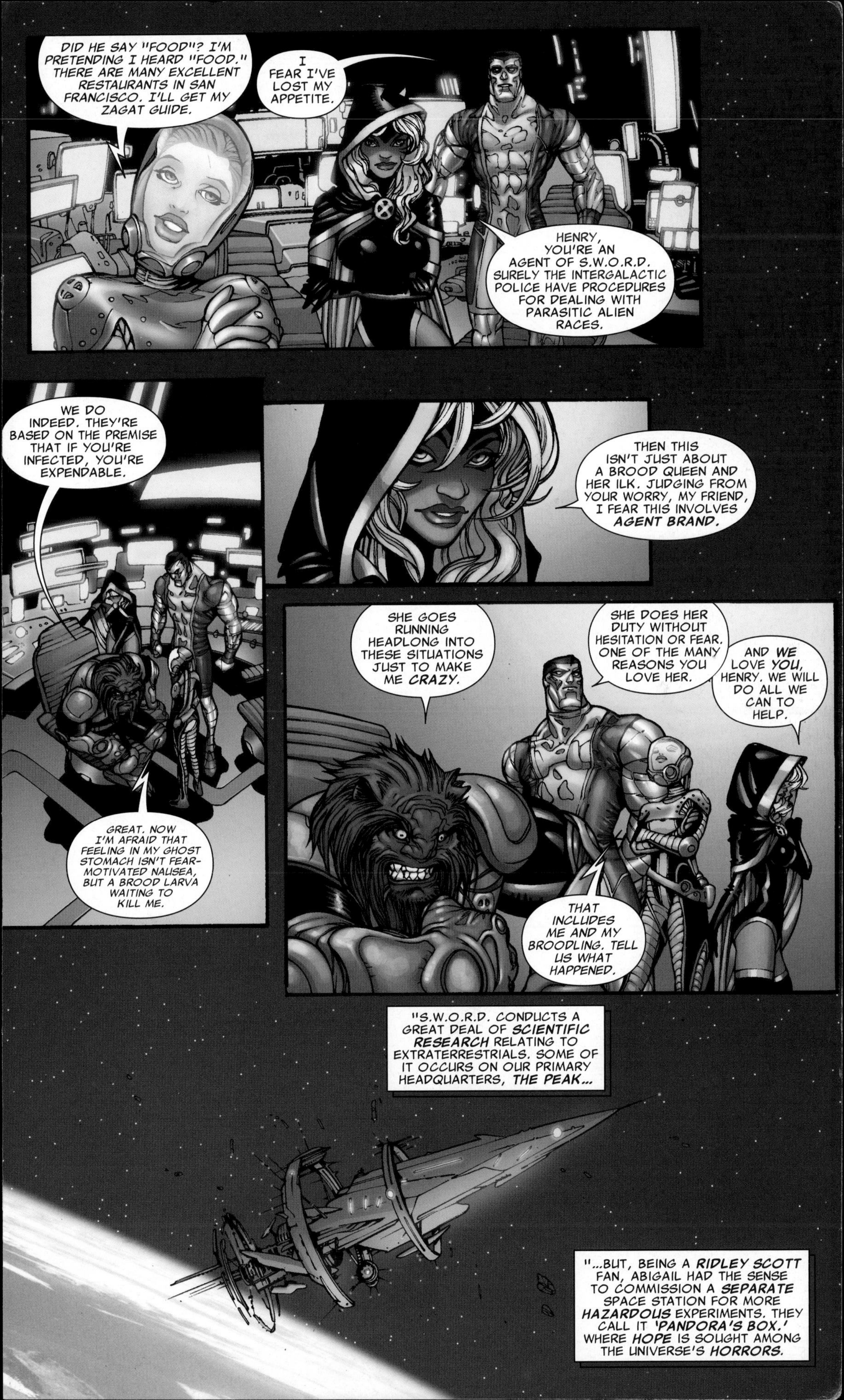
DID HE SAY "FOOD"? I'M PRETENDING I HEARD "FOOD." THERE ARE MANY EXCELLENT RESTAURANTS IN SAN FRANCISCO. I'LL GET MY ZAGAT GUIDE.
I FEAR I'VE LOST MY APPETITE.
HENRY, YOU'RE AN AGENT OF S.W.O.R.D. SURELY THE INTERGALACTIC POLICE HAVE PROCEDURES FOR DEALING WITH PARASITIC ALIEN RACES.
WE DO INDEED. THEY'RE BASED ON THE PREMISE THAT IF YOU'RE INFECTED, YOU'RE EXPENDABLE.
GREAT. NOW I'M AFRAID THAT FEELING IN MY GHOST STOMACH ISN'T FEAR-MOTIVATED NAUSEA, BUT A BROOD LARVA WAITING TO KILL ME.
THEN THIS ISN'T JUST ABOUT A BROOD QUEEN AND HER ILK. JUDGING FROM YOUR WORRY, MY FRIEND, I FEAR THIS INVOLVES AGENT BRAND.
SHE GOES RUNNING HEADLONG INTO THESE SITUATIONS JUST TO MAKE ME CRAZY.
SHE DOES HER DUTY WITHOUT HESITATION OR FEAR. ONE OF THE MANY REASONS YOU LOVE HER.
AND WE LOVE YOU, HENRY. WE WILL DO ALL WE CAN TO HELP.
THAT INCLUDES ME AND MY BROODLING. TELL US WHAT HAPPENED.
"S.W.O.R.D. CONDUCTS A GREAT DEAL OF SCIENTIFIC RESEARCH RELATING TO EXTRATERRESTRIALS. SOME OF IT OCCURS ON OUR PRIMARY HEADQUARTERS, THE PEAK...
"...BUT, BEING A RIDLEY SCOTT FAN, ABIGAIL HAD THE SENSE TO COMMISSION A SEPARATE SPACE STATION FOR MORE HAZARDOUS EXPERIMENTS. THEY CALL IT 'PANDORA'S BOX,' WHERE HOPE IS SOUGHT AMONG THE UNIVERSE'S HORRORS.

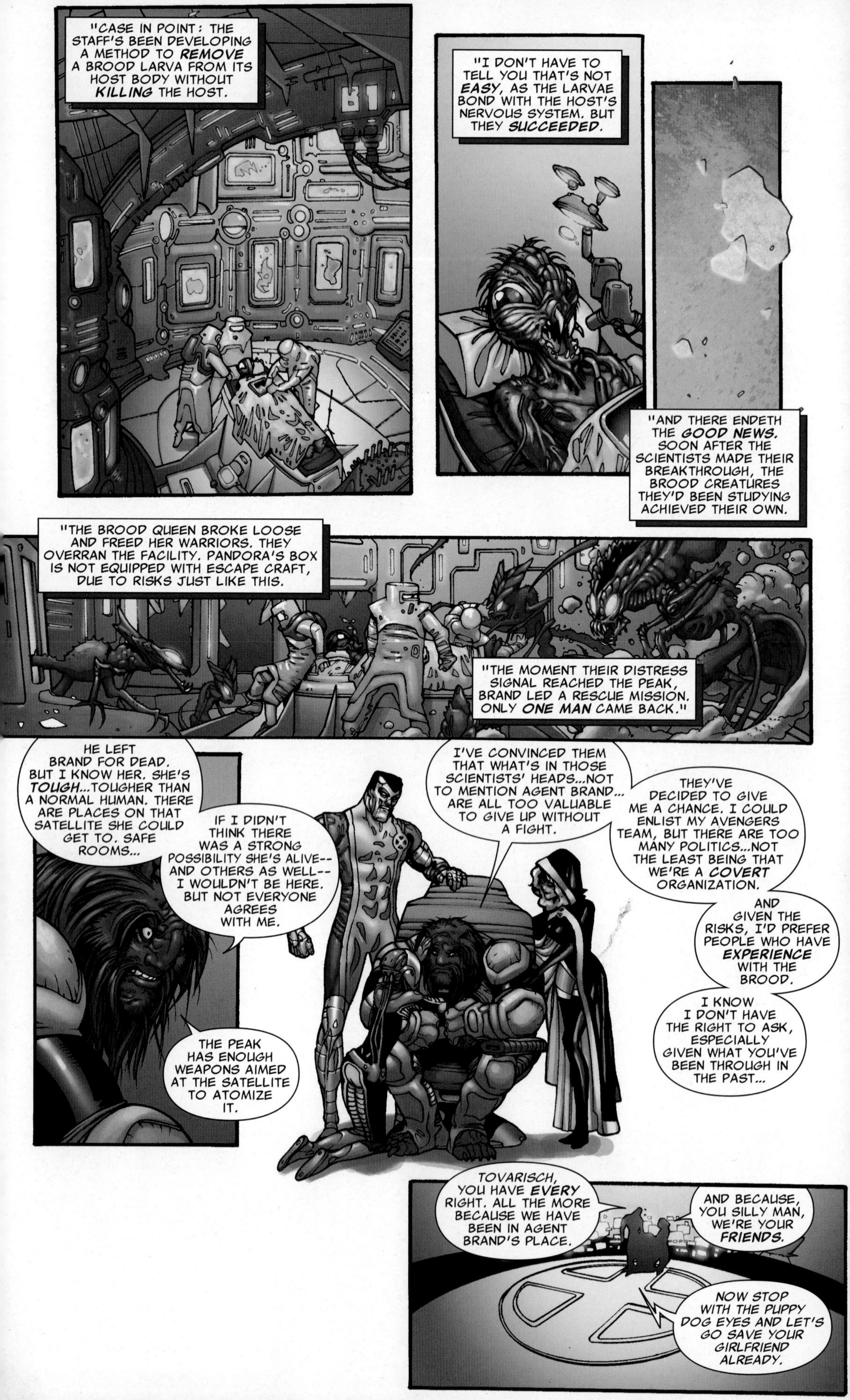

"CASE IN POINT: THE STAFF'S BEEN DEVELOPING A METHOD TO REMOVE A BROOD LARVA FROM ITS HOST BODY WITHOUT KILLING THE HOST.
"I DON'T HAVE TO TELL YOU THAT'S NOT EASY, AS THE LARVAE BOND WITH THE HOST'S NERVOUS SYSTEM. BUT THEY SUCCEEDED.
"AND THERE ENDETH THE GOOD NEWS. SOON AFTER THE SCIENTISTS MADE THEIR BREAKTHROUGH, THE BROOD CREATURES THEY'D BEEN STUDYING ACHIEVED THEIR OWN.
"THE BROOD QUEEN BROKE LOOSE AND FREED HER WARRIORS. THEY OVERRAN THE FACILITY. PANDORA'S BOX IS NOT EQUIPPED WITH ESCAPE CRAFT, DUE TO RISKS JUST LIKE THIS.
"THE MOMENT THEIR DISTRESS SIGNAL REACHED THE PEAK, BRAND LED A RESCUE MISSION. ONLY ONE MAN CAME BACK."
HE LEFT BRAND FOR DEAD. BUT I KNOW HER. SHE'S TOUGH...TOUGHER THAN A NORMAL HUMAN. THERE ARE PLACES ON THAT SATELLITE SHE COULD GET TO. SAFE ROOMS...
IF I DIDN'T THINK THERE WAS A STRONG POSSIBILITY SHE'S ALIVE--AND OTHERS AS WELL--I WOULDN'T BE HERE. BUT NOT EVERYONE AGREES WITH ME.
THE PEAK HAS ENOUGH WEAPONS AIMED AT THE SATELLITE TO ATOMIZE IT.
I'VE CONVINCED THEM THAT WHAT'S IN THOSE SCIENTISTS' HEADS...NOT TO MENTION AGENT BRAND... ARE ALL TOO VALUABLE TO GIVE UP WITHOUT A FIGHT.
THEY'VE DECIDED TO GIVE ME A CHANCE. I COULD ENLIST MY AVENGERS TEAM, BUT THERE ARE TOO MANY POLITICS...NOT THE LEAST BEING THAT WE'RE A COVERT ORGANIZATION.
AND GIVEN THE RISKS, I'D PREFER PEOPLE WHO HAVE EXPERIENCE WITH THE BROOD.
I KNOW I DON'T HAVE THE RIGHT TO ASK, ESPECIALLY GIVEN WHAT YOU'VE BEEN THROUGH IN THE PAST...
TOVARISCH, YOU HAVE EVERY RIGHT. ALL THE MORE BECAUSE WE HAVE BEEN IN AGENT BRAND'S PLACE.
AND BECAUSE, YOU SILLY MAN, WE'RE YOUR FRIENDS.
NOW STOP WITH THE PUPPY DOG EYES AND LET'S GO SAVE YOUR GIRLFRIEND ALREADY.

THE PEAK.
ORBITAL HEADQUARTERS OF S.W.O.R.D.

KITTY? ARE YOU ALL RIGHT?

I DON'T WANT TO MAKE YOU UNCOMFORTABLE, BUT HE HAS MORE EXPERIENCE FIGHTING THE BROOD THAN ANYONE.

HE SURVIVED ALONE ON THEIR HOME PLANET FOR YEARS, HUNTING THEM. THEY'RE *TERRIFIED* OF HIM.

I JUST ASSUMED YOU'D BEEN IN TOUCH... YOU REALLY HAVEN'T SPOKEN AT *ALL* SINCE YOU RETURNED TO EARTH?

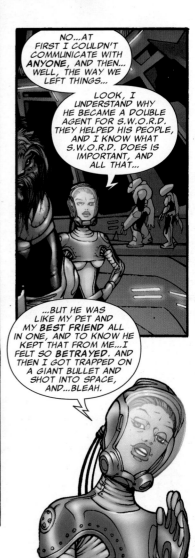

NO...AT FIRST I COULDN'T COMMUNICATE WITH *ANYONE*, AND THEN... WELL, THE WAY WE LEFT THINGS...

LOOK, I UNDERSTAND WHY HE BECAME A DOUBLE AGENT FOR S.W.O.R.D. THEY HELPED HIS PEOPLE, AND I KNOW WHAT S.W.O.R.D. DOES IS IMPORTANT, AND ALL THAT...

...BUT HE WAS LIKE MY PET AND MY *BEST FRIEND* ALL IN ONE, AND TO KNOW HE KEPT THAT FROM ME...I FELT SO *BETRAYED*. AND THEN I GOT TRAPPED ON A GIANT BULLET AND SHOT INTO SPACE, AND...BLEAH.

I GUESS IT'S TIME TO PUT ON MY BIG GIRL PANTS AND DO THIS, HUH?

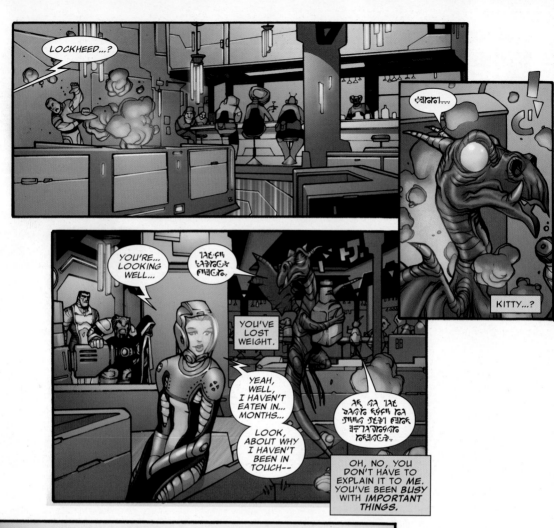

LOCKHEED...?

ᔕᕈᓮᖑᐁᔱ....

KITTY...?

YOU'RE... LOOKING WELL...

ᔱᐱᓬᖴᑊᔱ ᒷᔱᐱᔰᐁᓬ ᕮᒷᒷᔱᓬ....

YOU'VE LOST WEIGHT.

YEAH, WELL, I HAVEN'T EATEN IN... MONTHS...

LOOK, ABOUT WHY I HAVEN'T BEEN IN TOUCH--

ᐱᔰ ᓬᐱ ᓬᐱᔰ ᕮᐱᕮᔱᓬᓬᕮ ᔰᐱᓬᓬᓬ ᒷᕮᔱᕮ ᕮᐁᑊᐁᕮ. ᕮᓬᓬᓬᓬᒷᓬᔱᒷᓬᕮ ᓬᕮᕮᐁᑊᕮᓬᔱ.

OH, NO, YOU DON'T HAVE TO EXPLAIN IT TO ME. YOU'VE BEEN *BUSY* WITH *IMPORTANT THINGS.*

NOW WAIT JUST A MINUTE, MISTER! I'M *TRAPPED* IN AN INTANGIBLE STATE! I'VE BEEN *STUCK* IN A TUBE, NOT OUT *CLUBBING!*

AND WHAT ABOUT *YOU?* THEY DON'T HAVE *E-MAIL* ON THE WORLD'S MOST ADVANCED SPACE STATION?

ᔱᔰᔰ ᐁᔱᒷᐁ ᔱᐱᔰᓬ ᐱᓬᔱᐁ ᕮᔰᐱ ᔱᐱᔰ ᕮᕮ ᔱᔰᔱᕮᔰᔱ ᕮᒷ ᐁ ᔱᔰᔰᕮ

I'M NOT THE ONE WHO GOT ALL HUFFY ABOUT ME HAVING A LIFE THAT DIDN'T COMPLETELY REVOLVE AROUND *HER.*

NOW THAT IS *NOT FAIR* AND YOU KNOW--

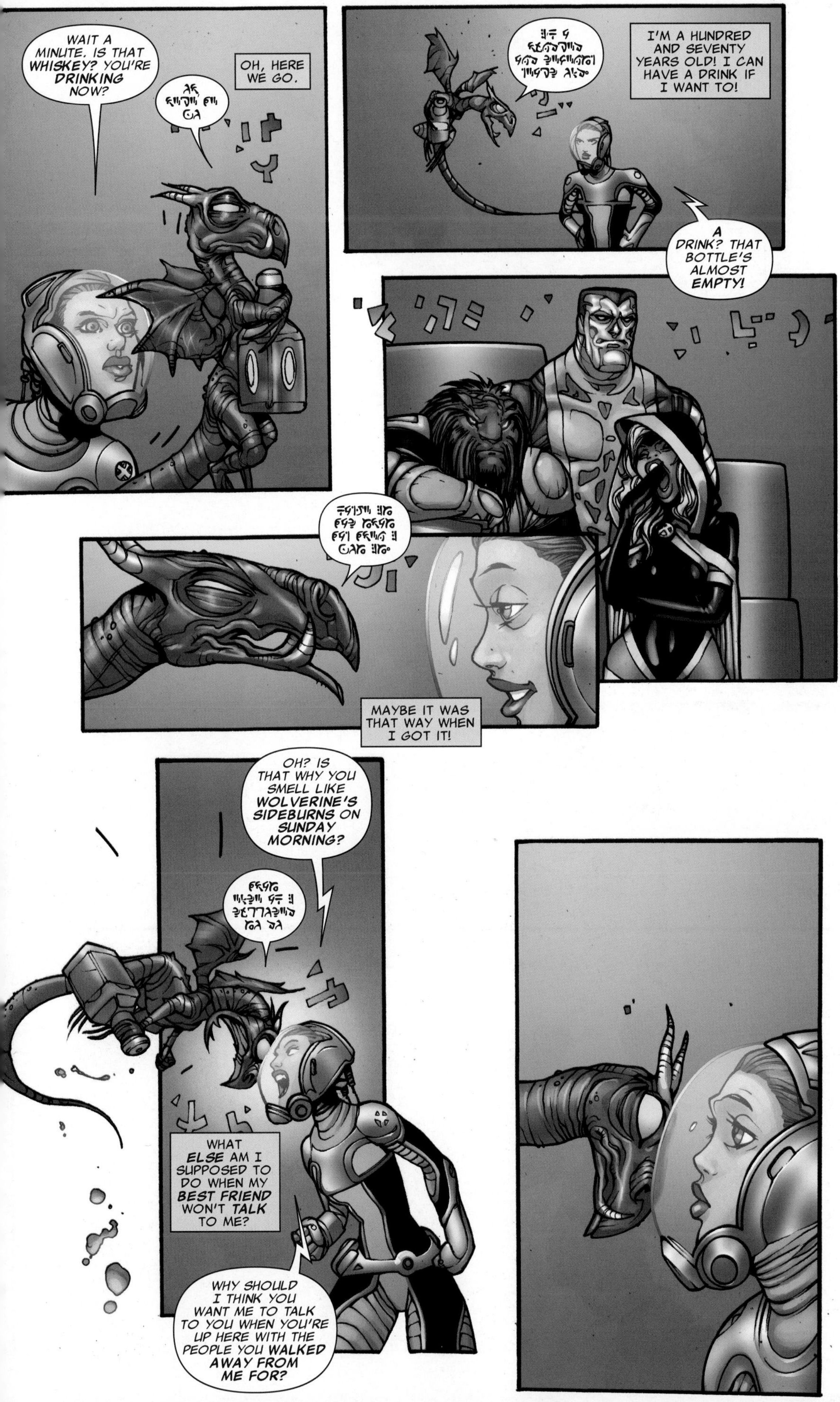
WAIT A MINUTE. IS THAT WHISKEY? YOU'RE DRINKING NOW?
OH, HERE WE GO.
I'M A HUNDRED AND SEVENTY YEARS OLD! I CAN HAVE A DRINK IF I WANT TO!
A DRINK? THAT BOTTLE'S ALMOST EMPTY!
MAYBE IT WAS THAT WAY WHEN I GOT IT!
OH? IS THAT WHY YOU SMELL LIKE WOLVERINE'S SIDEBURNS ON SUNDAY MORNING?
WHAT ELSE AM I SUPPOSED TO DO WHEN MY BEST FRIEND WON'T TALK TO ME?
WHY SHOULD I THINK YOU WANT ME TO TALK TO YOU WHEN YOU'RE UP HERE WITH THE PEOPLE YOU WALKED AWAY FROM ME FOR?

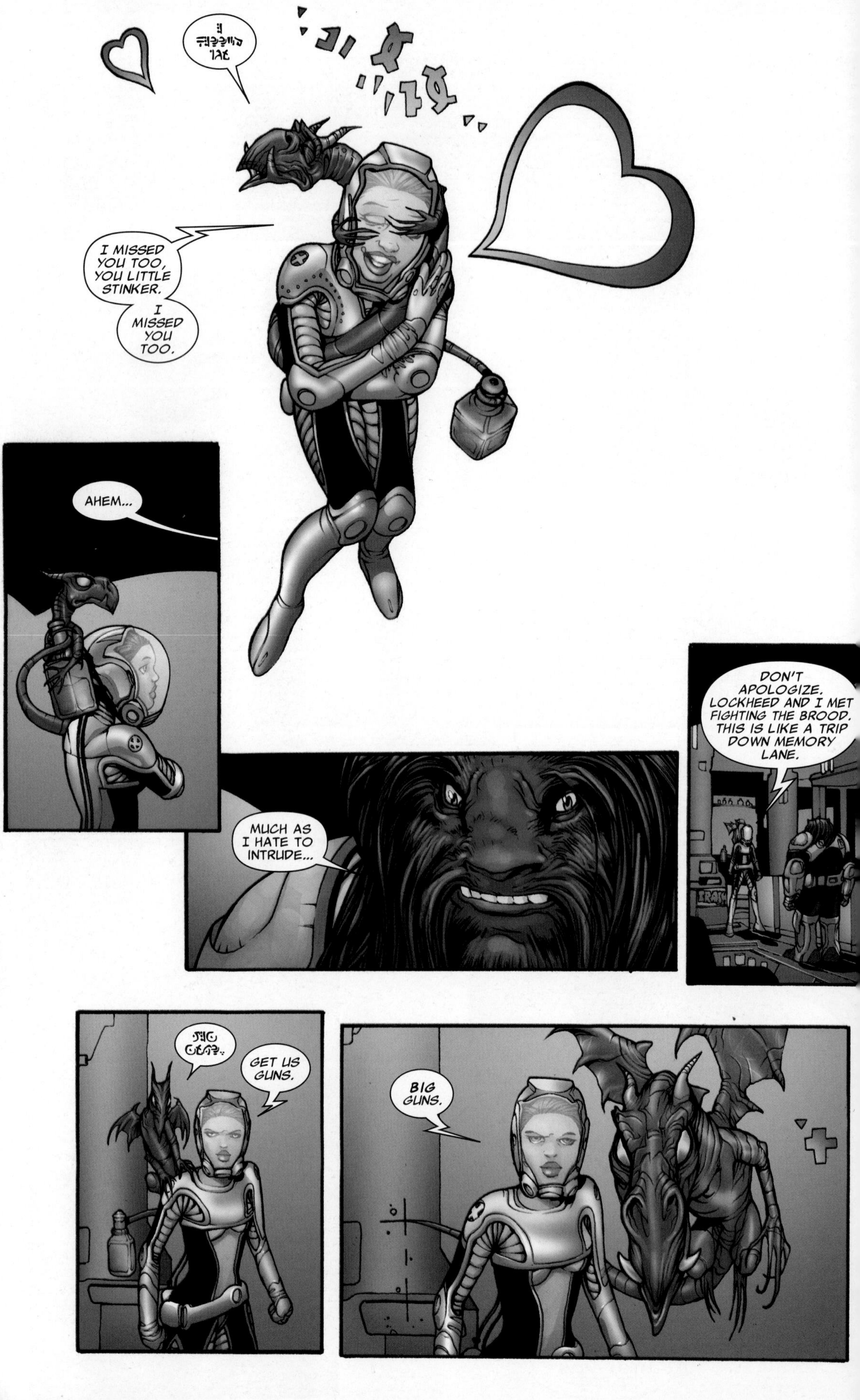
I MISSED YOU TOO, YOU LITTLE STINKER.
I MISSED YOU TOO.
AHEM...
MUCH AS I HATE TO INTRUDE...
DON'T APOLOGIZE. LOCKHEED AND I MET FIGHTING THE BROOD. THIS IS LIKE A TRIP DOWN MEMORY LANE.
GET US GUNS.
BIG GUNS.

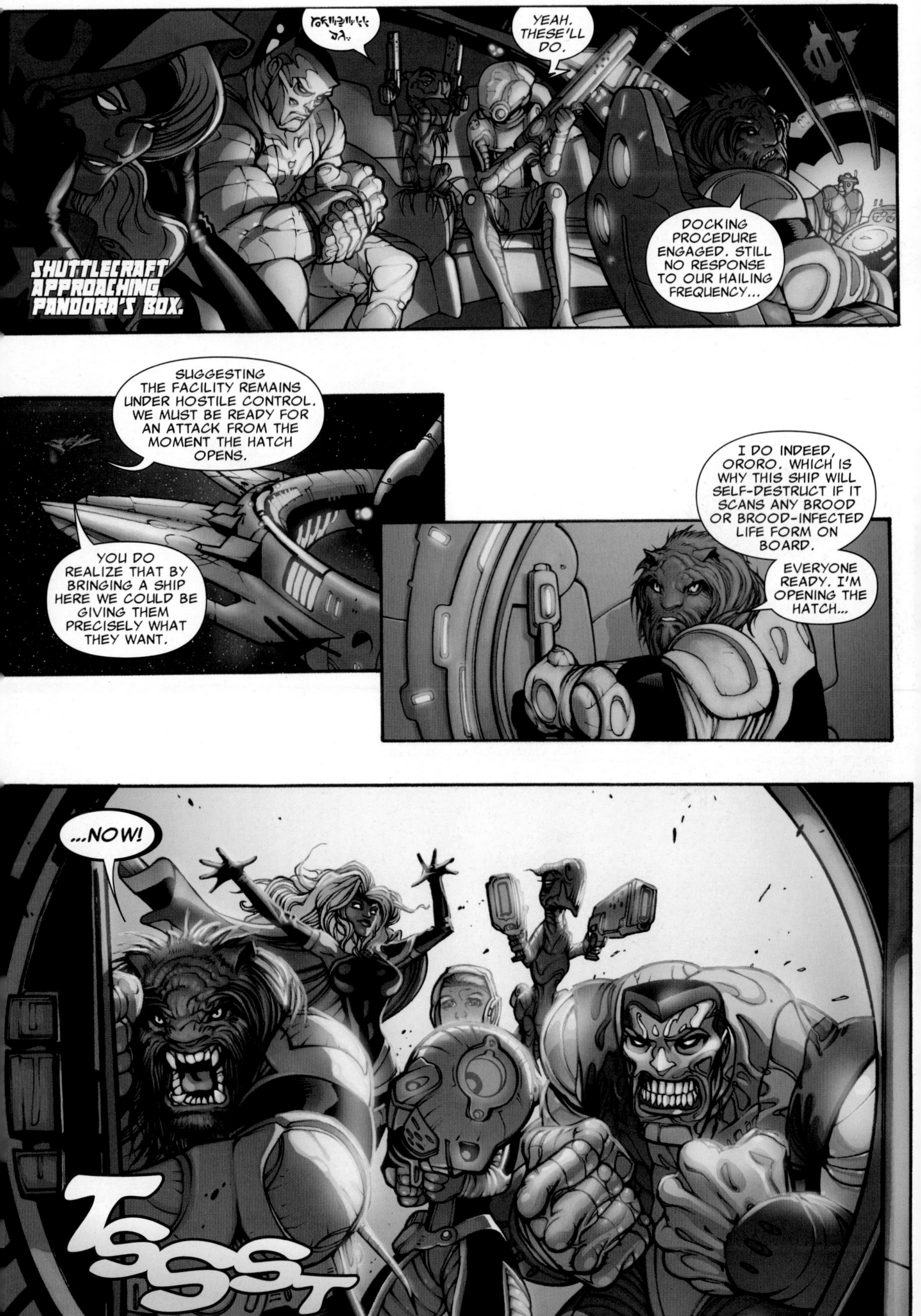
SHUTTLECRAFT APPROACHING PANDORA'S BOX.
YEAH. THESE'LL DO.
DOCKING PROCEDURE ENGAGED. STILL NO RESPONSE TO OUR HAILING FREQUENCY...
SUGGESTING THE FACILITY REMAINS UNDER HOSTILE CONTROL. WE MUST BE READY FOR AN ATTACK FROM THE MOMENT THE HATCH OPENS.
YOU DO REALIZE THAT BY BRINGING A SHIP HERE WE COULD BE GIVING THEM PRECISELY WHAT THEY WANT.
I DO INDEED, ORORO. WHICH IS WHY THIS SHIP WILL SELF-DESTRUCT IF IT SCANS ANY BROOD OR BROOD-INFECTED LIFE FORM ON BOARD.
EVERYONE READY. I'M OPENING THE HATCH...
...NOW!
TSSST

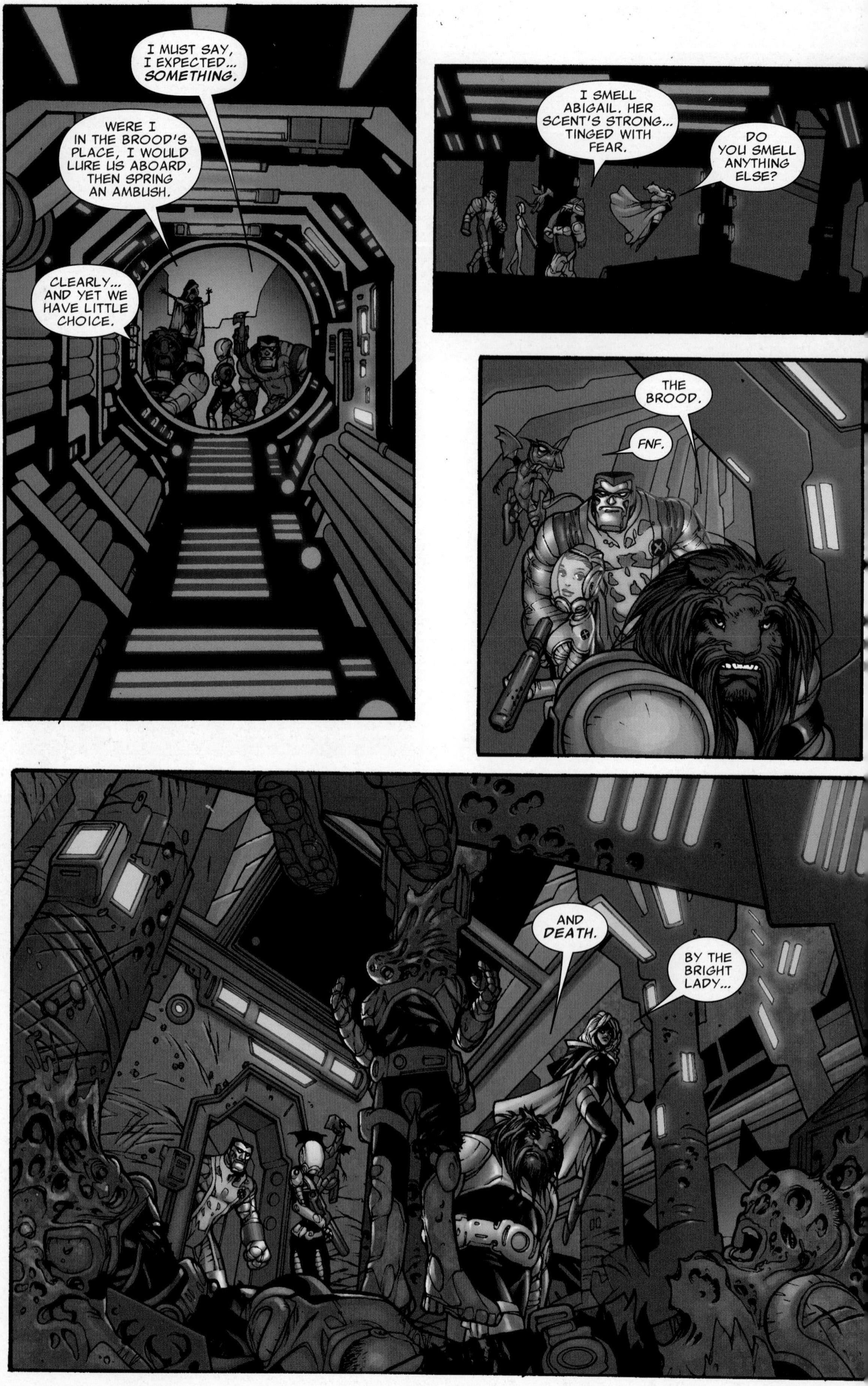
I MUST SAY, I EXPECTED... SOMETHING.
WERE I IN THE BROOD'S PLACE, I WOULD LURE US ABOARD, THEN SPRING AN AMBUSH.
CLEARLY... AND YET WE HAVE LITTLE CHOICE.
I SMELL ABIGAIL. HER SCENT'S STRONG... TINGED WITH FEAR.
DO YOU SMELL ANYTHING ELSE?
THE BROOD.
FNF.
AND DEATH.
BY THE BRIGHT LADY...

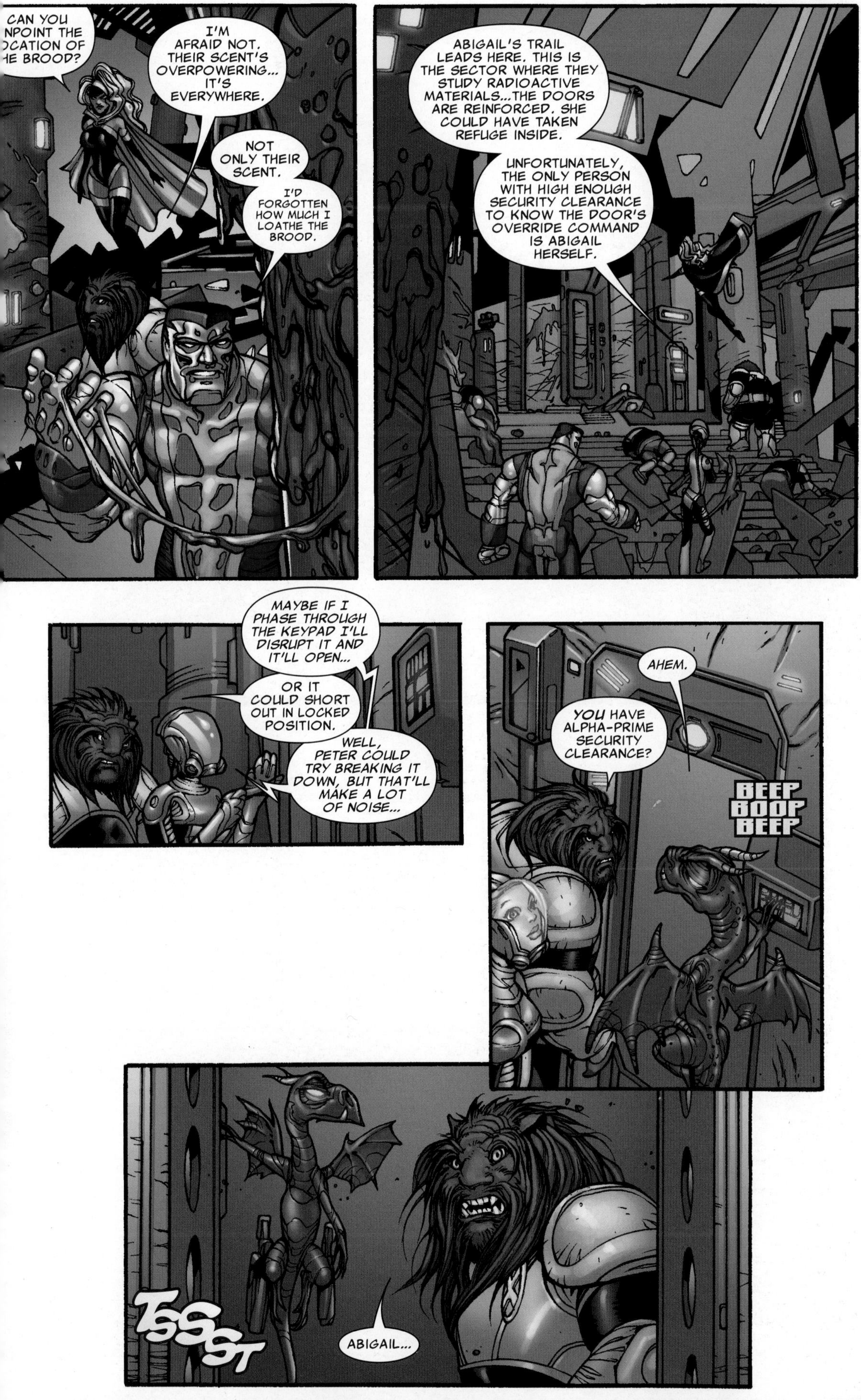
CAN YOU NPOINT THE OCATION OF HE BROOD?
I'M AFRAID NOT. THEIR SCENT'S OVERPOWERING... IT'S EVERYWHERE.
NOT ONLY THEIR SCENT.
I'D FORGOTTEN HOW MUCH I LOATHE THE BROOD.
ABIGAIL'S TRAIL LEADS HERE. THIS IS THE SECTOR WHERE THEY STUDY RADIOACTIVE MATERIALS...THE DOORS ARE REINFORCED. SHE COULD HAVE TAKEN REFUGE INSIDE.
UNFORTUNATELY, THE ONLY PERSON WITH HIGH ENOUGH SECURITY CLEARANCE TO KNOW THE DOOR'S OVERRIDE COMMAND IS ABIGAIL HERSELF.
MAYBE IF I PHASE THROUGH THE KEYPAD I'LL DISRUPT IT AND IT'LL OPEN...
OR IT COULD SHORT OUT IN LOCKED POSITION.
WELL, PETER COULD TRY BREAKING IT DOWN, BUT THAT'LL MAKE A LOT OF NOISE...
AHEM.
YOU HAVE ALPHA-PRIME SECURITY CLEARANCE?
BEEP BOOP BEEP
TSSST
ABIGAIL...

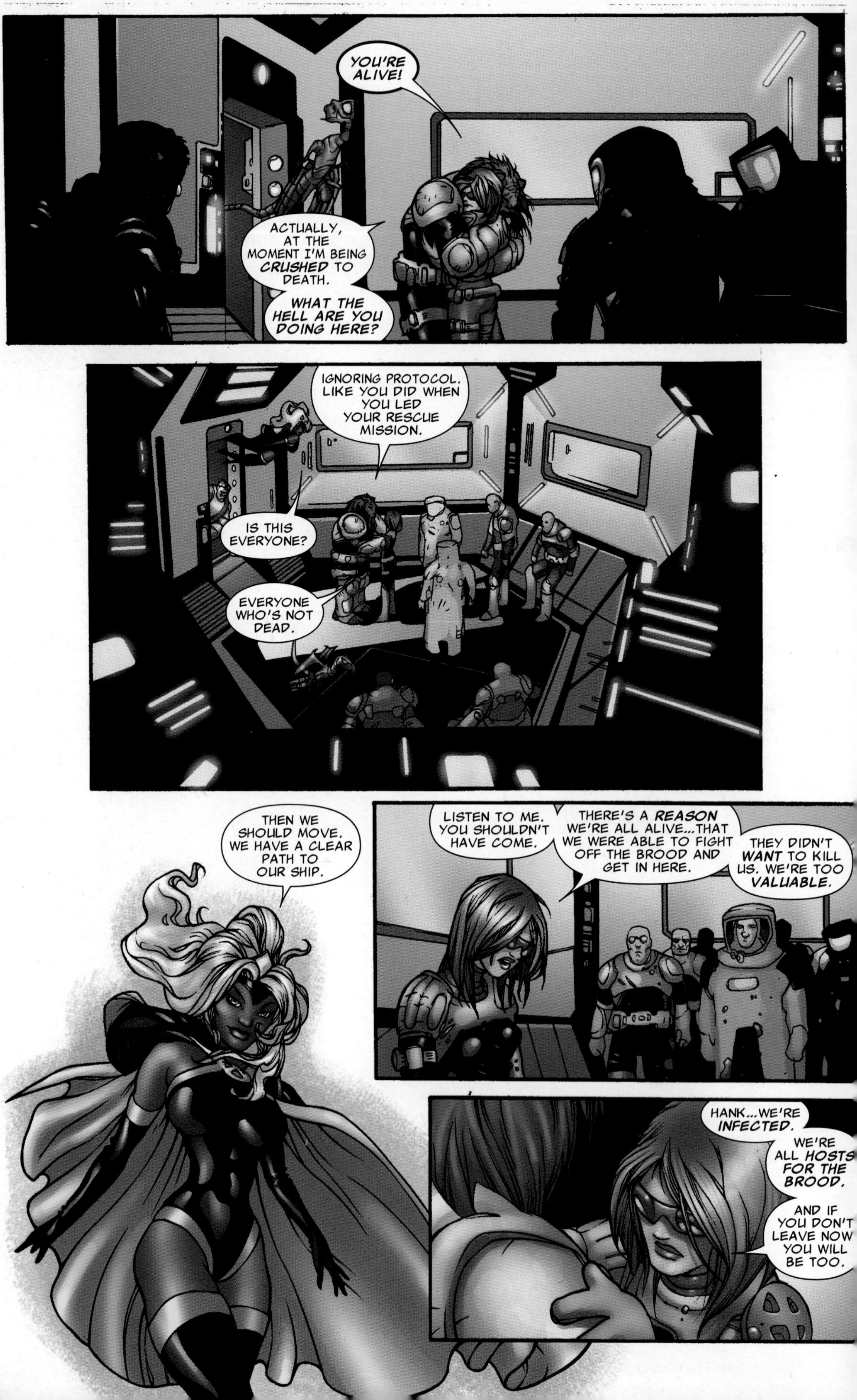
YOU'RE ALIVE!
ACTUALLY, AT THE MOMENT I'M BEING CRUSHED TO DEATH.
WHAT THE HELL ARE YOU DOING HERE?
IGNORING PROTOCOL. LIKE YOU DID WHEN YOU LED YOUR RESCUE MISSION.
IS THIS EVERYONE?
EVERYONE WHO'S NOT DEAD.
THEN WE SHOULD MOVE. WE HAVE A CLEAR PATH TO OUR SHIP.
LISTEN TO ME. YOU SHOULDN'T HAVE COME.
THERE'S A REASON WE'RE ALL ALIVE...THAT WE WERE ABLE TO FIGHT OFF THE BROOD AND GET IN HERE.
THEY DIDN'T WANT TO KILL US. WE'RE TOO VALUABLE.
HANK...WE'RE INFECTED.
WE'RE ALL HOSTS FOR THE BROOD.
AND IF YOU DON'T LEAVE NOW YOU WILL BE TOO.

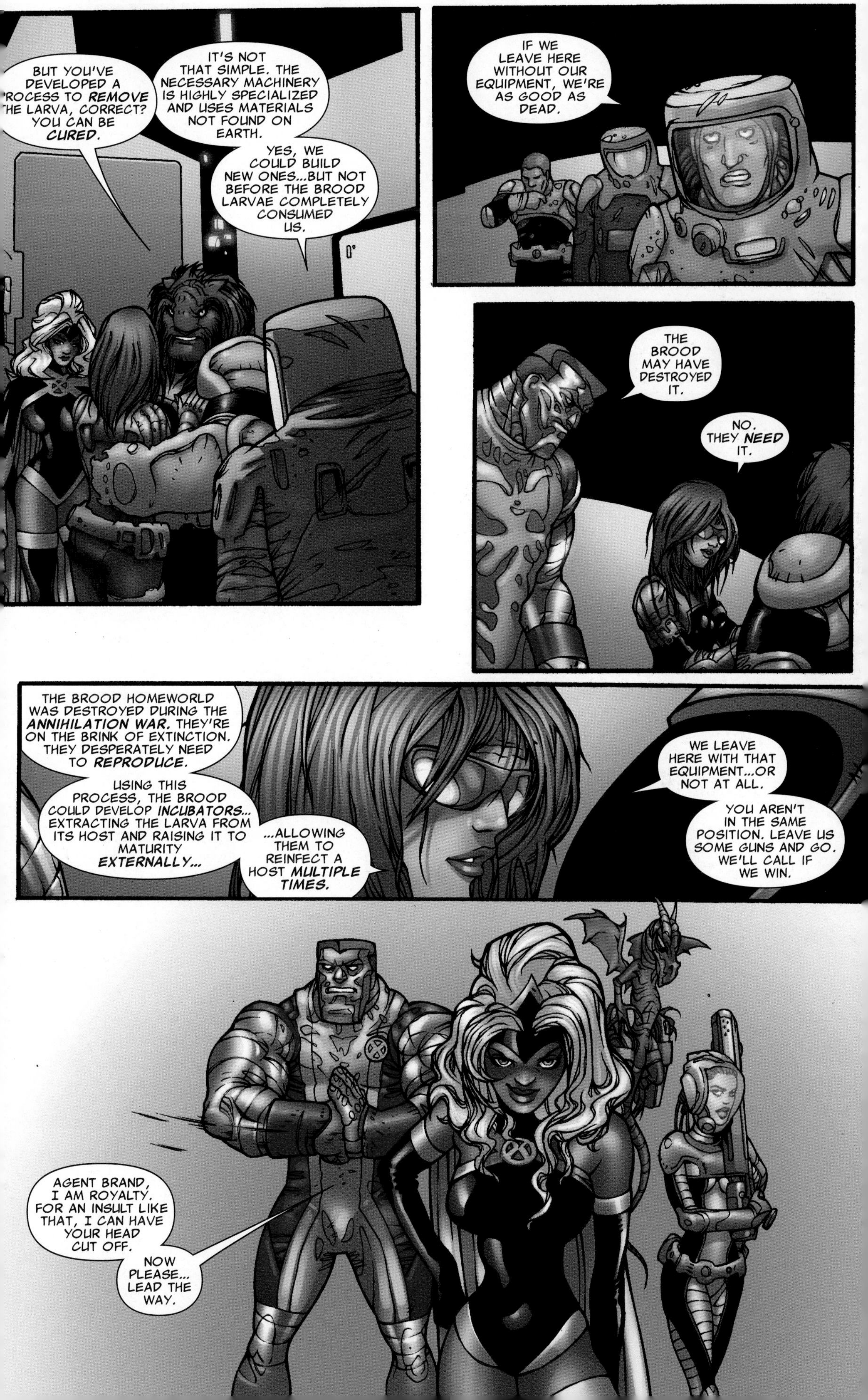
BUT YOU'VE DEVELOPED A PROCESS TO REMOVE THE LARVA, CORRECT? YOU CAN BE CURED.
IT'S NOT THAT SIMPLE. THE NECESSARY MACHINERY IS HIGHLY SPECIALIZED AND USES MATERIALS NOT FOUND ON EARTH.
YES, WE COULD BUILD NEW ONES...BUT NOT BEFORE THE BROOD LARVAE COMPLETELY CONSUMED US.
IF WE LEAVE HERE WITHOUT OUR EQUIPMENT, WE'RE AS GOOD AS DEAD.
THE BROOD MAY HAVE DESTROYED IT.
NO. THEY NEED IT.
THE BROOD HOMEWORLD WAS DESTROYED DURING THE ANNIHILATION WAR. THEY'RE ON THE BRINK OF EXTINCTION. THEY DESPERATELY NEED TO REPRODUCE.
USING THIS PROCESS, THE BROOD COULD DEVELOP INCUBATORS... EXTRACTING THE LARVA FROM ITS HOST AND RAISING IT TO MATURITY EXTERNALLY...
...ALLOWING THEM TO REINFECT A HOST MULTIPLE TIMES.
WE LEAVE HERE WITH THAT EQUIPMENT...OR NOT AT ALL.
YOU AREN'T IN THE SAME POSITION. LEAVE US SOME GUNS AND GO. WE'LL CALL IF WE WIN.
AGENT BRAND, I AM ROYALTY. FOR AN INSULT LIKE THAT, I CAN HAVE YOUR HEAD CUT OFF.
NOW PLEASE... LEAD THE WAY.

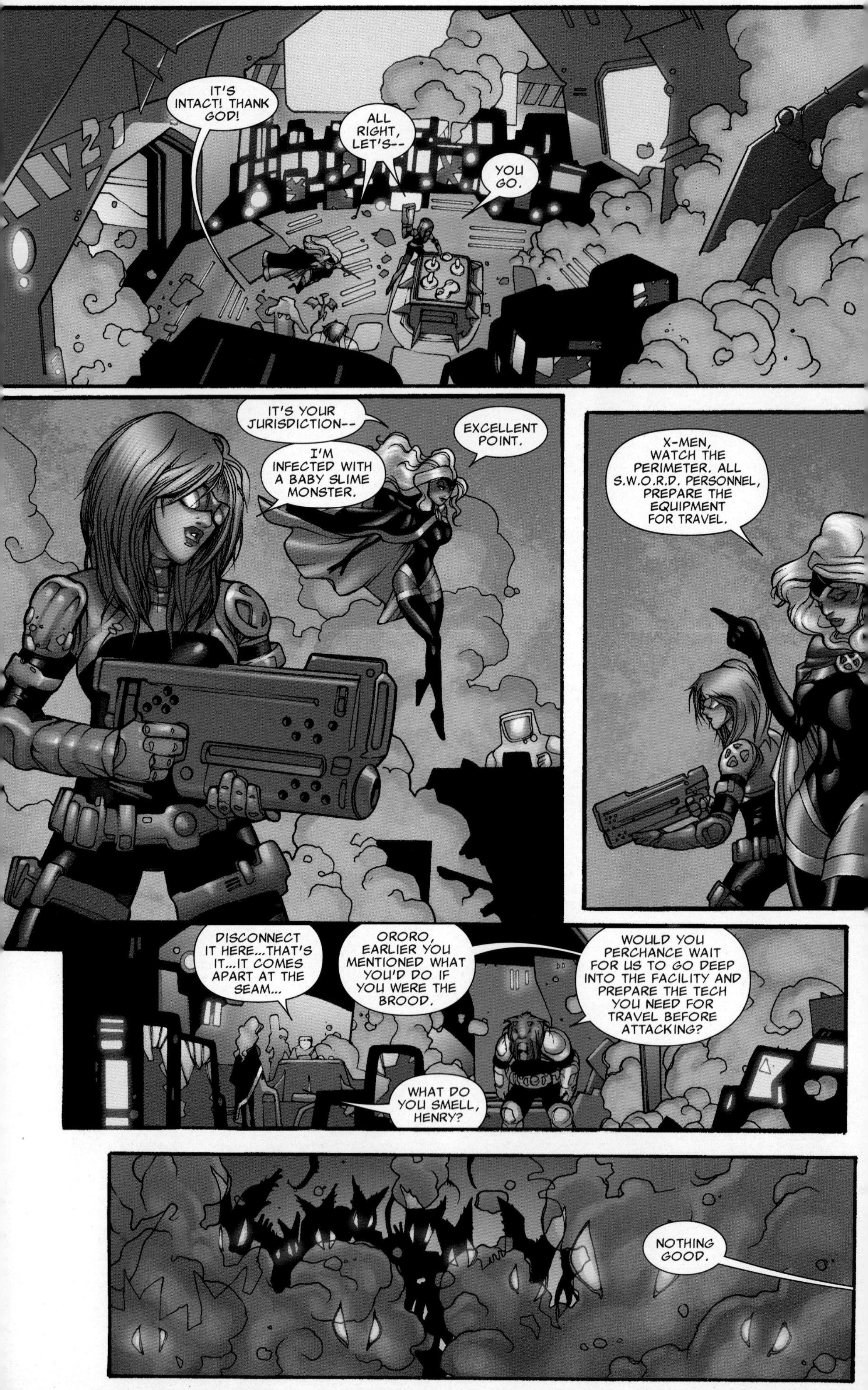
IT'S INTACT! THANK GOD!
ALL RIGHT, LET'S--
YOU GO.
IT'S YOUR JURISDICTION--
I'M INFECTED WITH A BABY SLIME MONSTER.
EXCELLENT POINT.
X-MEN, WATCH THE PERIMETER. ALL S.W.O.R.D. PERSONNEL, PREPARE THE EQUIPMENT FOR TRAVEL.
DISCONNECT IT HERE...THAT'S IT...IT COMES APART AT THE SEAM...
ORORO, EARLIER YOU MENTIONED WHAT YOU'D DO IF YOU WERE THE BROOD.
WOULD YOU PERCHANCE WAIT FOR US TO GO DEEP INTO THE FACILITY AND PREPARE THE TECH YOU NEED FOR TRAVEL BEFORE ATTACKING?
WHAT DO YOU SMELL, HENRY?
NOTHING GOOD.

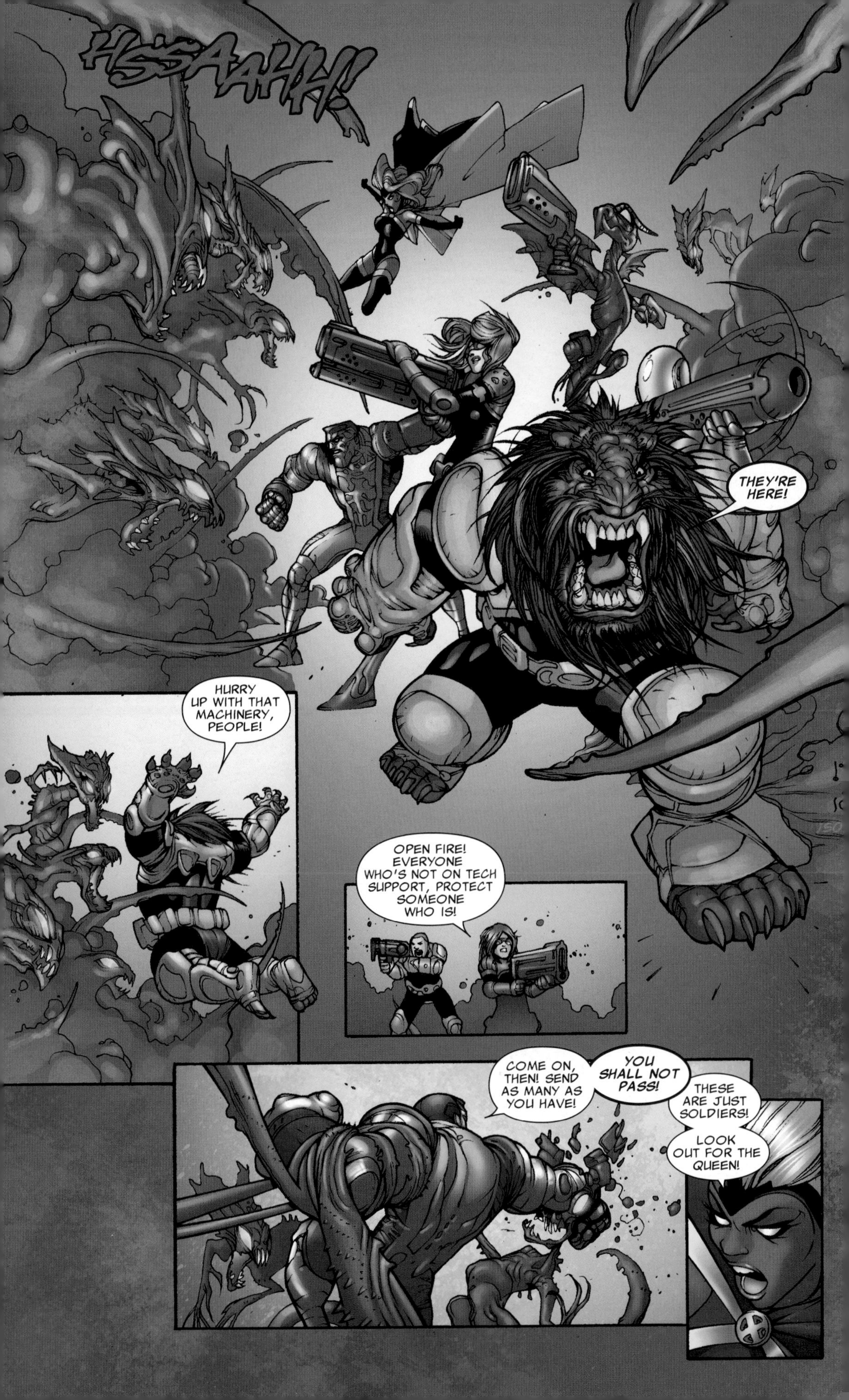
H'SSAAHH!
THEY'RE HERE!
HURRY UP WITH THAT MACHINERY, PEOPLE!
OPEN FIRE! EVERYONE WHO'S NOT ON TECH SUPPORT, PROTECT SOMEONE WHO IS!
COME ON, THEN! SEND AS MANY AS YOU HAVE!
YOU SHALL NOT PASS!
THESE ARE JUST SOLDIERS!
LOOK OUT FOR THE QUEEN!

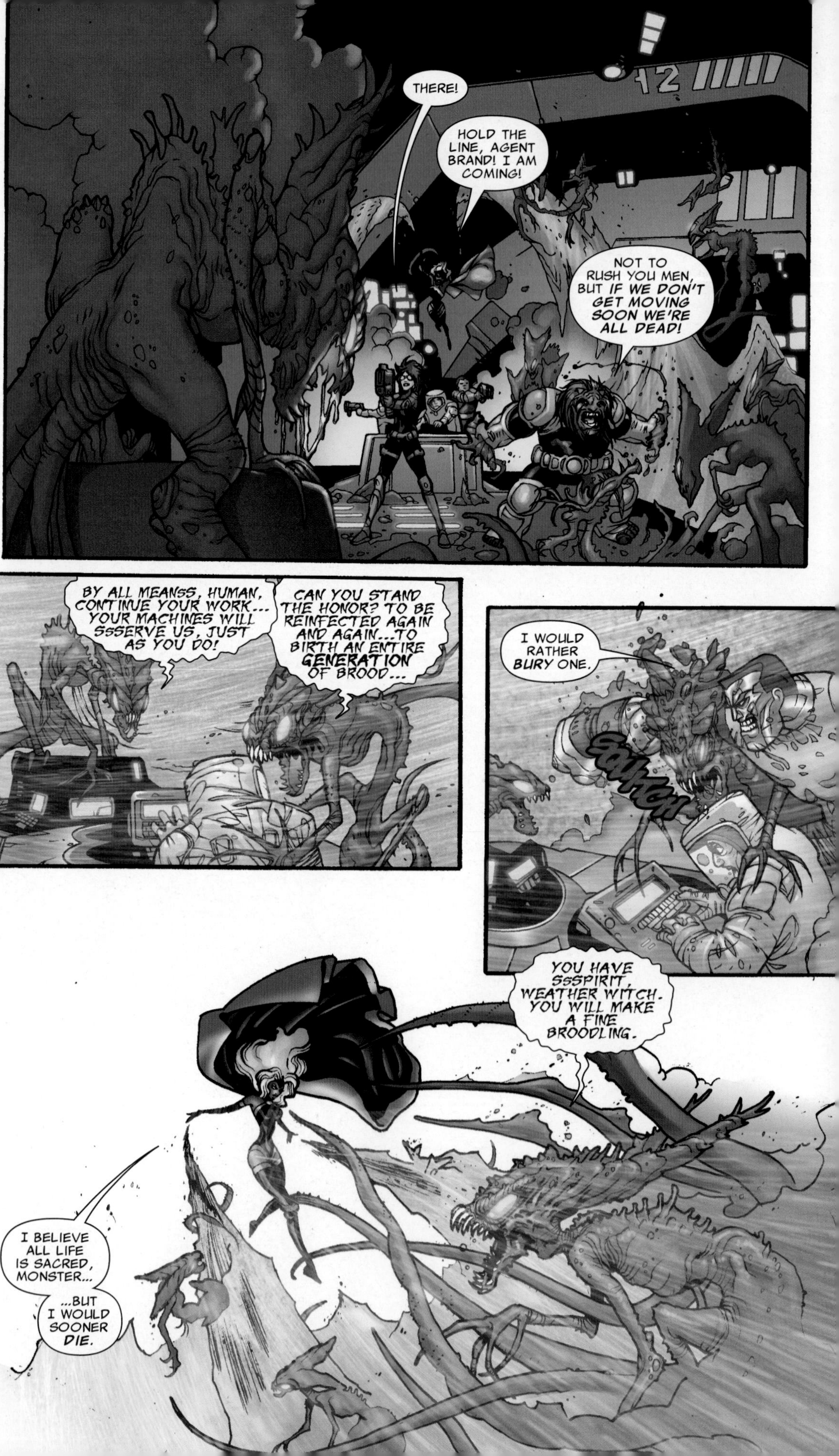
THERE!
HOLD THE LINE, AGENT BRAND! I AM COMING!
NOT TO RUSH YOU MEN, BUT IF WE DON'T GET MOVING SOON WE'RE ALL DEAD!
BY ALL MEANSS, HUMAN, CONTINUE YOUR WORK... YOUR MACHINES WILL SSSERVE US, JUST AS YOU DO!
CAN YOU STAND THE HONOR? TO BE REINFECTED AGAIN AND AGAIN...TO BIRTH AN ENTIRE GENERATION OF BROOD...
I WOULD RATHER BURY ONE.
YOU HAVE SSSPIRIT, WEATHER WITCH. YOU WILL MAKE A FINE BROODLING.
I BELIEVE ALL LIFE IS SACRED, MONSTER...
...BUT I WOULD SOONER DIE.

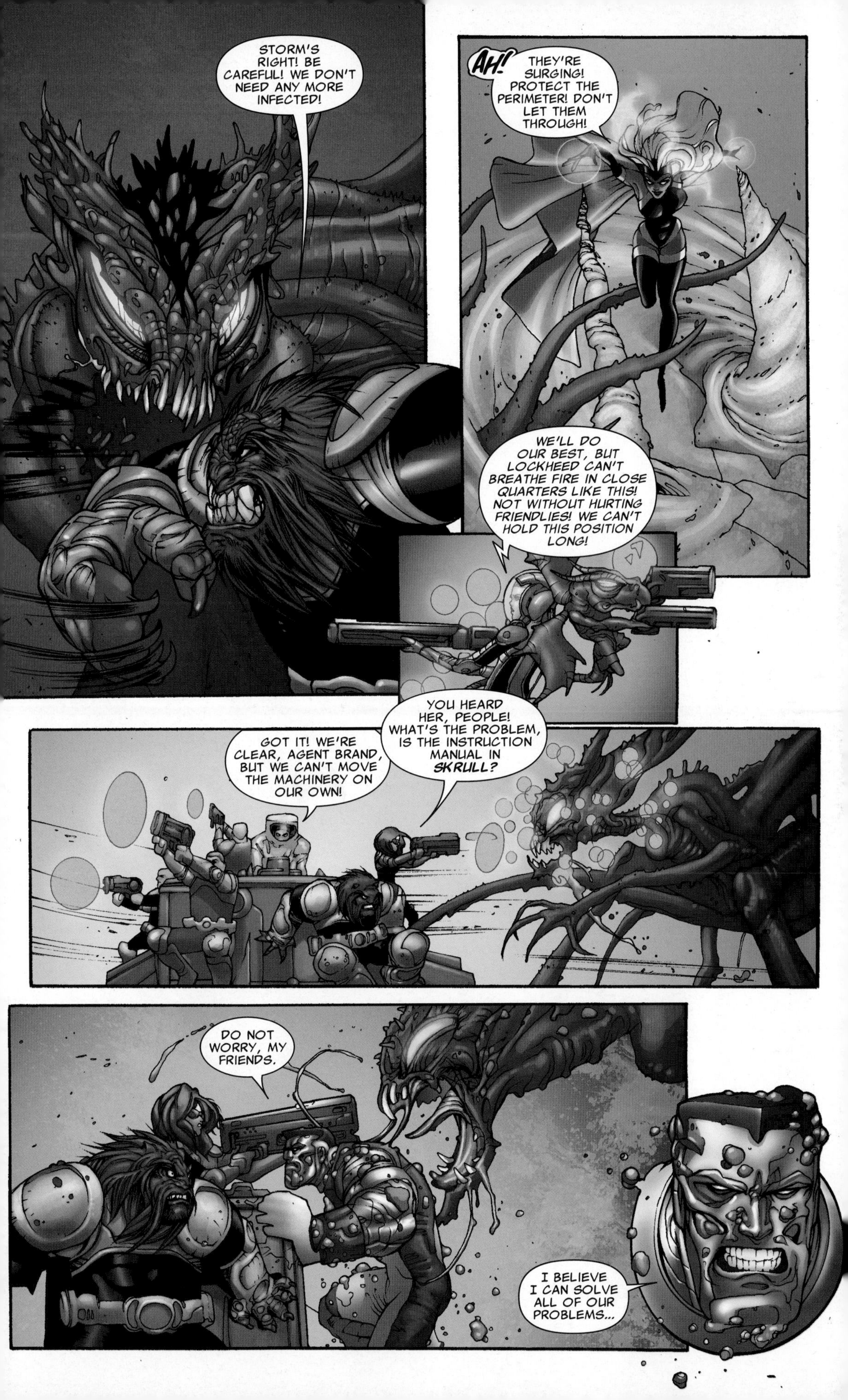
STORM'S RIGHT! BE CAREFUL! WE DON'T NEED ANY MORE INFECTED!
AH!
THEY'RE SURGING! PROTECT THE PERIMETER! DON'T LET THEM THROUGH!
WE'LL DO OUR BEST, BUT LOCKHEED CAN'T BREATHE FIRE IN CLOSE QUARTERS LIKE THIS! NOT WITHOUT HURTING FRIENDLIES! WE CAN'T HOLD THIS POSITION LONG!
GOT IT! WE'RE CLEAR, AGENT BRAND, BUT WE CAN'T MOVE THE MACHINERY ON OUR OWN!
YOU HEARD HER, PEOPLE! WHAT'S THE PROBLEM, IS THE INSTRUCTION MANUAL IN SKRULL?
DO NOT WORRY, MY FRIENDS.
I BELIEVE I CAN SOLVE ALL OF OUR PROBLEMS...

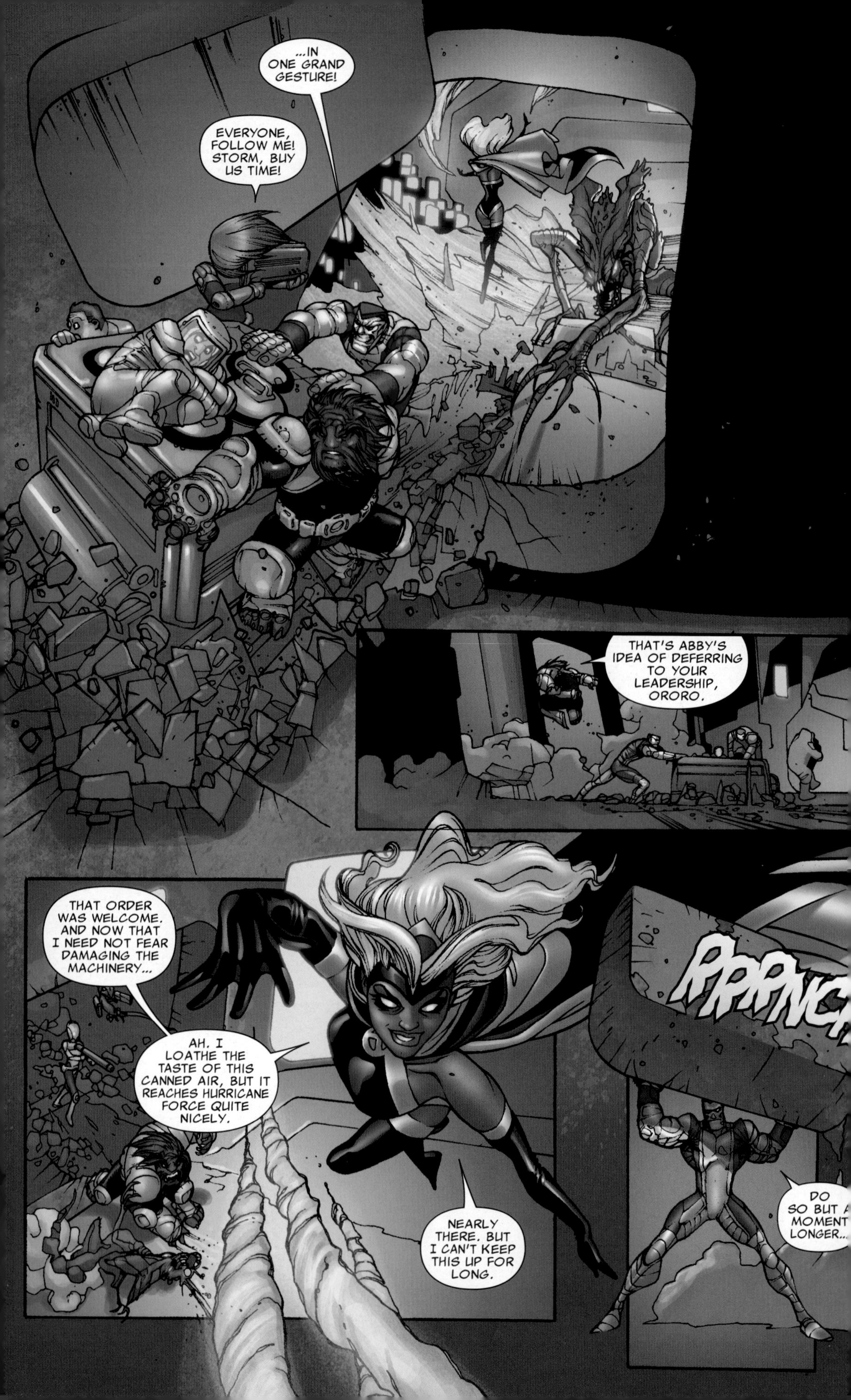
EVERYONE, FOLLOW ME! STORM, BUY US TIME!
...IN ONE GRAND GESTURE!
THAT'S ABBY'S IDEA OF DEFERRING TO YOUR LEADERSHIP, ORORO.
THAT ORDER WAS WELCOME. AND NOW THAT I NEED NOT FEAR DAMAGING THE MACHINERY...
AH. I LOATHE THE TASTE OF THIS CANNED AIR, BUT IT REACHES HURRICANE FORCE QUITE NICELY.
NEARLY THERE. BUT I CAN'T KEEP THIS UP FOR LONG.
RRRNCH
DO SO BUT A MOMENT LONGER...

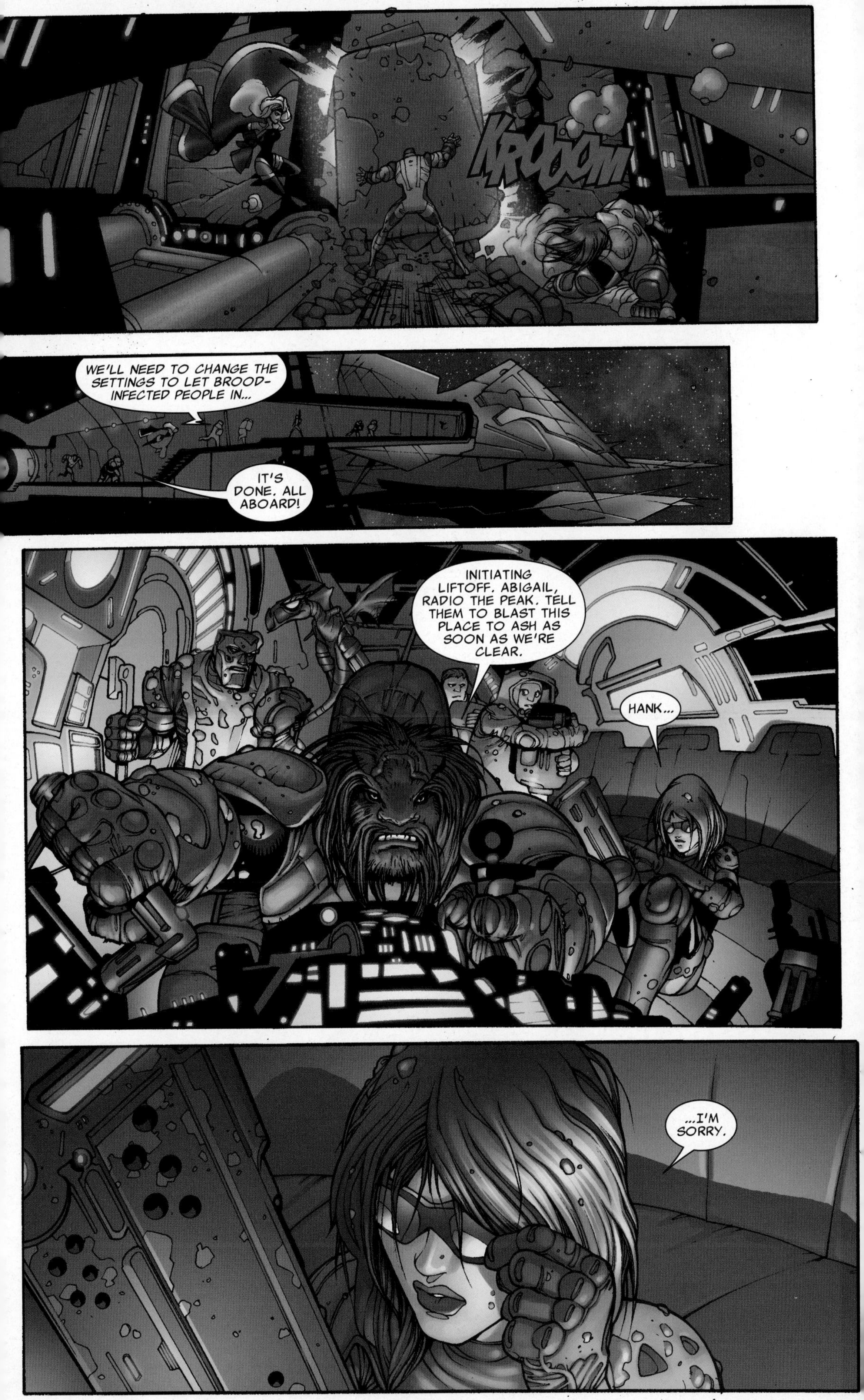
KROOOM
WE'LL NEED TO CHANGE THE SETTINGS TO LET BROOD-INFECTED PEOPLE IN...
IT'S DONE. ALL ABOARD!
INITIATING LIFTOFF. ABIGAIL, RADIO THE PEAK. TELL THEM TO BLAST THIS PLACE TO ASH AS SOON AS WE'RE CLEAR.
HANK...
...I'M SORRY.

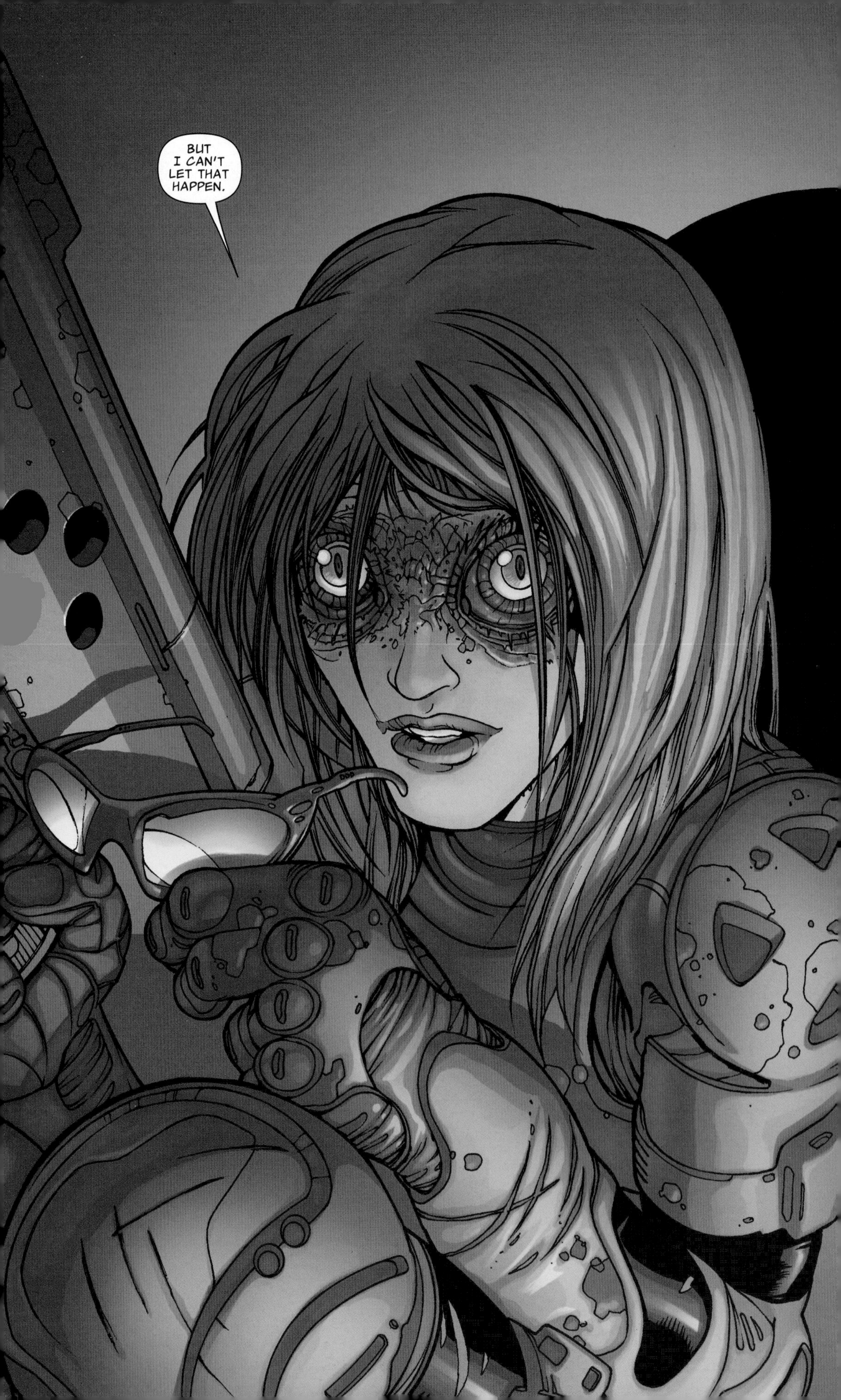
BUT I CAN'T LET THAT HAPPEN.

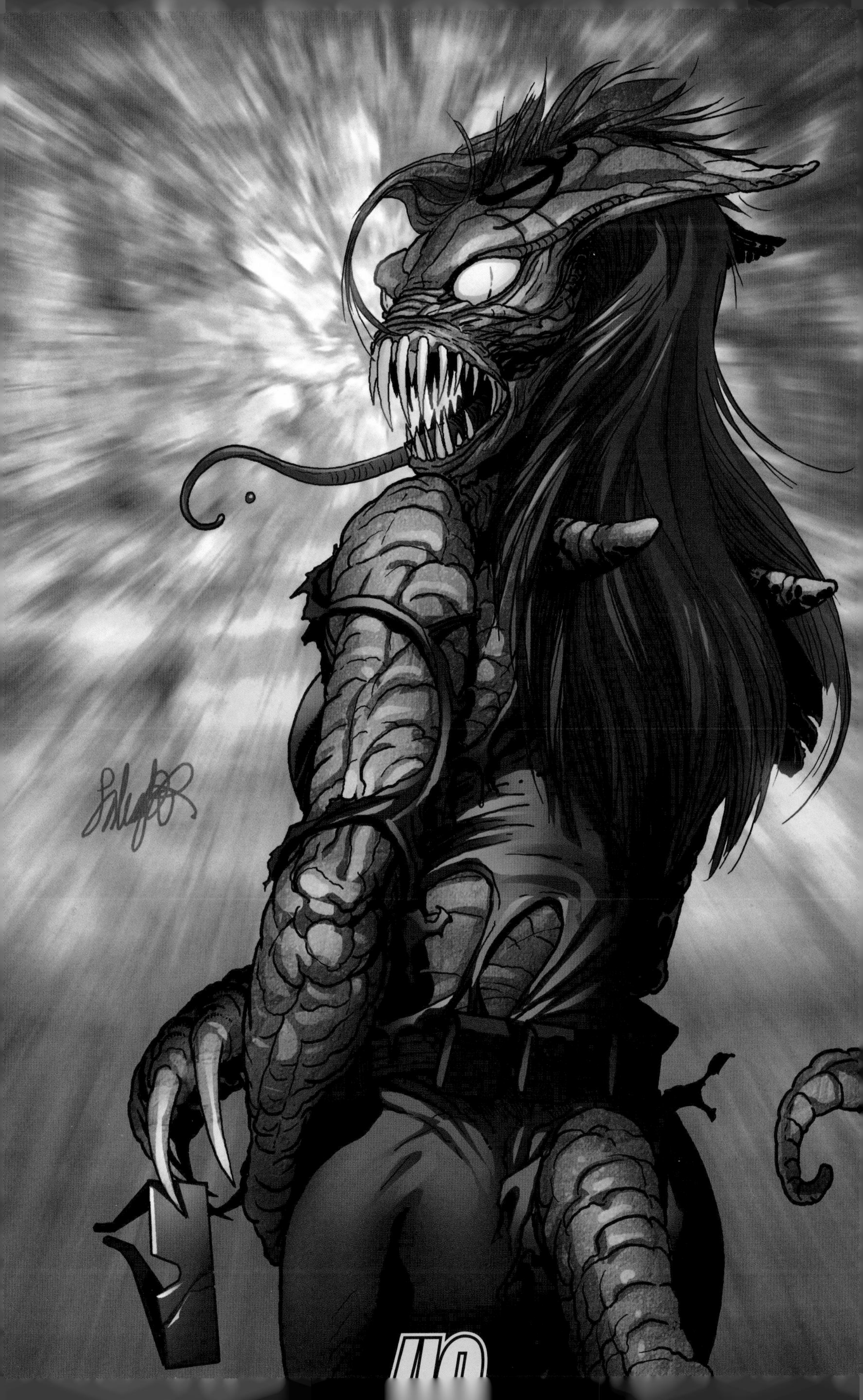

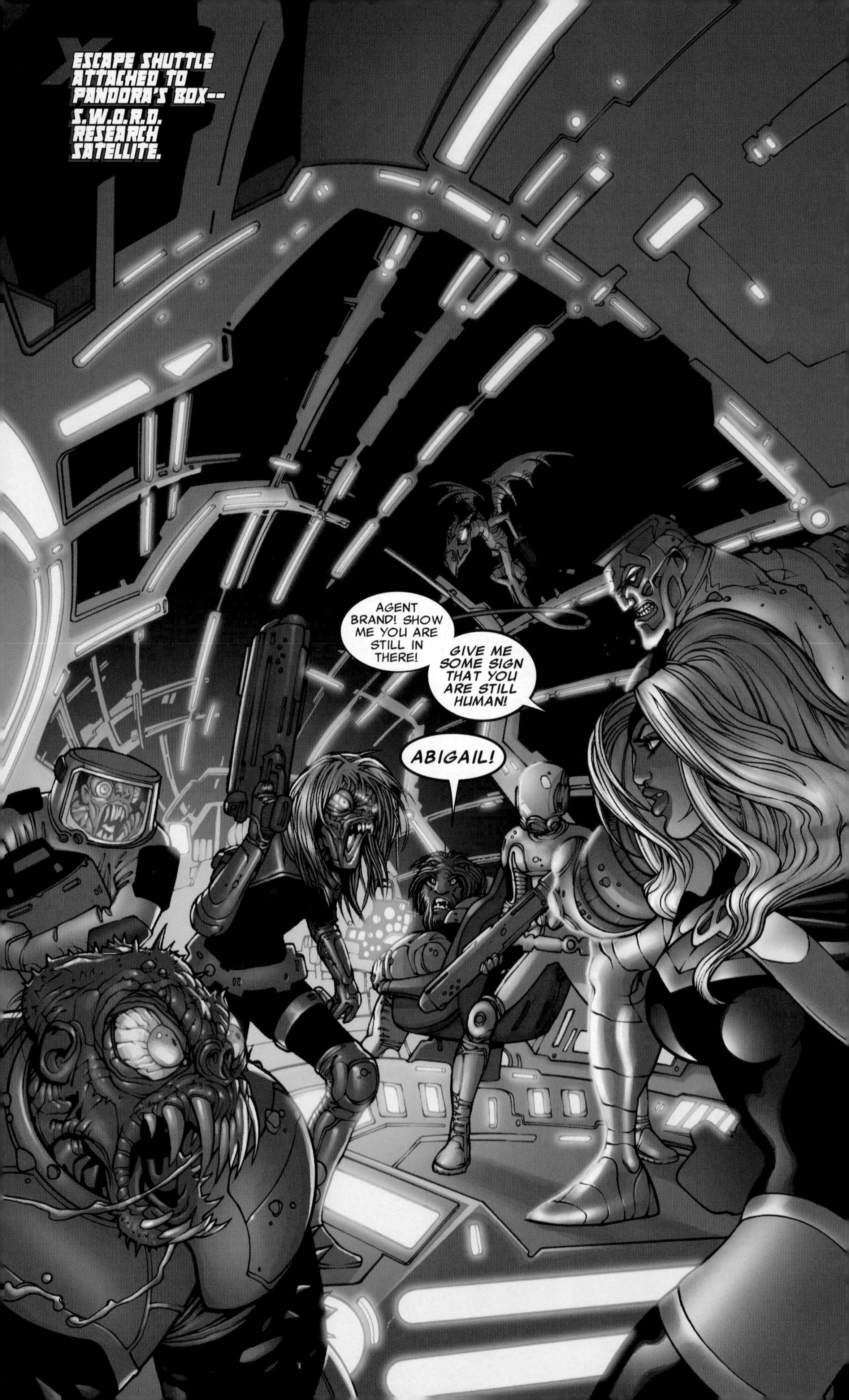
ESCAPE SHUTTLE ATTACHED TO PANDORA'S BOX--
S.W.O.R.D. RESEARCH SATELLITE.
AGENT BRAND! SHOW ME YOU ARE STILL IN THERE!
GIVE ME SOME SIGN THAT YOU ARE STILL HUMAN!
ABIGAIL!

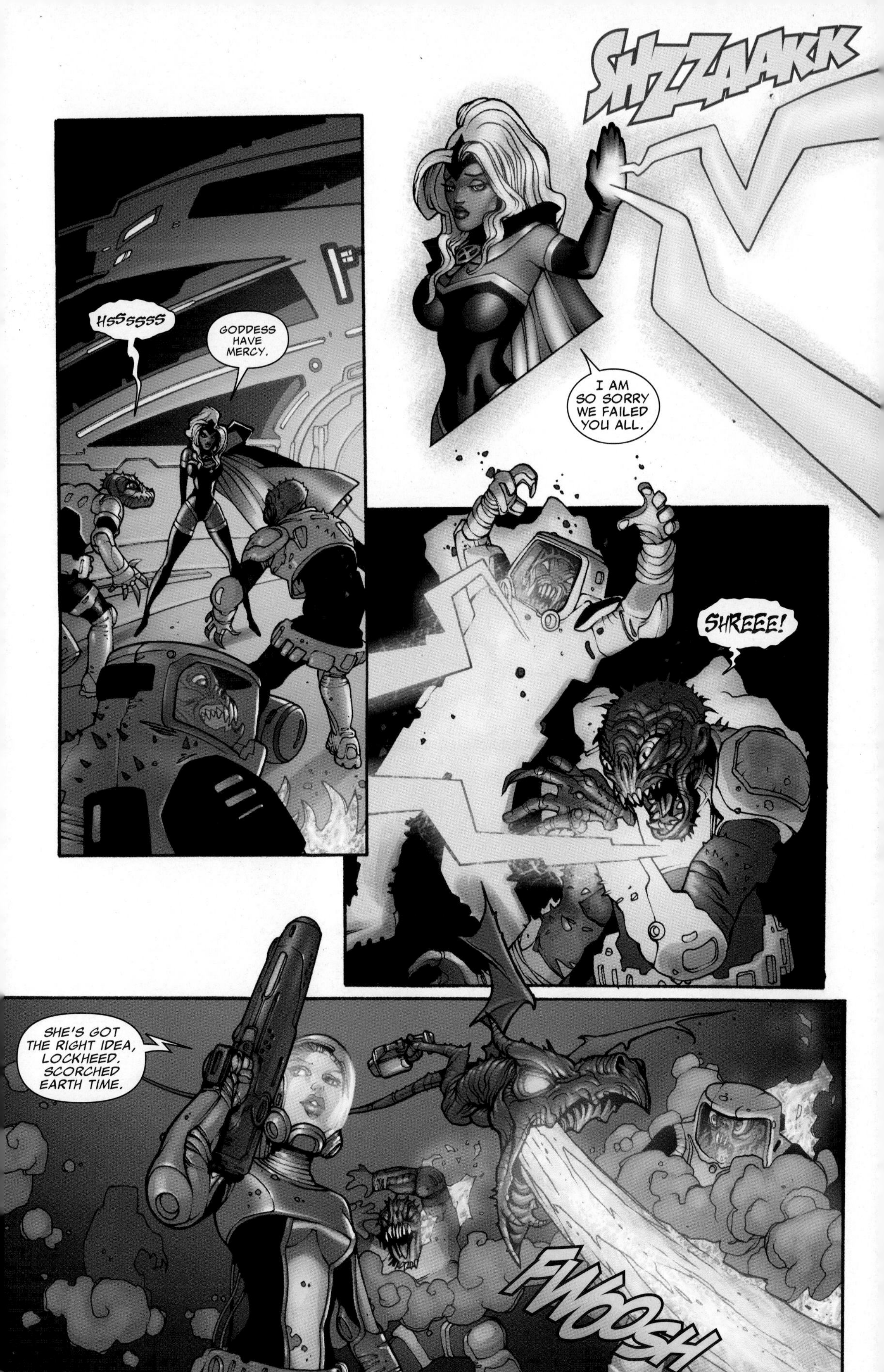
SHZZAAKK
HSSSSSS
GODDESS HAVE MERCY.
I AM SO SORRY WE FAILED YOU ALL.
SHREEE!
SHE'S GOT THE RIGHT IDEA, LOCKHEED. SCORCHED EARTH TIME.
FWOOSH

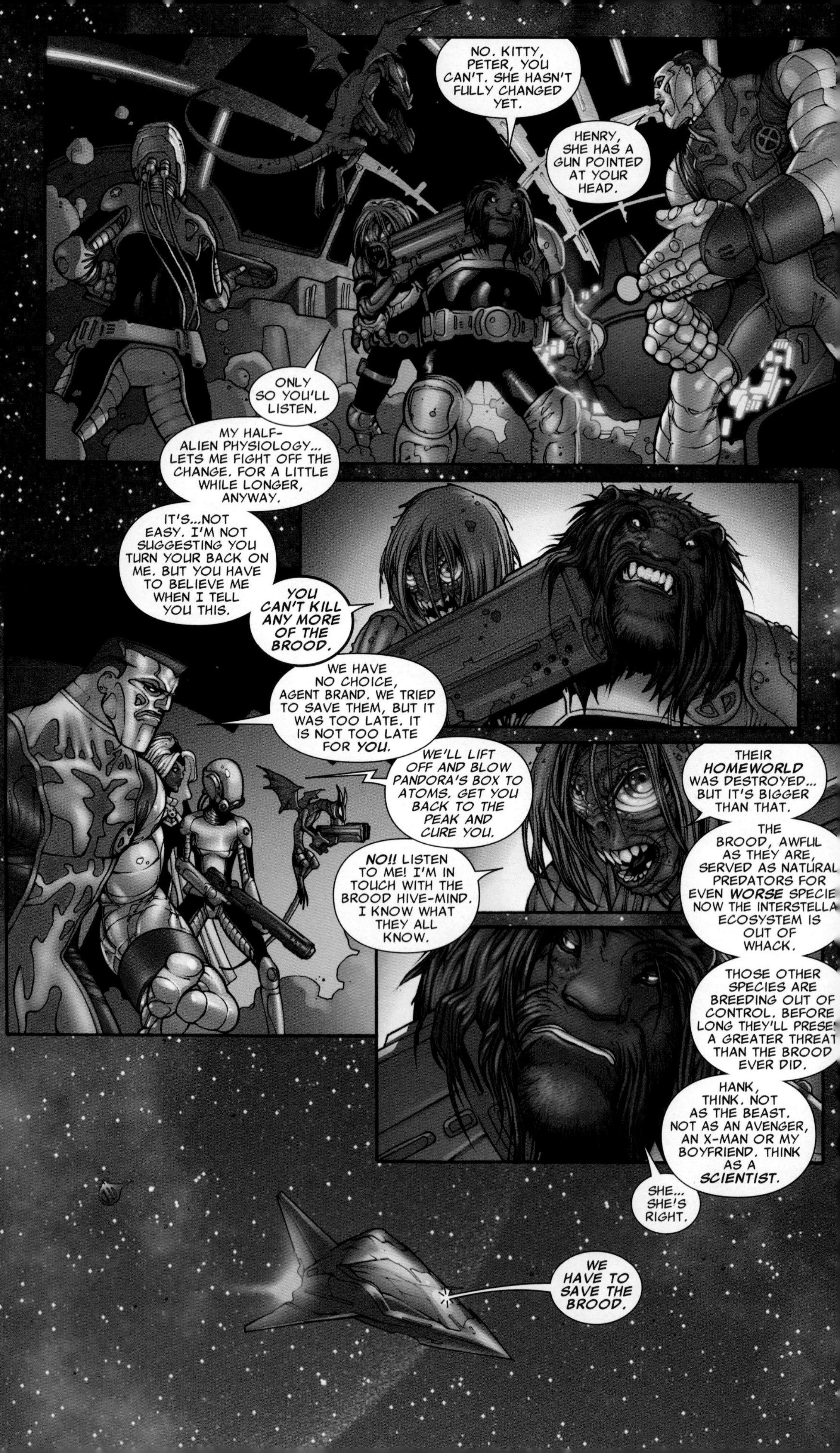
NO. KITTY, PETER, YOU CAN'T. SHE HASN'T FULLY CHANGED YET.
HENRY, SHE HAS A GUN POINTED AT YOUR HEAD.
ONLY SO YOU'LL LISTEN.
MY HALF-ALIEN PHYSIOLOGY... LETS ME FIGHT OFF THE CHANGE. FOR A LITTLE WHILE LONGER, ANYWAY.
IT'S...NOT EASY. I'M NOT SUGGESTING YOU TURN YOUR BACK ON ME. BUT YOU HAVE TO BELIEVE ME WHEN I TELL YOU THIS.
YOU CAN'T KILL ANY MORE OF THE BROOD.
WE HAVE NO CHOICE, AGENT BRAND. WE TRIED TO SAVE THEM, BUT IT WAS TOO LATE. IT IS NOT TOO LATE FOR YOU.
WE'LL LIFT OFF AND BLOW PANDORA'S BOX TO ATOMS. GET YOU BACK TO THE PEAK AND CURE YOU.
NO!! LISTEN TO ME! I'M IN TOUCH WITH THE BROOD HIVE-MIND. I KNOW WHAT THEY ALL KNOW.
THEIR HOMEWORLD WAS DESTROYED... BUT IT'S BIGGER THAN THAT.
THE BROOD, AWFUL AS THEY ARE, SERVED AS NATURAL PREDATORS FOR EVEN WORSE SPECIE NOW THE INTERSTELLA ECOSYSTEM IS OUT OF WHACK.
THOSE OTHER SPECIES ARE BREEDING OUT OF CONTROL. BEFORE LONG THEY'LL PRESE A GREATER THREAT THAN THE BROOD EVER DID.
HANK, THINK. NOT AS THE BEAST. NOT AS AN AVENGER, AN X-MAN OR MY BOYFRIEND. THINK AS A SCIENTIST.
SHE... SHE'S RIGHT.
WE HAVE TO SAVE THE BROOD.

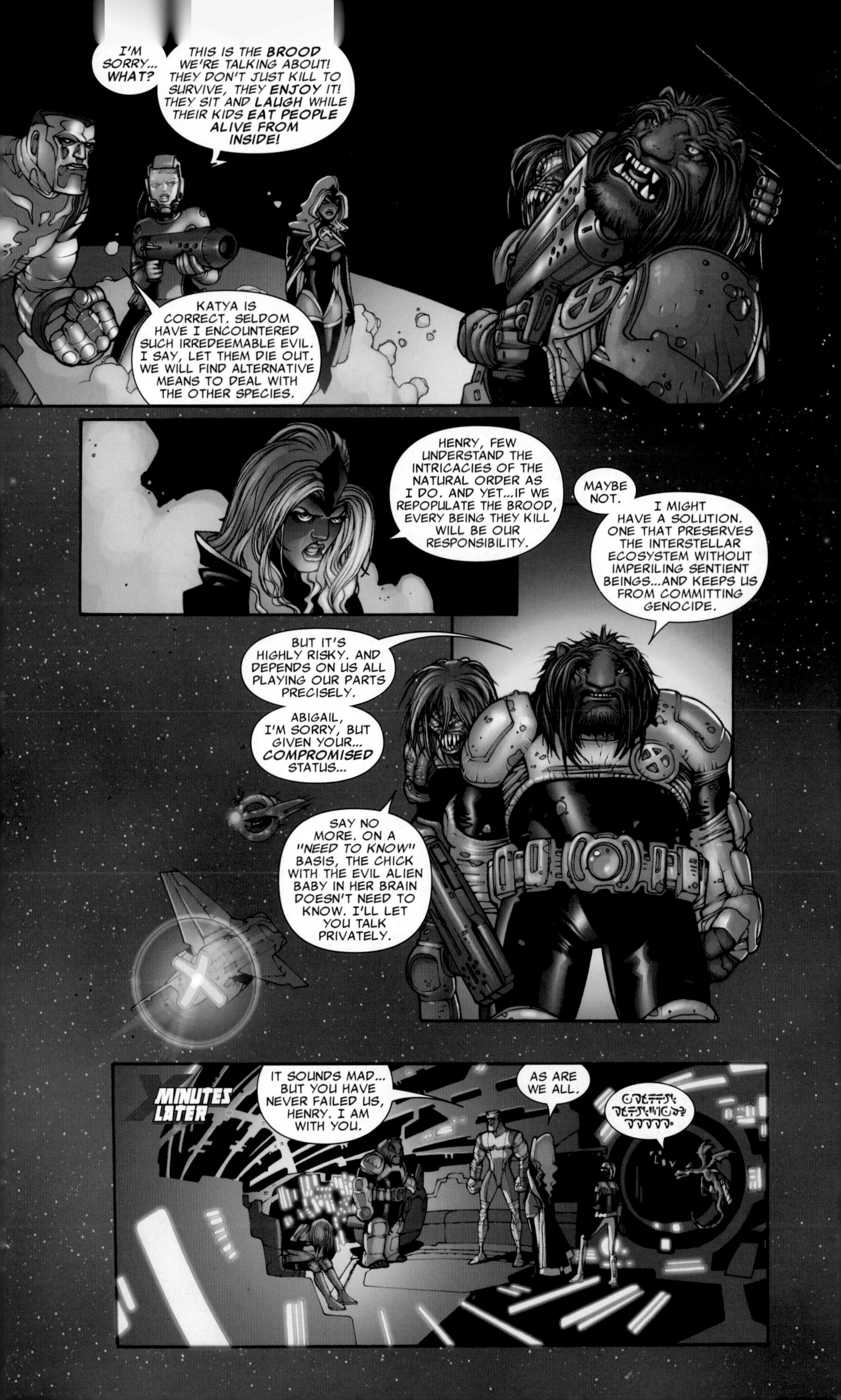

I'M SORRY... WHAT?
THIS IS THE BROOD WE'RE TALKING ABOUT! THEY DON'T JUST KILL TO SURVIVE, THEY ENJOY IT! THEY SIT AND LAUGH WHILE THEIR KIDS EAT PEOPLE ALIVE FROM INSIDE!
KATYA IS CORRECT. SELDOM HAVE I ENCOUNTERED SUCH IRREDEEMABLE EVIL. I SAY, LET THEM DIE OUT. WE WILL FIND ALTERNATIVE MEANS TO DEAL WITH THE OTHER SPECIES.
HENRY, FEW UNDERSTAND THE INTRICACIES OF THE NATURAL ORDER AS I DO. AND YET...IF WE REPOPULATE THE BROOD, EVERY BEING THEY KILL WILL BE OUR RESPONSIBILITY.
MAYBE NOT.
I MIGHT HAVE A SOLUTION. ONE THAT PRESERVES THE INTERSTELLAR ECOSYSTEM WITHOUT IMPERILING SENTIENT BEINGS...AND KEEPS US FROM COMMITTING GENOCIDE.
BUT IT'S HIGHLY RISKY. AND DEPENDS ON US ALL PLAYING OUR PARTS PRECISELY.
ABIGAIL, I'M SORRY, BUT GIVEN YOUR... COMPROMISED STATUS...
SAY NO MORE. ON A "NEED TO KNOW" BASIS, THE CHICK WITH THE EVIL ALIEN BABY IN HER BRAIN DOESN'T NEED TO KNOW. I'LL LET YOU TALK PRIVATELY.
MINUTES LATER
IT SOUNDS MAD... BUT YOU HAVE NEVER FAILED US, HENRY. I AM WITH YOU.
AS ARE WE ALL.

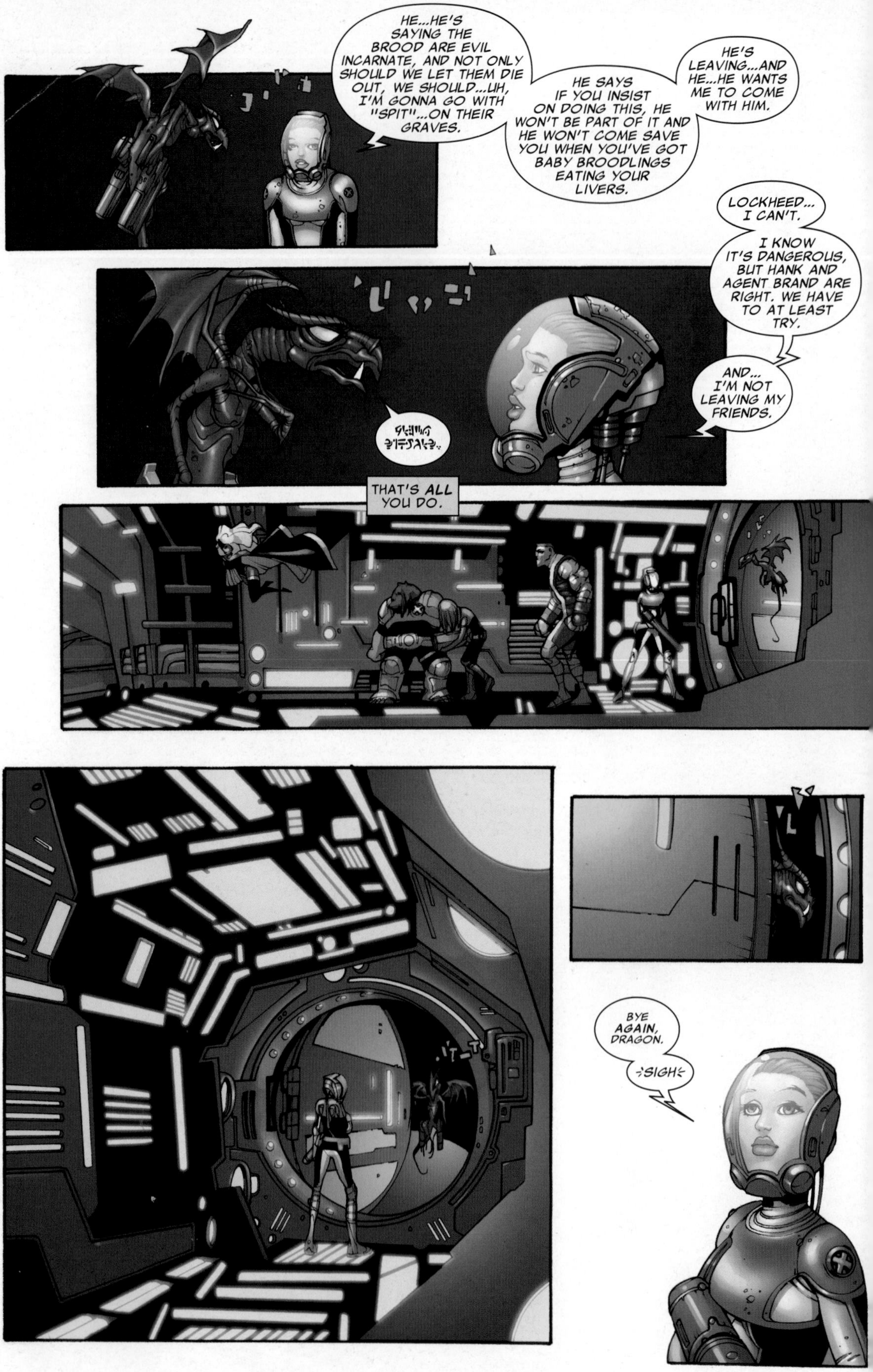
HE...HE'S SAYING THE BROOD ARE EVIL INCARNATE, AND NOT ONLY SHOULD WE LET THEM DIE OUT, WE SHOULD...UH, I'M GONNA GO WITH "SPIT"...ON THEIR GRAVES.
HE SAYS IF YOU INSIST ON DOING THIS, HE WON'T BE PART OF IT AND HE WON'T COME SAVE YOU WHEN YOU'VE GOT BABY BROODLINGS EATING YOUR LIVERS.
HE'S LEAVING...AND HE...HE WANTS ME TO COME WITH HIM.
LOCKHEED... I CAN'T.
I KNOW IT'S DANGEROUS, BUT HANK AND AGENT BRAND ARE RIGHT. WE HAVE TO AT LEAST TRY.
AND... I'M NOT LEAVING MY FRIENDS.
THAT'S ALL YOU DO.
BYE AGAIN, DRAGON.
SIGH

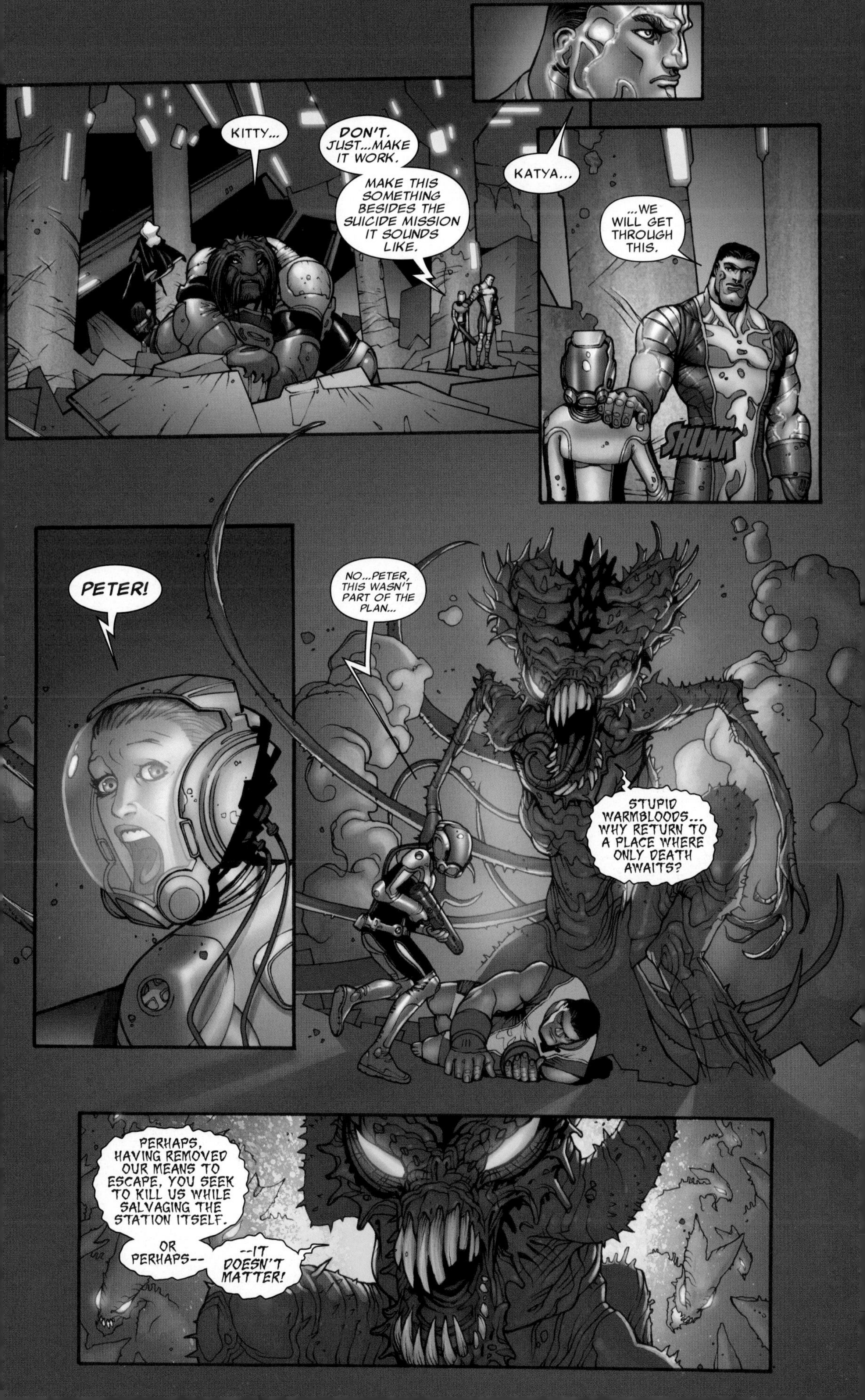
KITTY...
DON'T. JUST...MAKE IT WORK.
MAKE THIS SOMETHING BESIDES THE SUICIDE MISSION IT SOUNDS LIKE.
KATYA...
...WE WILL GET THROUGH THIS.
SHUNK
PETER!
NO...PETER, THIS WASN'T PART OF THE PLAN...
STUPID WARMBLOODS... WHY RETURN TO A PLACE WHERE ONLY DEATH AWAITS?
PERHAPS, HAVING REMOVED OUR MEANS TO ESCAPE, YOU SEEK TO KILL US WHILE SALVAGING THE STATION ITSELF.
OR PERHAPS--
--IT DOESN'T MATTER!

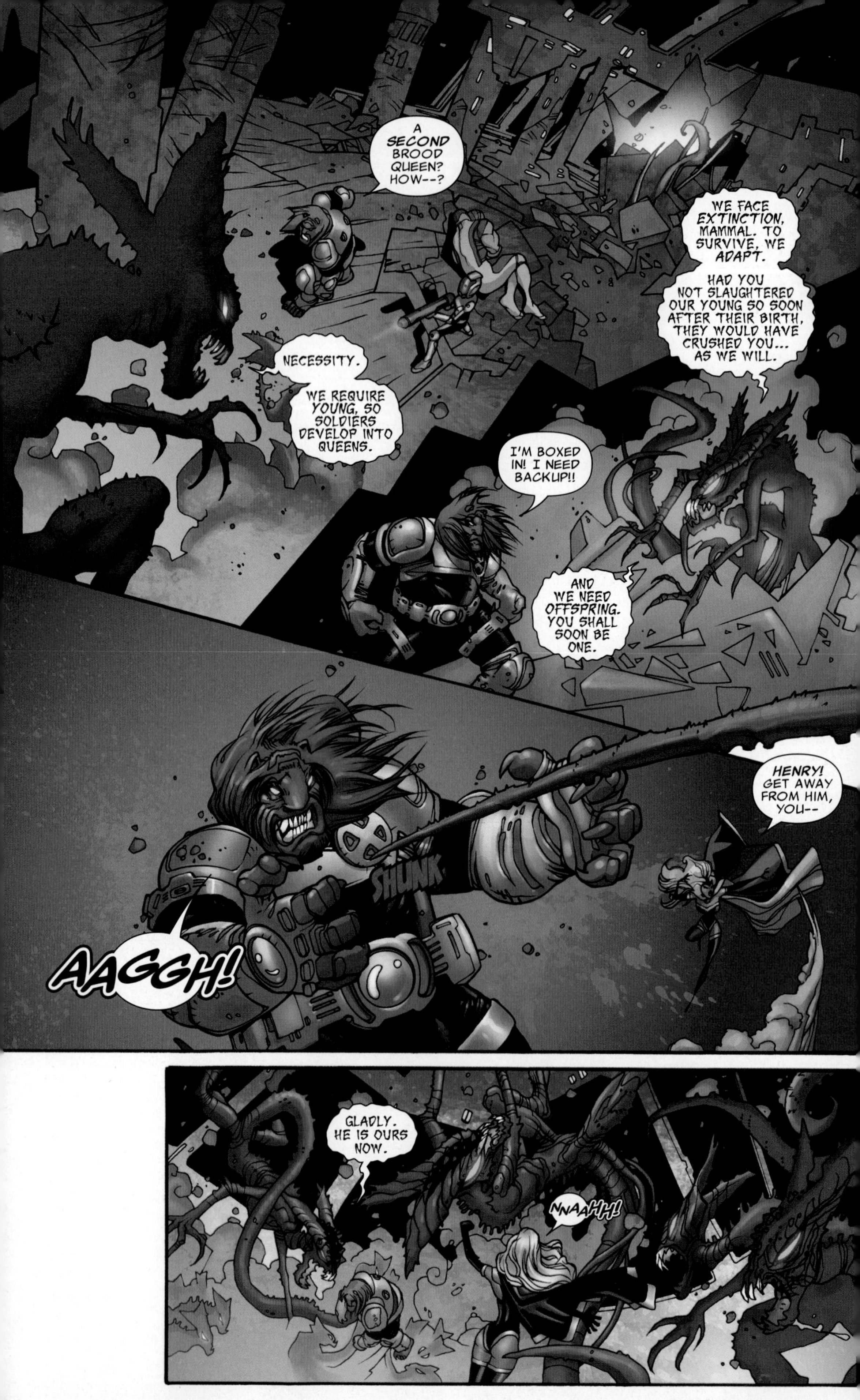

A SECOND BROOD QUEEN? HOW--?
NECESSITY.
WE REQUIRE YOUNG, SO SOLDIERS DEVELOP INTO QUEENS.
WE FACE EXTINCTION, MAMMAL. TO SURVIVE, WE ADAPT.
HAD YOU NOT SLAUGHTERED OUR YOUNG SO SOON AFTER THEIR BIRTH, THEY WOULD HAVE CRUSHED YOU... AS WE WILL.
I'M BOXED IN! I NEED BACKUP!!
AND WE NEED OFFSPRING. YOU SHALL SOON BE ONE.
SHUNK
AAGGH!
HENRY! GET AWAY FROM HIM, YOU--
GLADLY. HE IS OURS NOW.
NNAAHH!

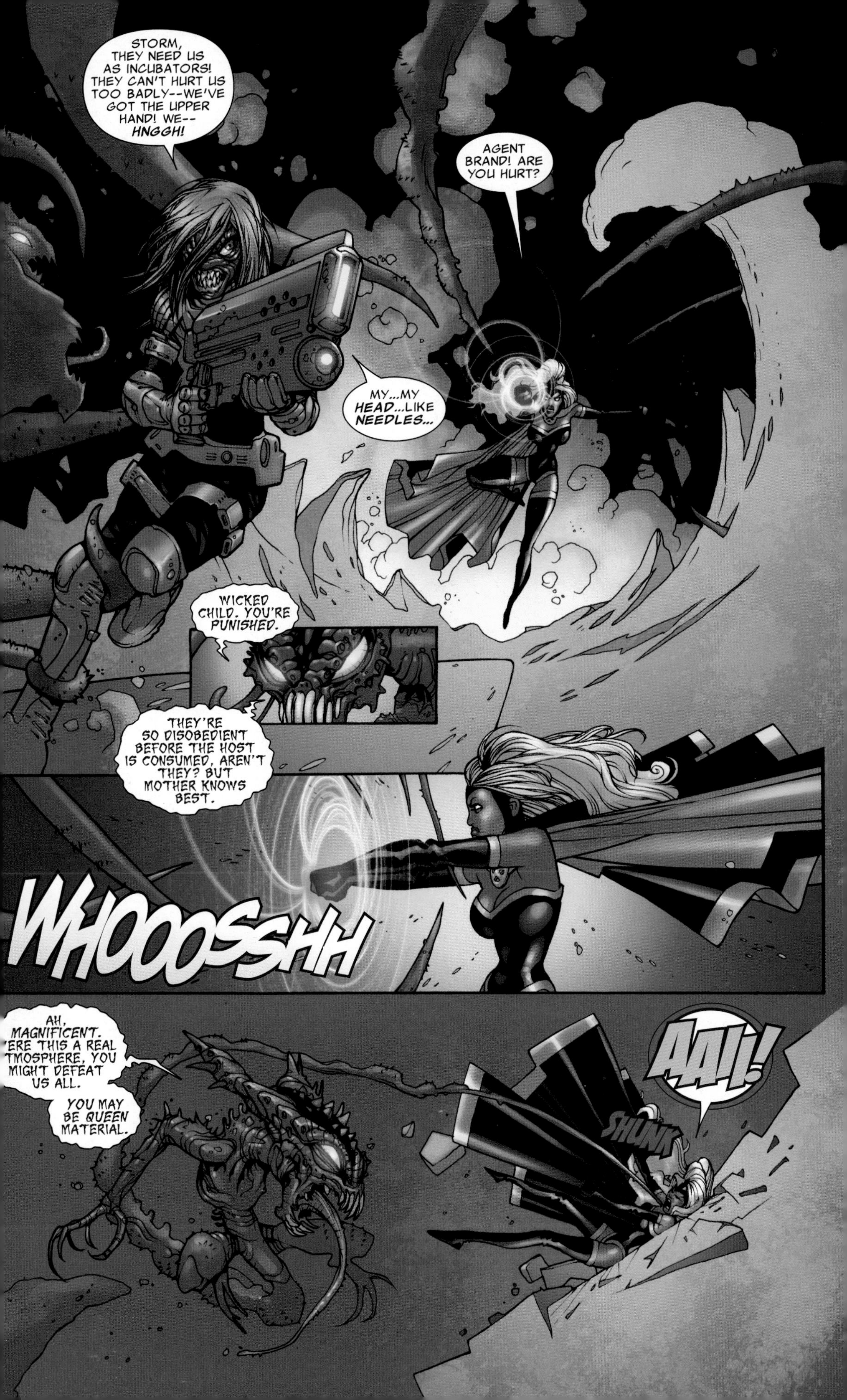
STORM, THEY NEED US AS INCUBATORS! THEY CAN'T HURT US TOO BADLY--WE'VE GOT THE UPPER HAND! WE-- HNGGH!
AGENT BRAND! ARE YOU HURT?
MY...MY HEAD...LIKE NEEDLES...
WICKED CHILD. YOU'RE PUNISHED.
THEY'RE SO DISOBEDIENT BEFORE THE HOST IS CONSUMED, AREN'T THEY? BUT MOTHER KNOWS BEST.
WHOOOSSHH
AH, MAGNIFICENT. 'ERE THIS A REAL TMOSPHERE, YOU MIGHT DEFEAT US ALL.
YOU MAY BE QUEEN MATERIAL.
AAII!
SHUNK

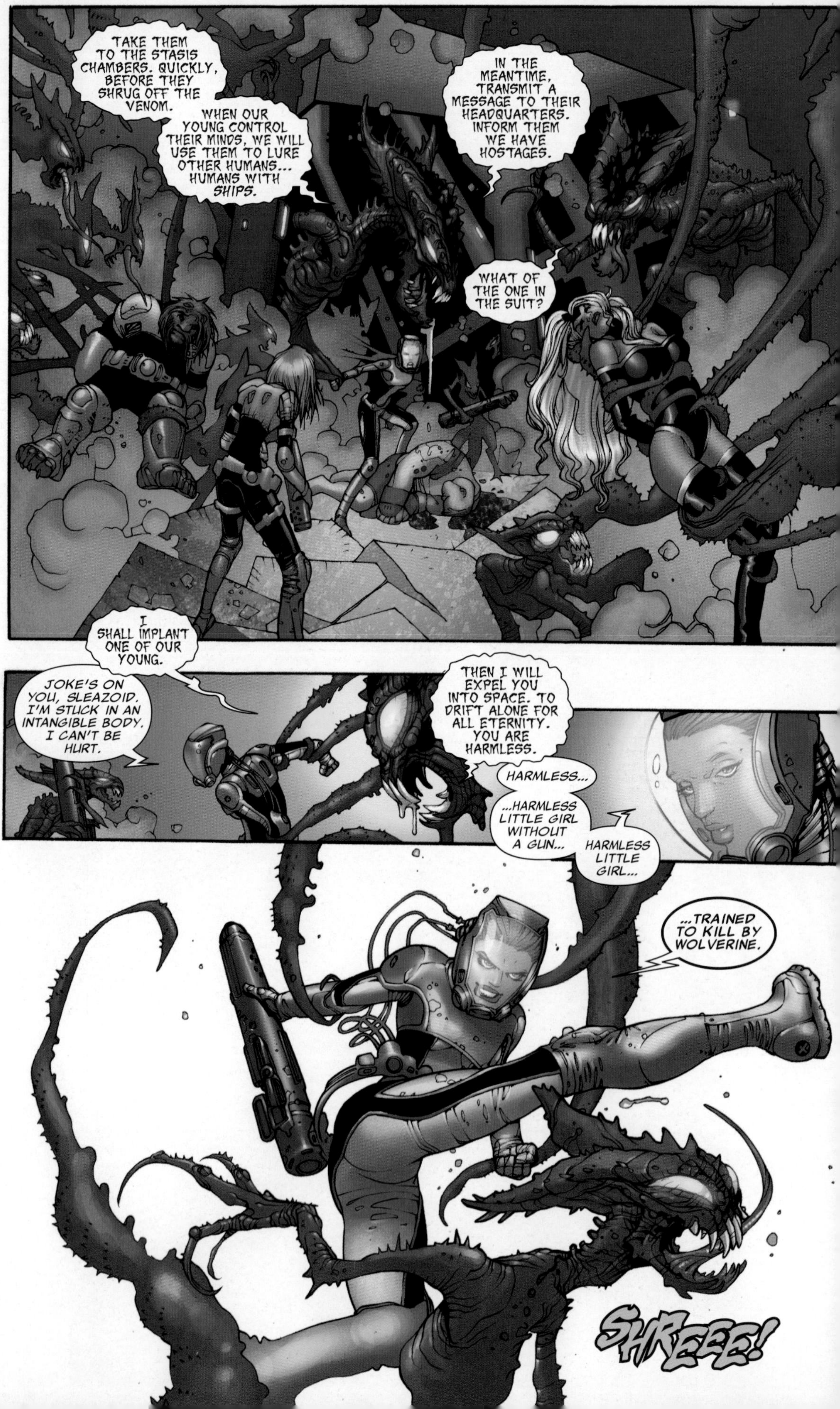
TAKE THEM TO THE STASIS CHAMBERS. QUICKLY, BEFORE THEY SHRUG OFF THE VENOM.
WHEN OUR YOUNG CONTROL THEIR MINDS, WE WILL USE THEM TO LURE OTHER HUMANS... HUMANS WITH SHIPS.
IN THE MEANTIME, TRANSMIT A MESSAGE TO THEIR HEADQUARTERS. INFORM THEM WE HAVE HOSTAGES.
WHAT OF THE ONE IN THE SUIT?
I SHALL IMPLANT ONE OF OUR YOUNG.
JOKE'S ON YOU, SLEAZOID. I'M STUCK IN AN INTANGIBLE BODY. I CAN'T BE HURT.
THEN I WILL EXPEL YOU INTO SPACE. TO DRIFT ALONE FOR ALL ETERNITY. YOU ARE HARMLESS.
HARMLESS...
...HARMLESS LITTLE GIRL WITHOUT A GUN...
HARMLESS LITTLE GIRL...
...TRAINED TO KILL BY WOLVERINE.
SHREEE!

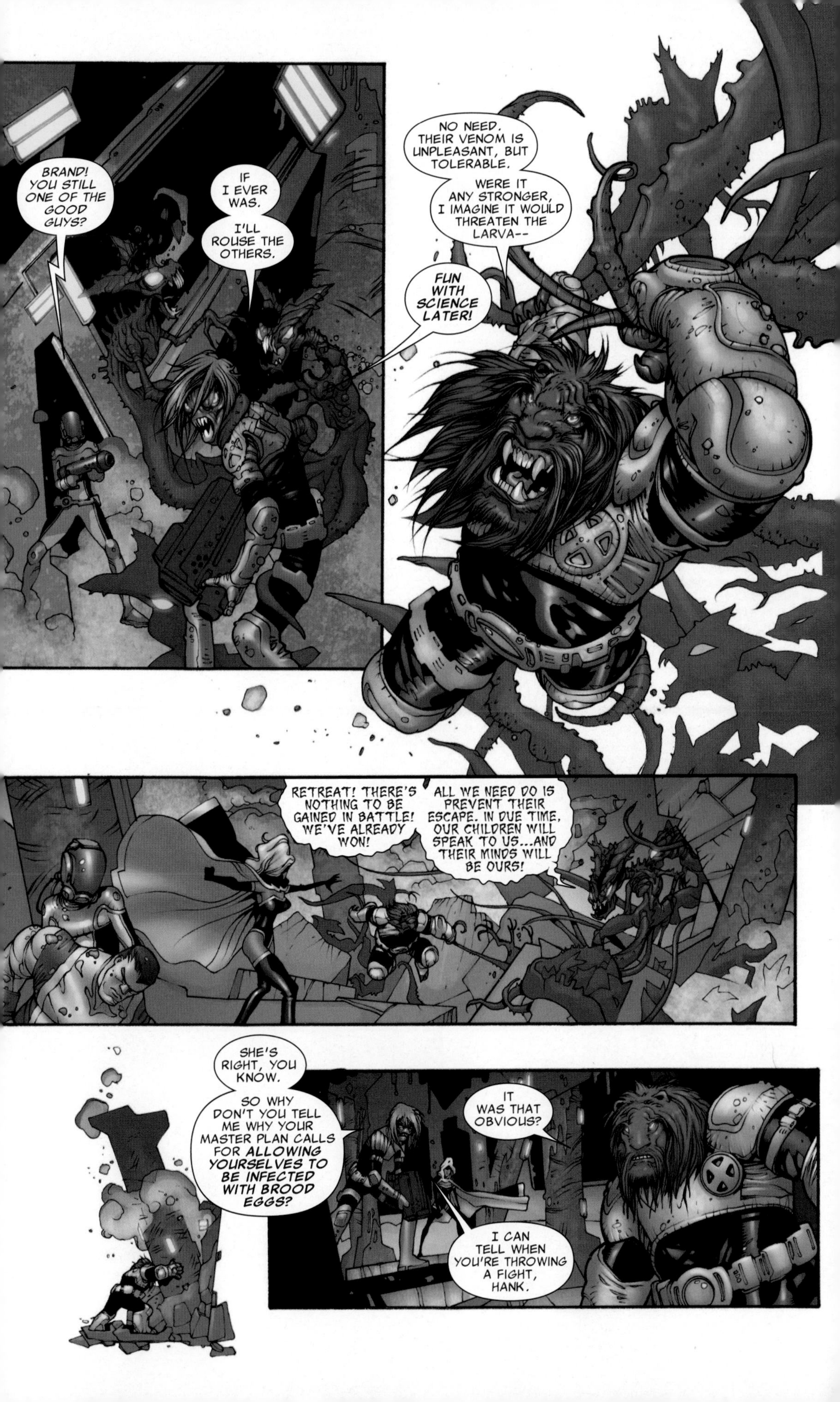
BRAND! YOU STILL ONE OF THE GOOD GUYS?
IF I EVER WAS.
I'LL ROUSE THE OTHERS.
NO NEED. THEIR VENOM IS UNPLEASANT, BUT TOLERABLE.
WERE IT ANY STRONGER, I IMAGINE IT WOULD THREATEN THE LARVA--
FUN WITH SCIENCE LATER!
RETREAT! THERE'S NOTHING TO BE GAINED IN BATTLE! WE'VE ALREADY WON!
ALL WE NEED DO IS PREVENT THEIR ESCAPE. IN DUE TIME, OUR CHILDREN WILL SPEAK TO US...AND THEIR MINDS WILL BE OURS!
SHE'S RIGHT, YOU KNOW.
SO WHY DON'T YOU TELL ME WHY YOUR MASTER PLAN CALLS FOR ALLOWING YOURSELVES TO BE INFECTED WITH BROOD EGGS?
IT WAS THAT OBVIOUS?
I CAN TELL WHEN YOU'RE THROWING A FIGHT, HANK.

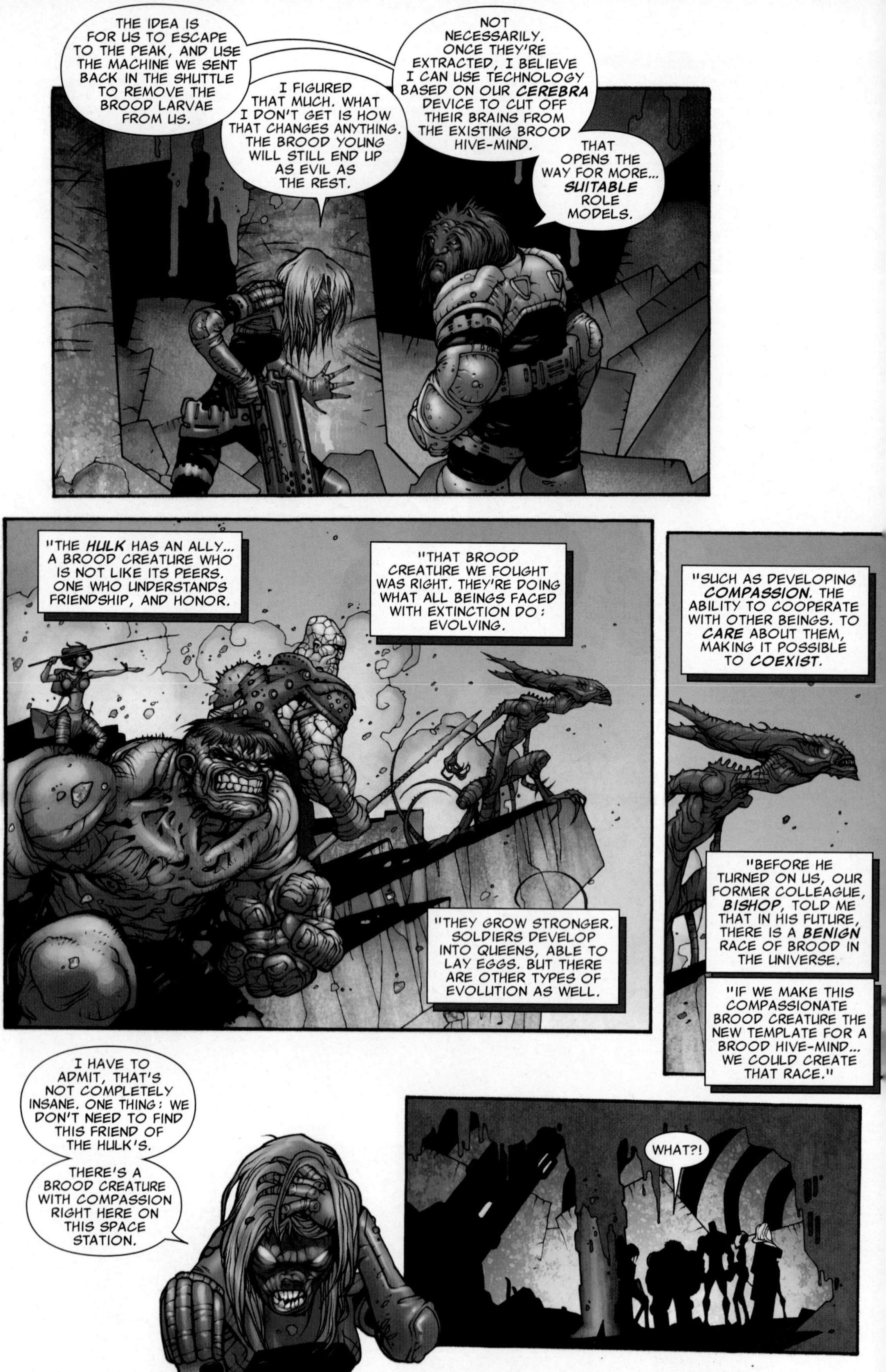
THE IDEA IS FOR US TO ESCAPE TO THE PEAK, AND USE THE MACHINE WE SENT BACK IN THE SHUTTLE TO REMOVE THE BROOD LARVAE FROM US.
I FIGURED THAT MUCH. WHAT I DON'T GET IS HOW THAT CHANGES ANYTHING. THE BROOD YOUNG WILL STILL END UP AS EVIL AS THE REST.
NOT NECESSARILY. ONCE THEY'RE EXTRACTED, I BELIEVE I CAN USE TECHNOLOGY BASED ON OUR CEREBRA DEVICE TO CUT OFF THEIR BRAINS FROM THE EXISTING BROOD HIVE-MIND.
THAT OPENS THE WAY FOR MORE... SUITABLE ROLE MODELS.
"THE HULK HAS AN ALLY... A BROOD CREATURE WHO IS NOT LIKE ITS PEERS. ONE WHO UNDERSTANDS FRIENDSHIP, AND HONOR.
"THAT BROOD CREATURE WE FOUGHT WAS RIGHT. THEY'RE DOING WHAT ALL BEINGS FACED WITH EXTINCTION DO: EVOLVING.
"THEY GROW STRONGER. SOLDIERS DEVELOP INTO QUEENS, ABLE TO LAY EGGS. BUT THERE ARE OTHER TYPES OF EVOLUTION AS WELL.
"SUCH AS DEVELOPING COMPASSION. THE ABILITY TO COOPERATE WITH OTHER BEINGS. TO CARE ABOUT THEM, MAKING IT POSSIBLE TO COEXIST.
"BEFORE HE TURNED ON US, OUR FORMER COLLEAGUE, BISHOP, TOLD ME THAT IN HIS FUTURE, THERE IS A BENIGN RACE OF BROOD IN THE UNIVERSE.
"IF WE MAKE THIS COMPASSIONATE BROOD CREATURE THE NEW TEMPLATE FOR A BROOD HIVE-MIND... WE COULD CREATE THAT RACE."
I HAVE TO ADMIT, THAT'S NOT COMPLETELY INSANE. ONE THING: WE DON'T NEED TO FIND THIS FRIEND OF THE HULK'S.
THERE'S A BROOD CREATURE WITH COMPASSION RIGHT HERE ON THIS SPACE STATION.
WHAT?!

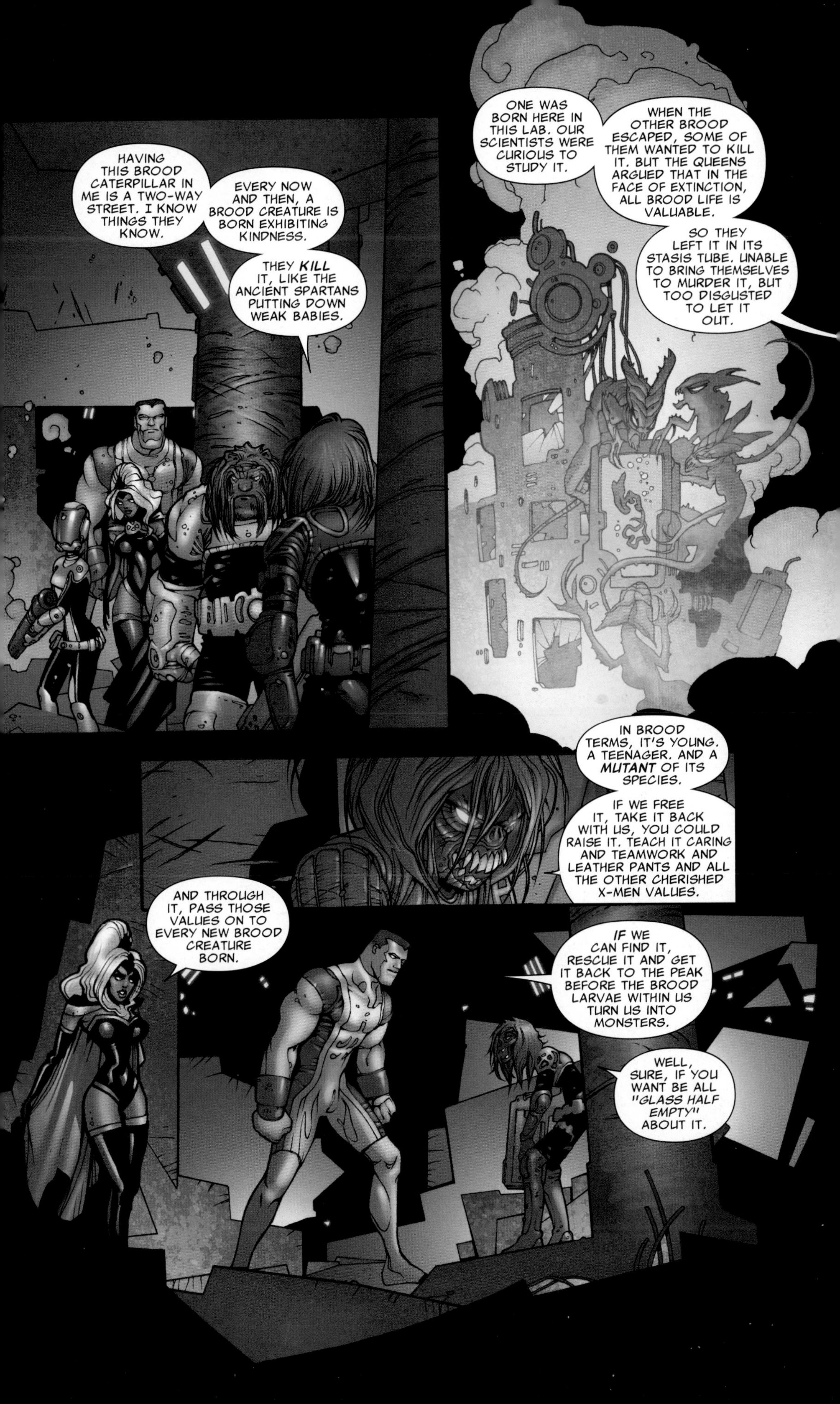
HAVING THIS BROOD CATERPILLAR IN ME IS A TWO-WAY STREET. I KNOW THINGS THEY KNOW.
EVERY NOW AND THEN, A BROOD CREATURE IS BORN EXHIBITING KINDNESS.
THEY KILL IT, LIKE THE ANCIENT SPARTANS PUTTING DOWN WEAK BABIES.
ONE WAS BORN HERE IN THIS LAB. OUR SCIENTISTS WERE CURIOUS TO STUDY IT.
WHEN THE OTHER BROOD ESCAPED, SOME OF THEM WANTED TO KILL IT. BUT THE QUEENS ARGUED THAT IN THE FACE OF EXTINCTION, ALL BROOD LIFE IS VALUABLE.
SO THEY LEFT IT IN ITS STASIS TUBE. UNABLE TO BRING THEMSELVES TO MURDER IT, BUT TOO DISGUSTED TO LET IT OUT.
IN BROOD TERMS, IT'S YOUNG. A TEENAGER. AND A MUTANT OF ITS SPECIES.
IF WE FREE IT, TAKE IT BACK WITH US, YOU COULD RAISE IT. TEACH IT CARING AND TEAMWORK AND LEATHER PANTS AND ALL THE OTHER CHERISHED X-MEN VALUES.
AND THROUGH IT, PASS THOSE VALUES ON TO EVERY NEW BROOD CREATURE BORN.
IF WE CAN FIND IT, RESCUE IT AND GET IT BACK TO THE PEAK BEFORE THE BROOD LARVAE WITHIN US TURN US INTO MONSTERS.
WELL, SURE, IF YOU WANT BE ALL "GLASS HALF EMPTY" ABOUT IT.

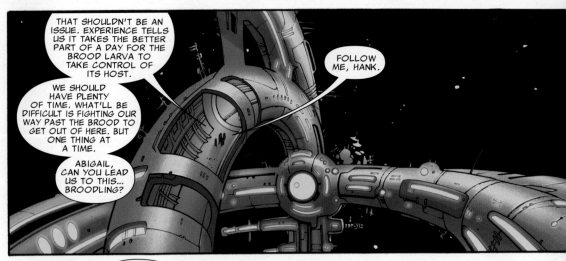

THAT SHOULDN'T BE AN ISSUE. EXPERIENCE TELLS US IT TAKES THE BETTER PART OF A DAY FOR THE BROOD LARVA TO TAKE CONTROL OF ITS HOST.

FOLLOW ME, HANK.

WE SHOULD HAVE PLENTY OF TIME. WHAT'LL BE DIFFICULT IS FIGHTING OUR WAY PAST THE BROOD TO GET OUT OF HERE. BUT ONE THING AT A TIME.

ABIGAIL, CAN YOU LEAD US TO THIS... BROODLING?

I SEE IT, JUST AHEAD... STILL IN STASIS.

THAT MIGHT JUST MEAN IT SAYS "THANK YOU" BEFORE CHOWING DOWN ON YOUR SPLEEN.

OKAY, BEFORE WE DO SOMETHING WE'LL REGRET... LET'S REMEMBER THIS IS A BROOD CREATURE. IT'S COMPASSIONATE BY THE STANDARDS OF A BROOD CREATURE.

DO NOT WORRY, KATYA. IF IT IS HOSTILE, WE ARE MORE THAN A MATCH FOR A SINGLE YOUTH.

I GUESS...

UGH. EVEN WITHOUT A SOLID NOSE, THE SMELL MAKES ME WANT TO HURL.

GET READY, PEOPLE. THEY USUALLY GO FOR THE THROAT...

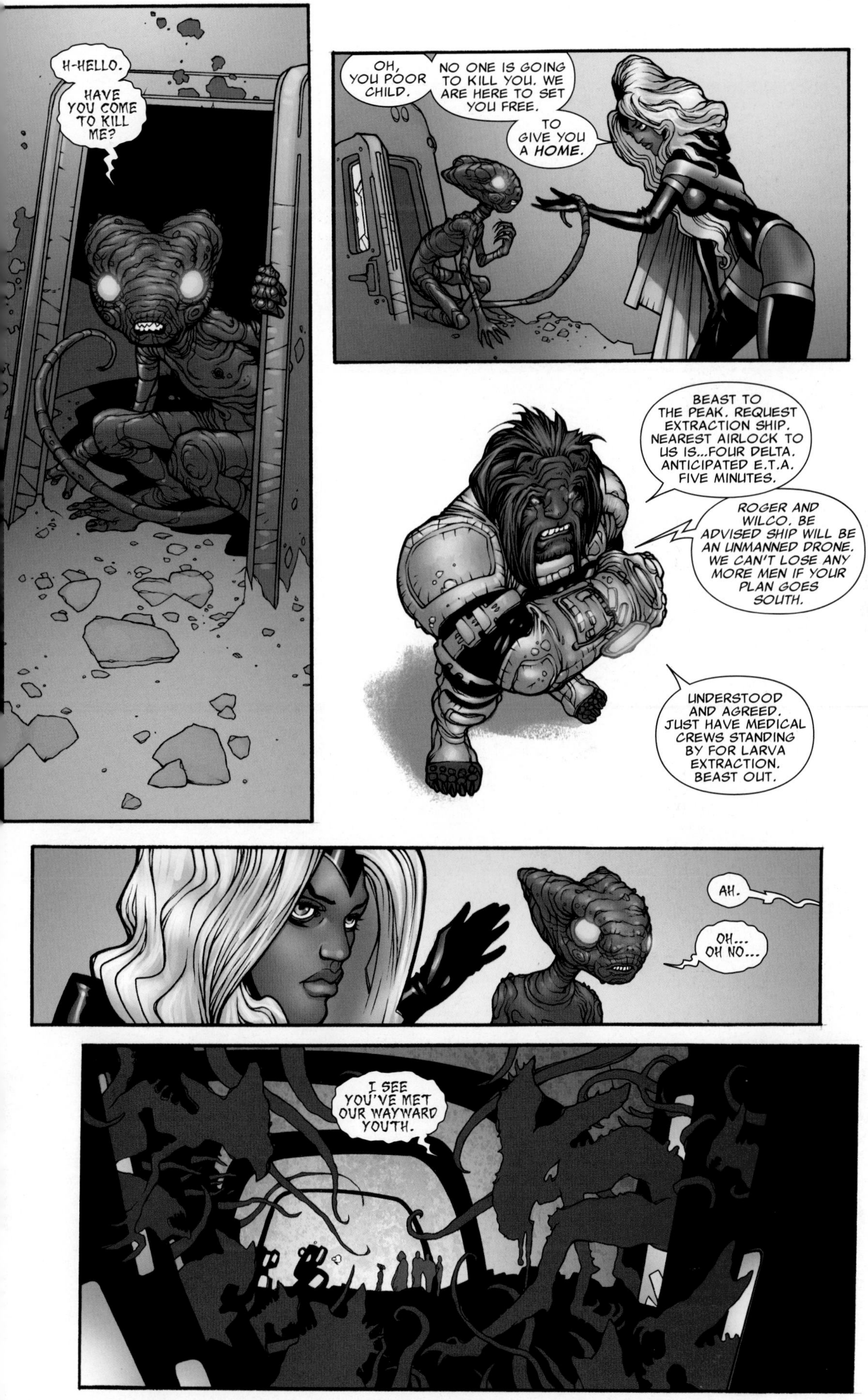
H-HELLO.
HAVE YOU COME TO KILL ME?
OH, YOU POOR CHILD.
NO ONE IS GOING TO KILL YOU. WE ARE HERE TO SET YOU FREE.
TO GIVE YOU A HOME.
BEAST TO THE PEAK. REQUEST EXTRACTION SHIP. NEAREST AIRLOCK TO US IS...FOUR DELTA. ANTICIPATED E.T.A. FIVE MINUTES.
ROGER AND WILCO. BE ADVISED SHIP WILL BE AN UNMANNED DRONE. WE CAN'T LOSE ANY MORE MEN IF YOUR PLAN GOES SOUTH.
UNDERSTOOD AND AGREED. JUST HAVE MEDICAL CREWS STANDING BY FOR LARVA EXTRACTION. BEAST OUT.
AH.
OH... OH NO...
I SEE YOU'VE MET OUR WAYWARD YOUTH.

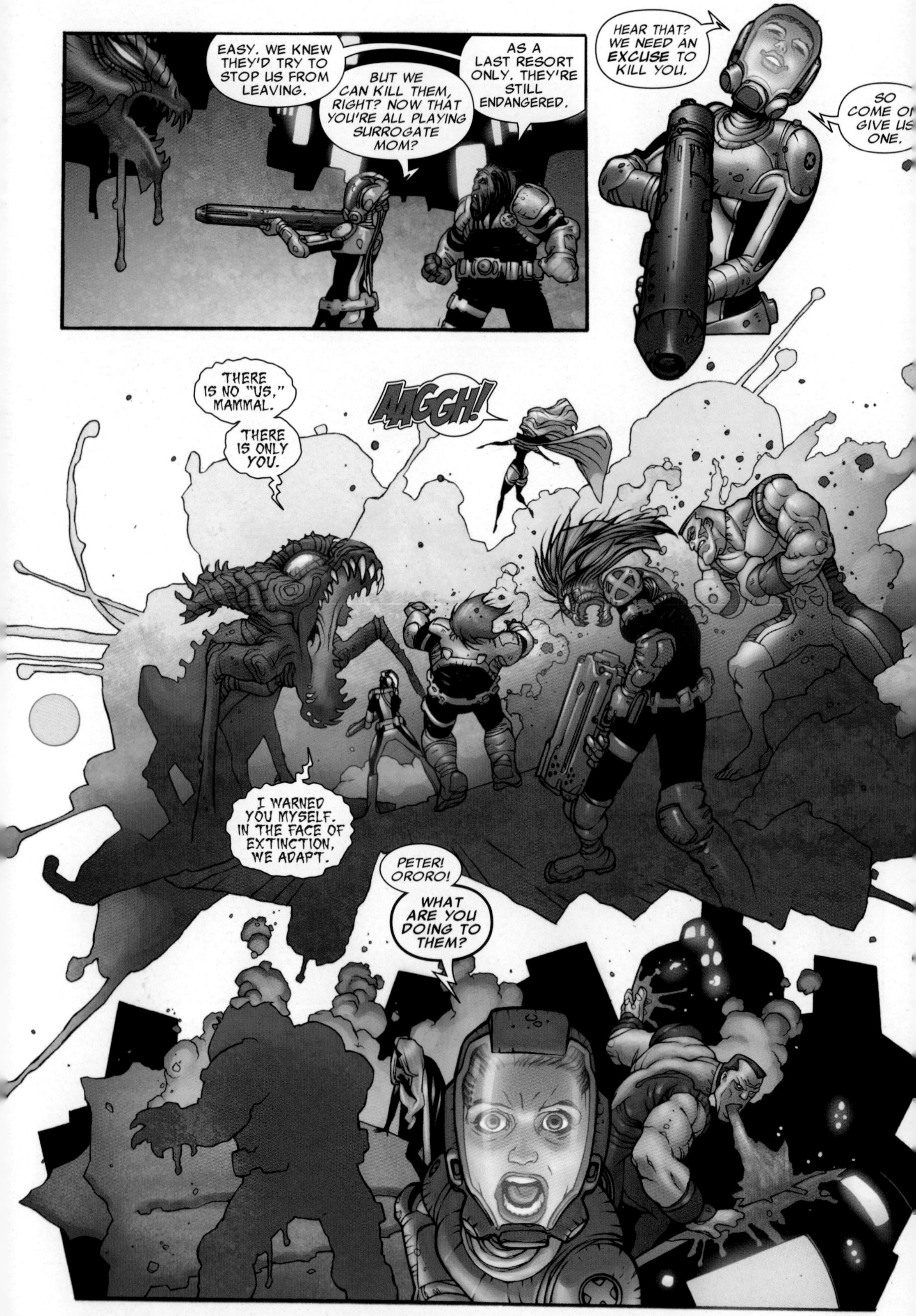
EASY. WE KNEW THEY'D TRY TO STOP US FROM LEAVING.
BUT WE CAN KILL THEM, RIGHT? NOW THAT YOU'RE ALL PLAYING SURROGATE MOM?
AS A LAST RESORT ONLY. THEY'RE STILL ENDANGERED.
HEAR THAT? WE NEED AN EXCUSE TO KILL YOU.
SO COME ON GIVE US ONE.
THERE IS NO "US," MAMMAL.
THERE IS ONLY YOU.
AAGGH!
I WARNED YOU MYSELF. IN THE FACE OF EXTINCTION, WE ADAPT.
PETER! ORORO!
WHAT ARE YOU DOING TO THEM?

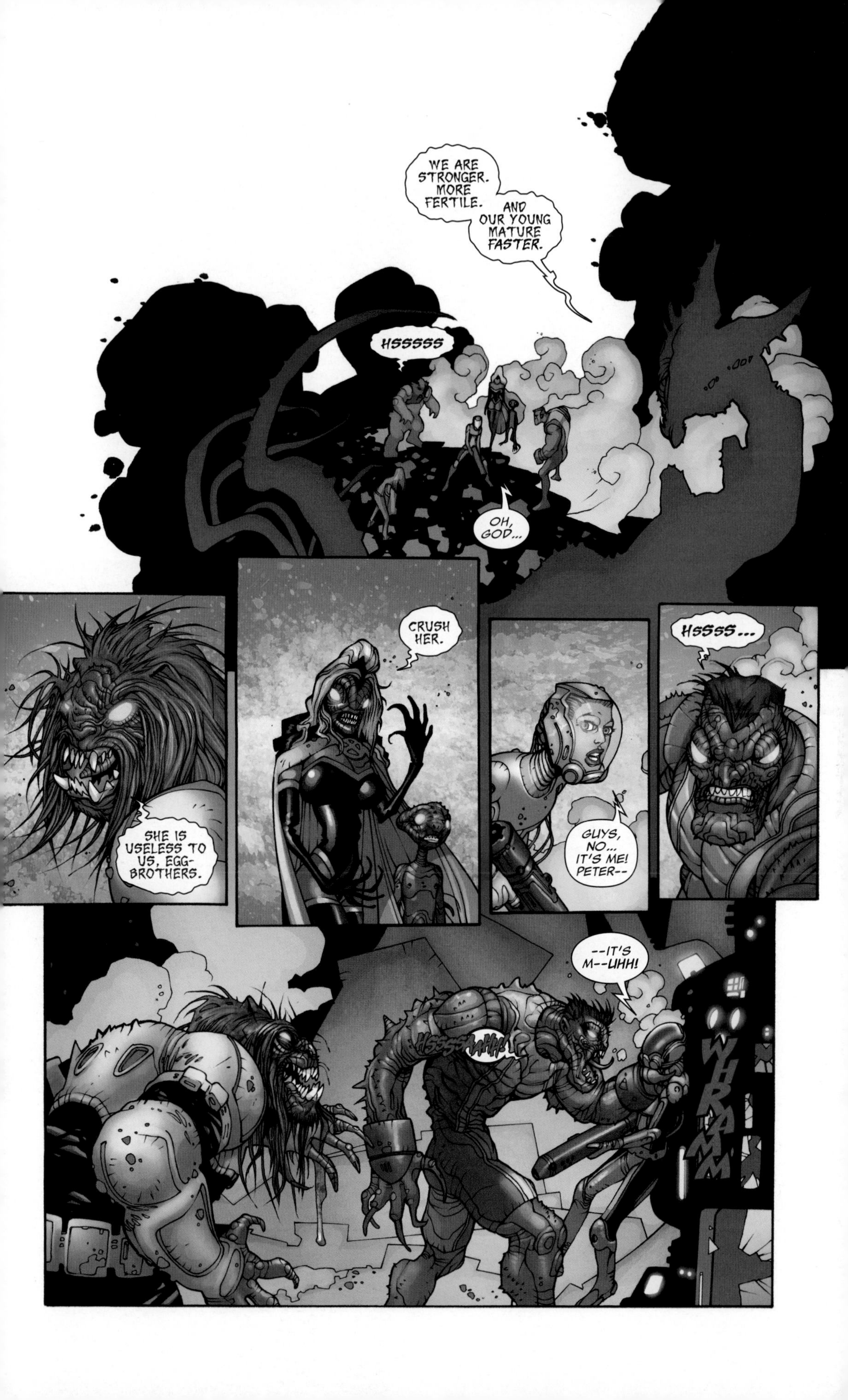
WE ARE STRONGER. MORE FERTILE.
AND OUR YOUNG MATURE FASTER.
HSSSSS
OH, GOD...
SHE IS USELESS TO US, EGG-BROTHERS.
CRUSH HER.
GUYS, NO... IT'S ME! PETER--
HSSSS...
--IT'S M--UHH!
HSSSSAHHH!
WHRRMM

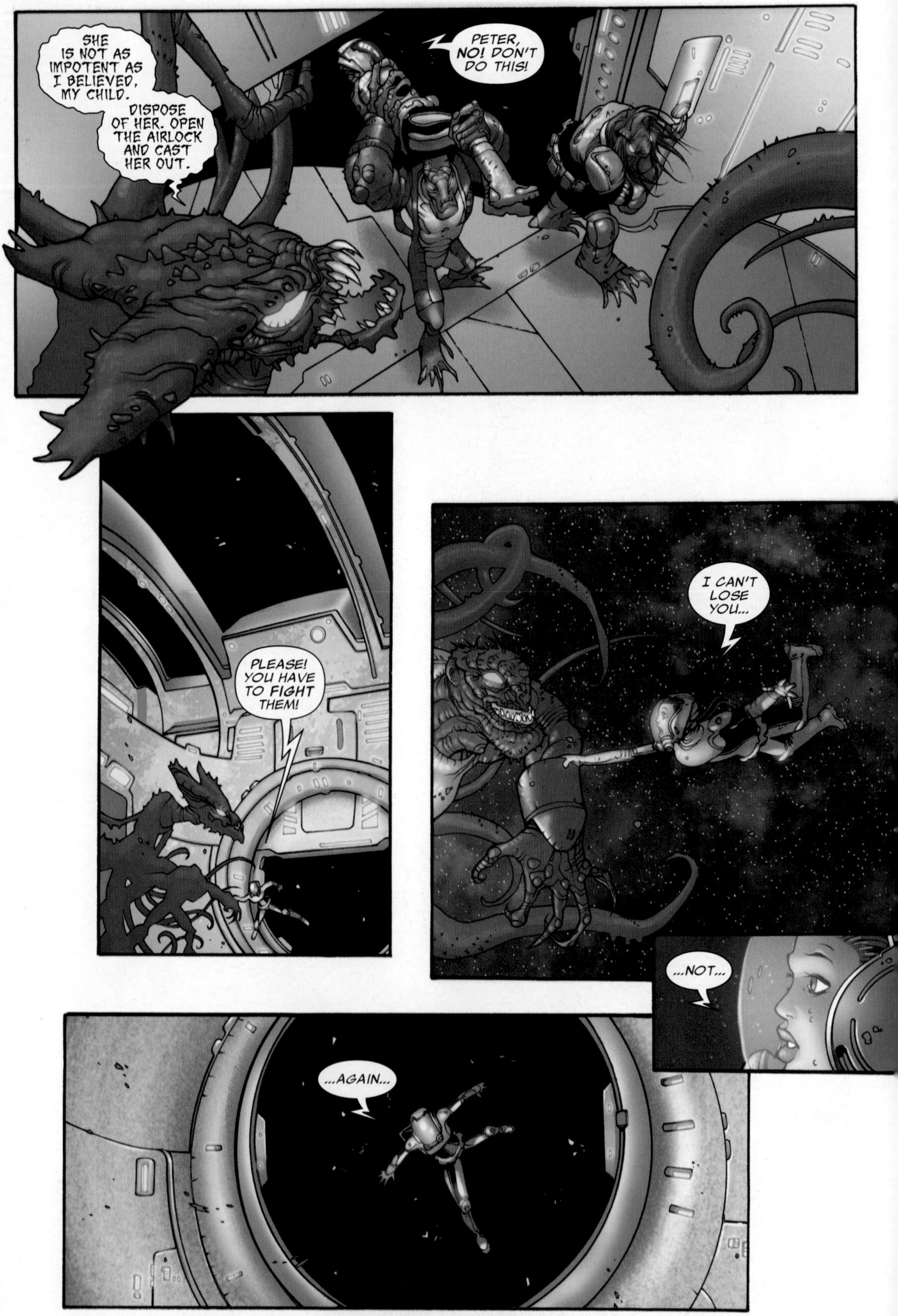
SHE IS NOT AS IMPOTENT AS I BELIEVED, MY CHILD.
DISPOSE OF HER. OPEN THE AIRLOCK AND CAST HER OUT.
PETER, NO! DON'T DO THIS!
PLEASE! YOU HAVE TO FIGHT THEM!
I CAN'T LOSE YOU...
...NOT...
...AGAIN...

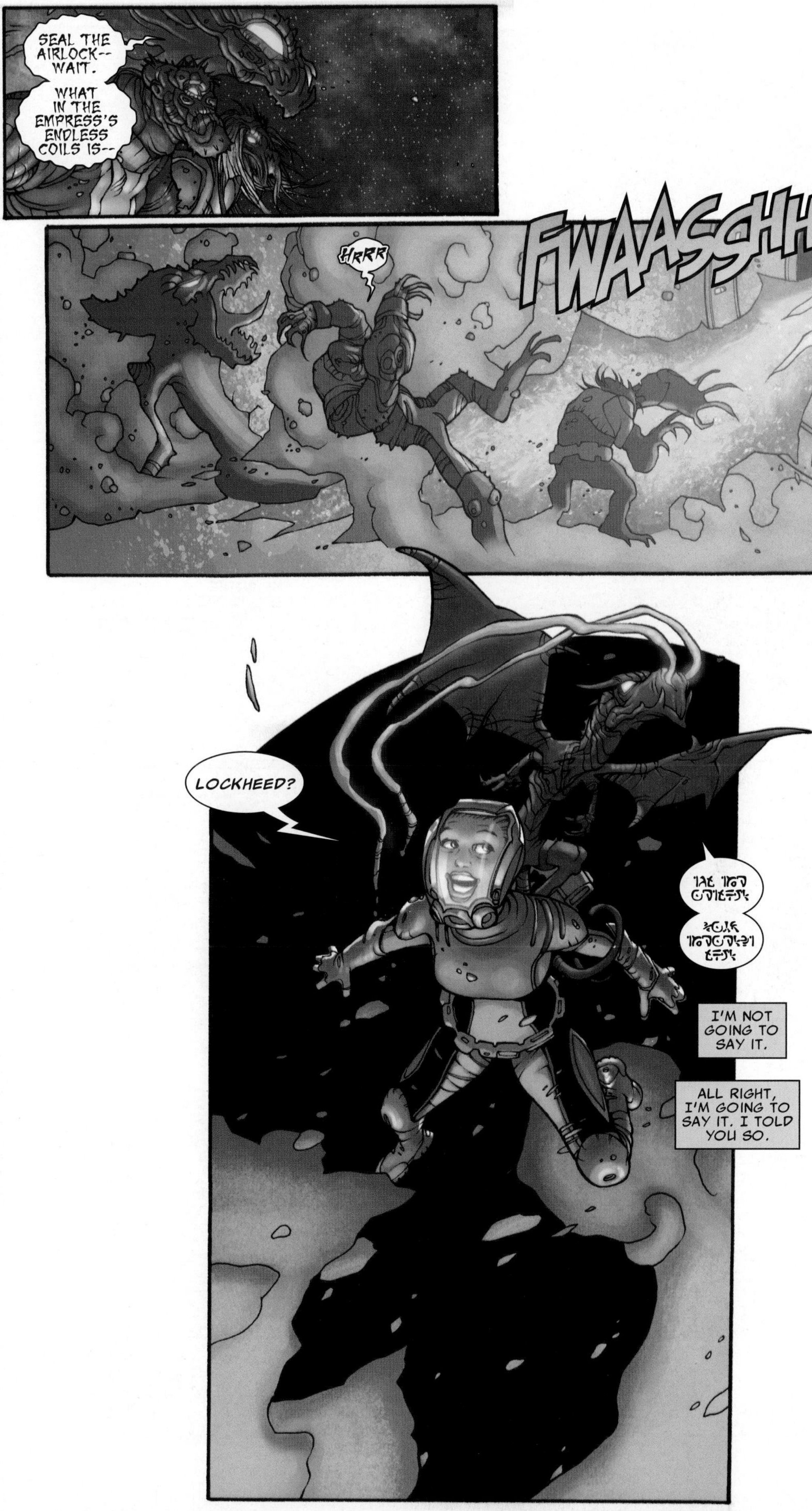
SEAL THE AIRLOCK-- WAIT.
WHAT IN THE EMPRESS'S ENDLESS COILS IS--
FWAASSHH
HRRR
LOCKHEED?
I'M NOT GOING TO SAY IT.
ALL RIGHT, I'M GOING TO SAY IT. I TOLD YOU SO.

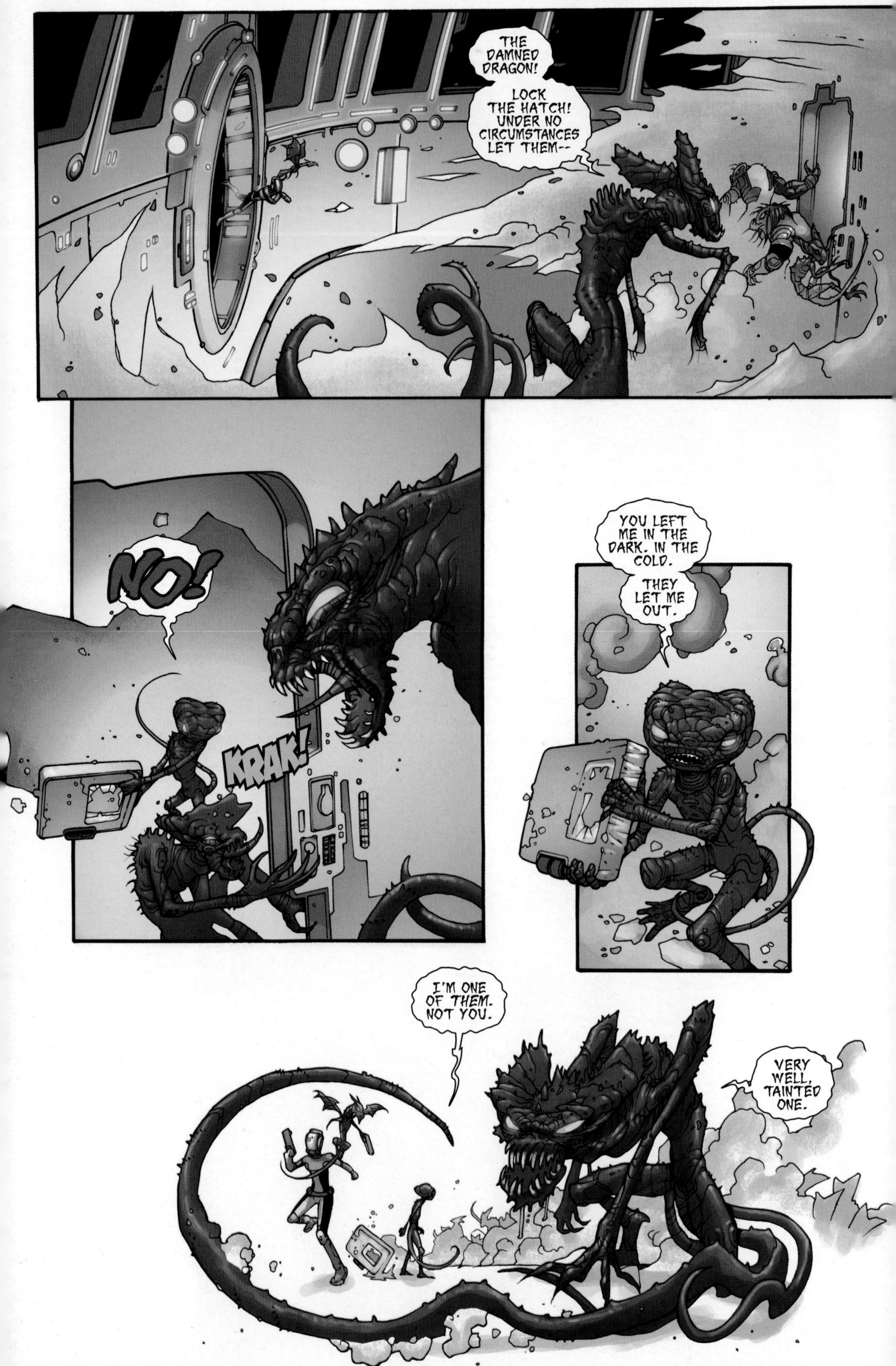
THE DAMNED DRAGON!
LOCK THE HATCH! UNDER NO CIRCUMSTANCES LET THEM--
NO!
KRAK!
YOU LEFT ME IN THE DARK. IN THE COLD.
THEY LET ME OUT.
I'M ONE OF THEM. NOT YOU.
VERY WELL, TAINTED ONE.

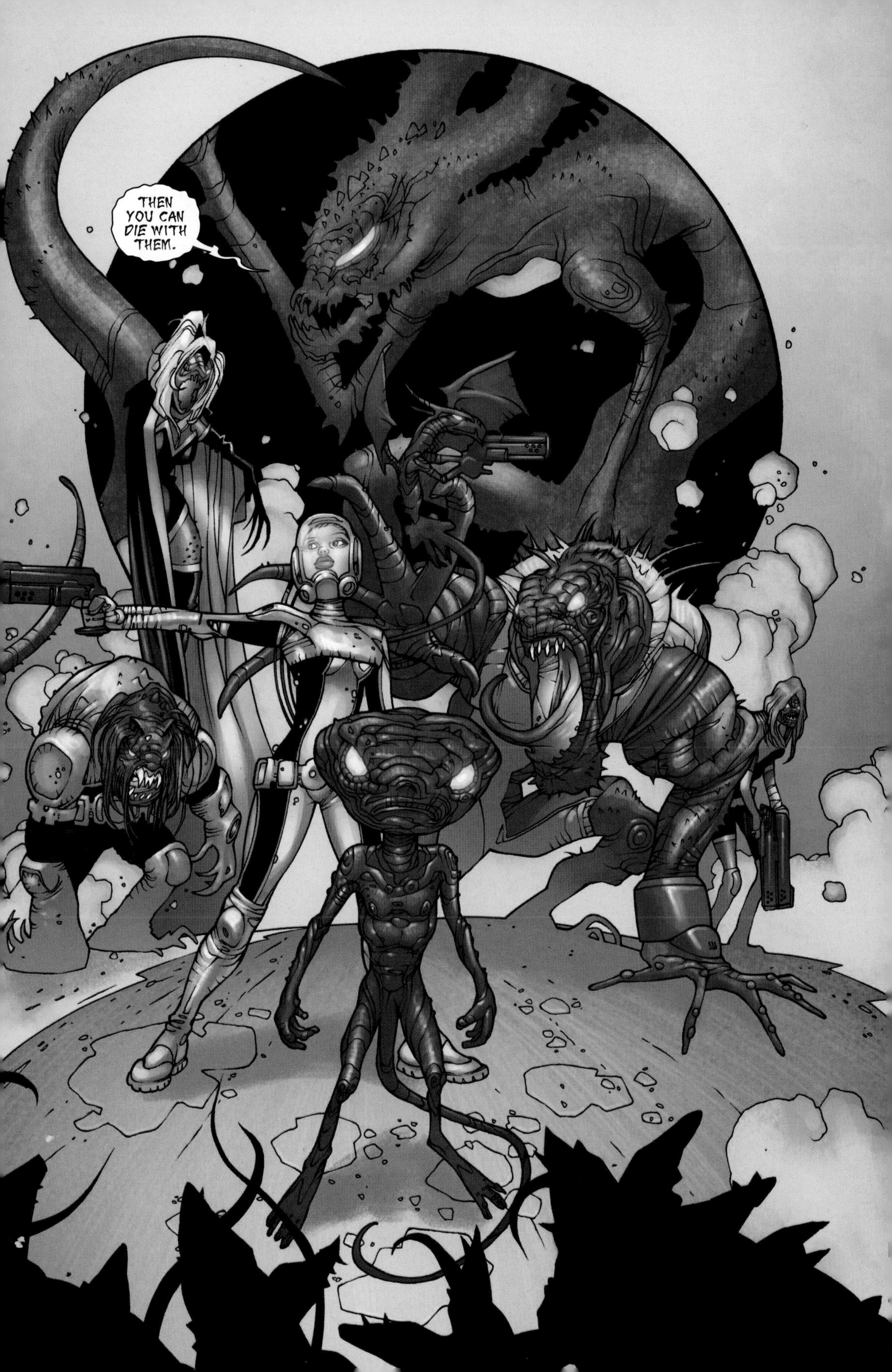
THEN YOU CAN DIE WITH THEM.

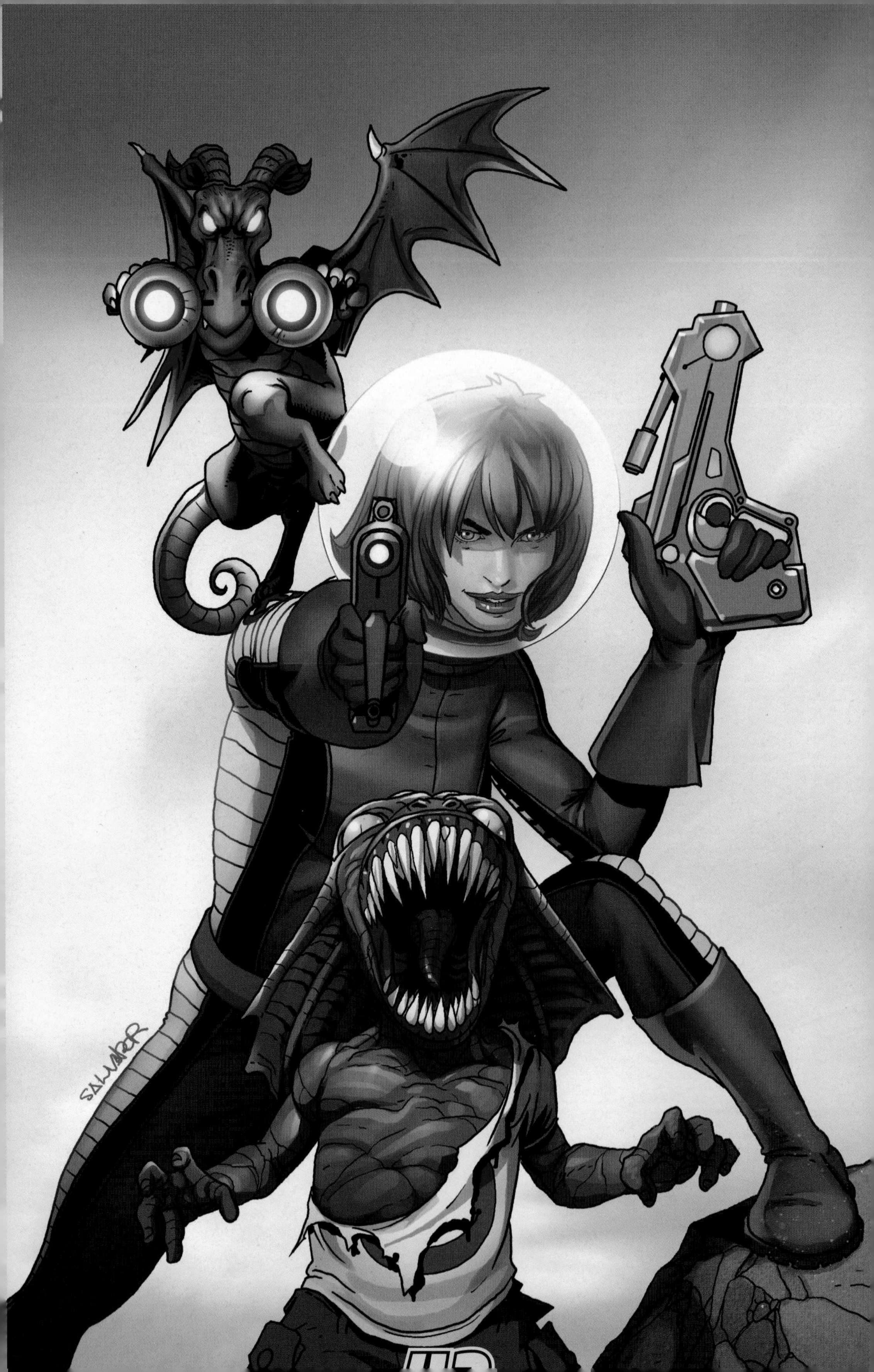

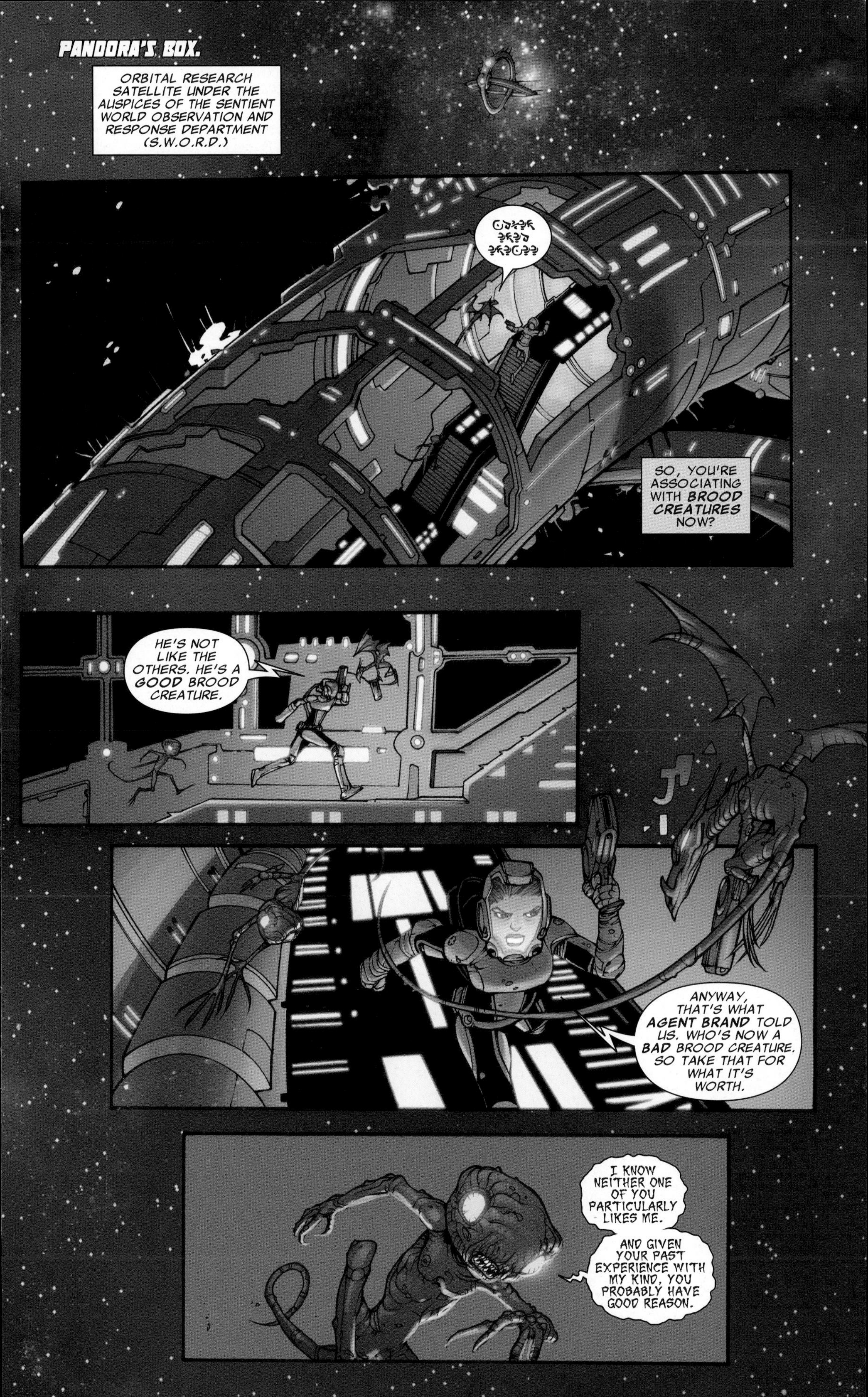
PANDORA'S BOX.
ORBITAL RESEARCH SATELLITE UNDER THE AUSPICES OF THE SENTIENT WORLD OBSERVATION AND RESPONSE DEPARTMENT (S.W.O.R.D.)
SO, YOU'RE ASSOCIATING WITH BROOD CREATURES NOW?
HE'S NOT LIKE THE OTHERS. HE'S A GOOD BROOD CREATURE.
ANYWAY, THAT'S WHAT AGENT BRAND TOLD US. WHO'S NOW A BAD BROOD CREATURE. SO TAKE THAT FOR WHAT IT'S WORTH.
I KNOW NEITHER ONE OF YOU PARTICULARLY LIKES ME.
AND GIVEN YOUR PAST EXPERIENCE WITH MY KIND, YOU PROBABLY HAVE GOOD REASON.

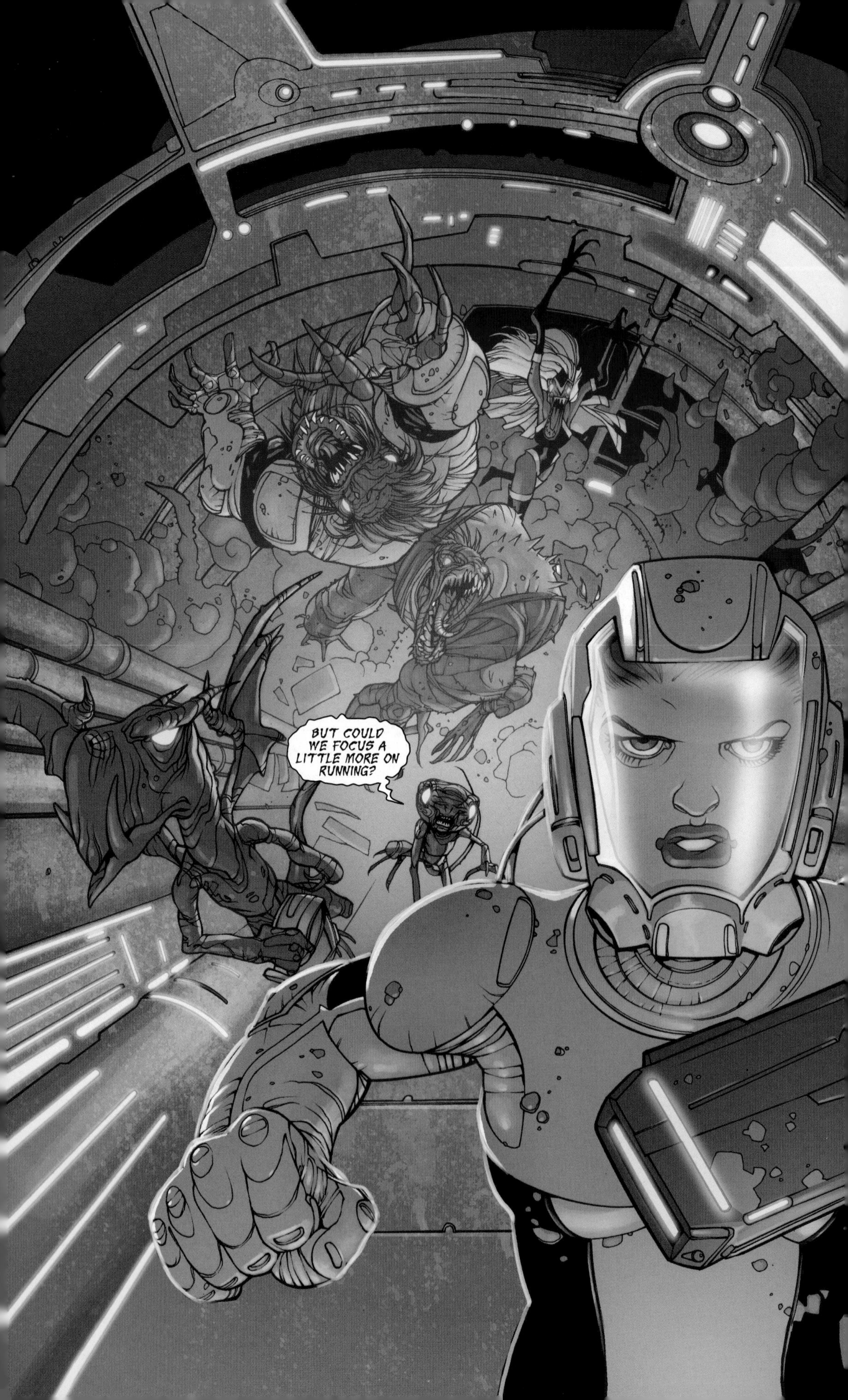
BUT COULD WE FOCUS A LITTLE MORE ON RUNNING?

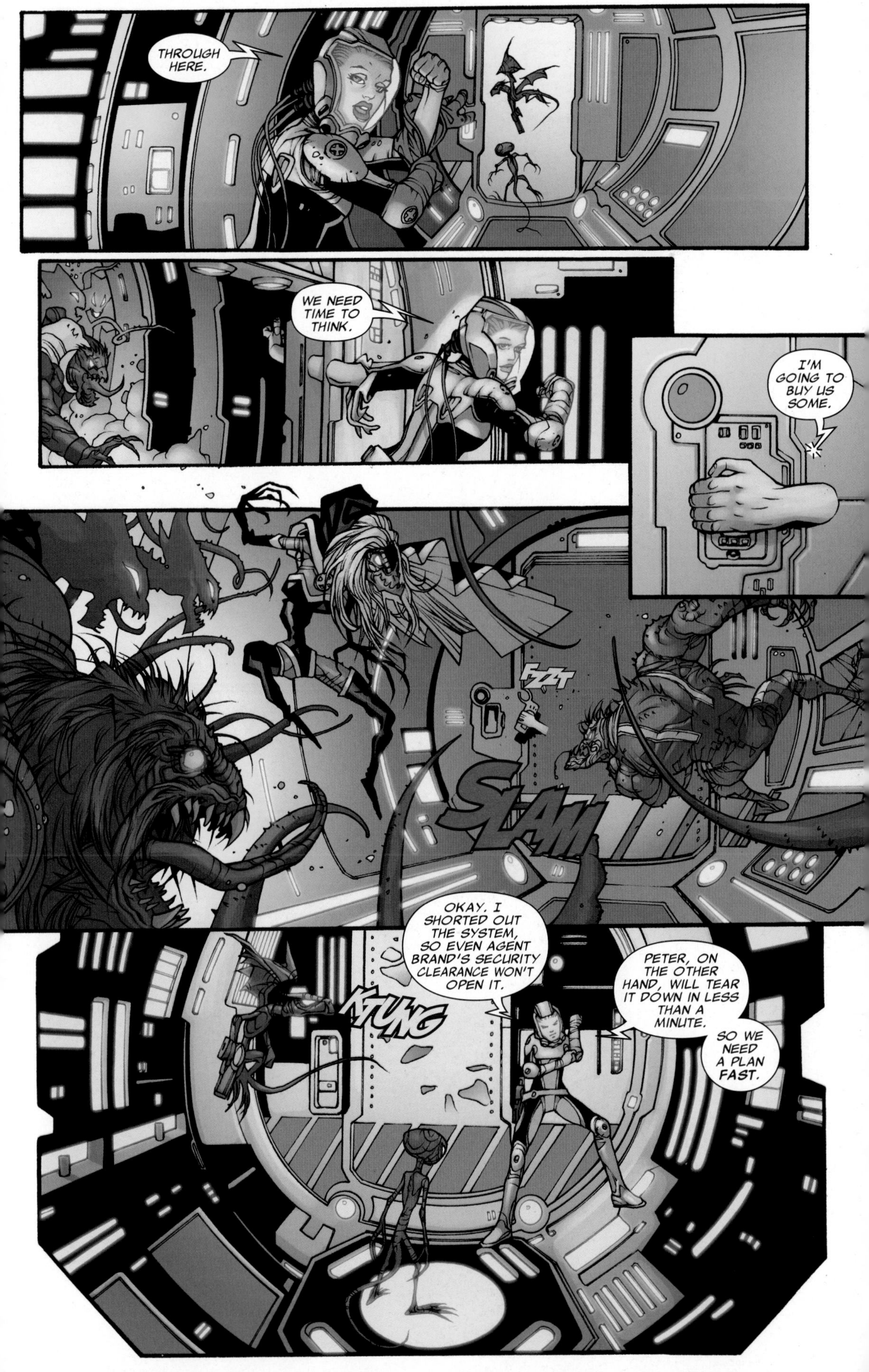
THROUGH HERE.
WE NEED TIME TO THINK.
I'M GOING TO BUY US SOME.
FZZT
SLAM
OKAY. I SHORTED OUT THE SYSTEM, SO EVEN AGENT BRAND'S SECURITY CLEARANCE WON'T OPEN IT.
KTUNG
PETER, ON THE OTHER HAND, WILL TEAR IT DOWN IN LESS THAN A MINUTE.
SO WE NEED A PLAN FAST.

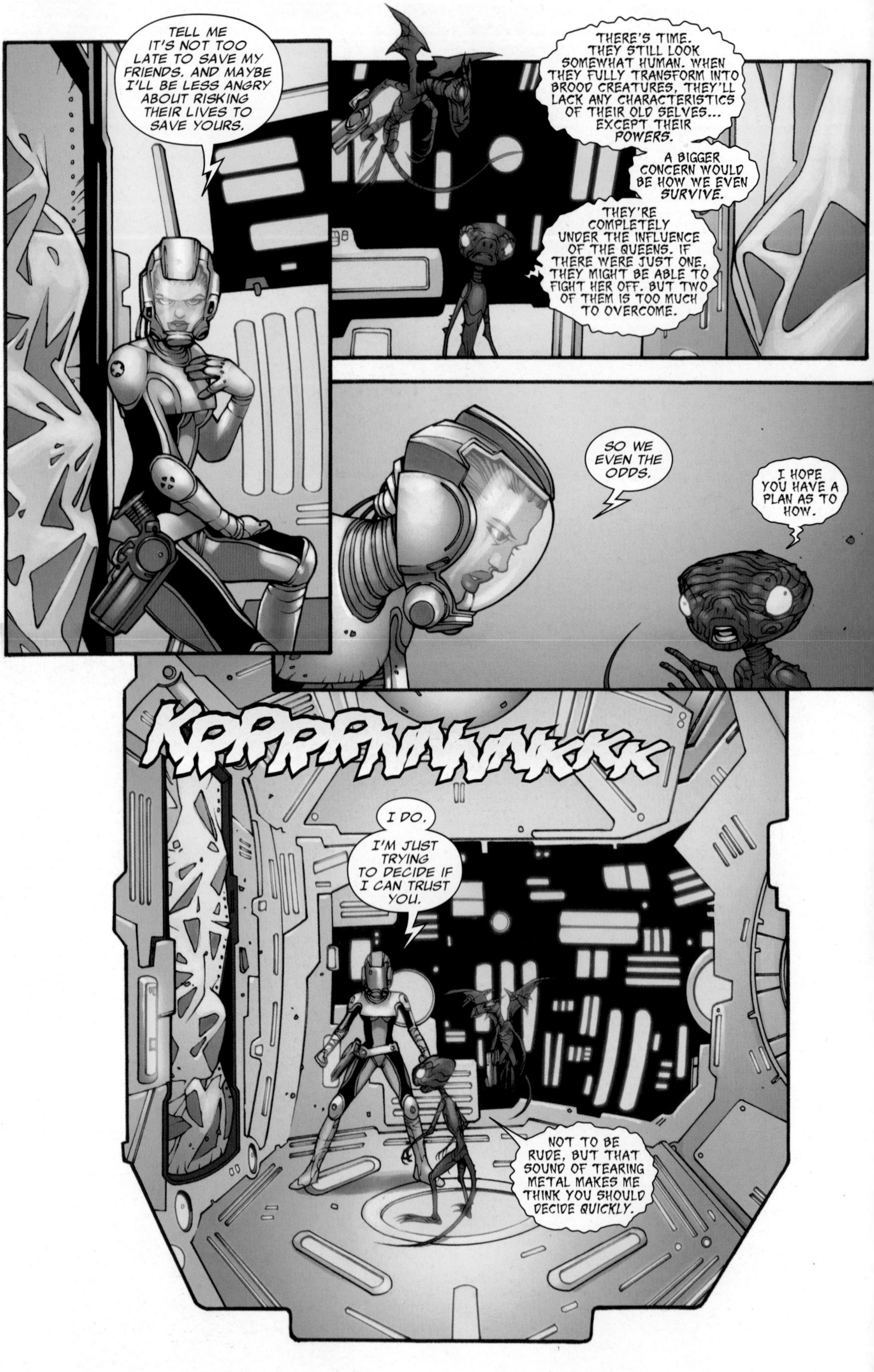
TELL ME IT'S NOT TOO LATE TO SAVE MY FRIENDS. AND MAYBE I'LL BE LESS ANGRY ABOUT RISKING THEIR LIVES TO SAVE YOURS.
THERE'S TIME. THEY STILL LOOK SOMEWHAT HUMAN. WHEN THEY FULLY TRANSFORM INTO BROOD CREATURES, THEY'LL LACK ANY CHARACTERISTICS OF THEIR OLD SELVES... EXCEPT THEIR POWERS.
A BIGGER CONCERN WOULD BE HOW WE EVEN SURVIVE.
THEY'RE COMPLETELY UNDER THE INFLUENCE OF THE QUEENS. IF THERE WERE JUST ONE, THEY MIGHT BE ABLE TO FIGHT HER OFF. BUT TWO OF THEM IS TOO MUCH TO OVERCOME.
SO WE EVEN THE ODDS.
I HOPE YOU HAVE A PLAN AS TO HOW.
KRRRRNNNNKKK
I DO.
I'M JUST TRYING TO DECIDE IF I CAN TRUST YOU.
NOT TO BE RUDE, BUT THAT SOUND OF TEARING METAL MAKES ME THINK YOU SHOULD DECIDE QUICKLY.

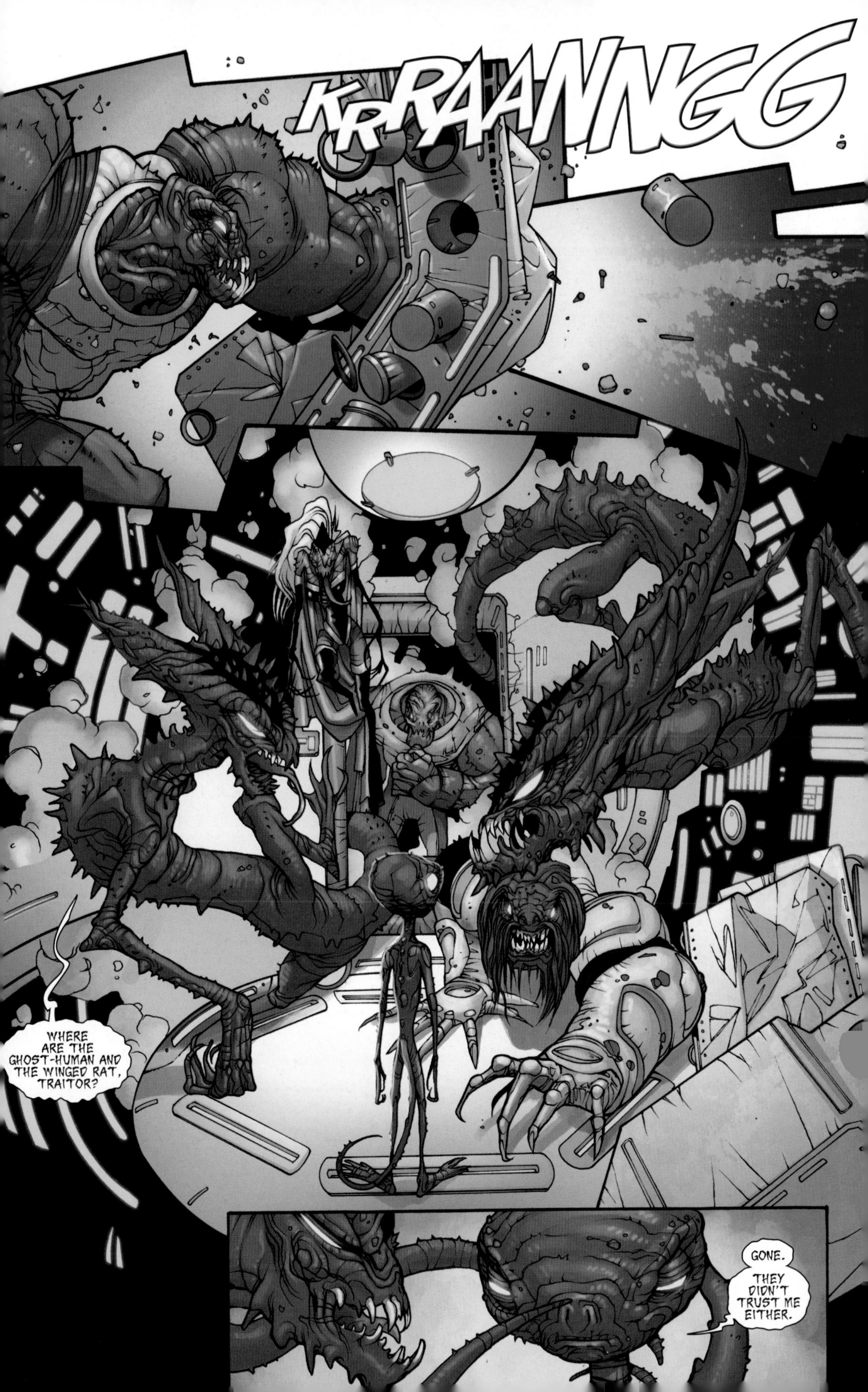
KRRAANNGG
WHERE ARE THE GHOST-HUMAN AND THE WINGED RAT, TRAITOR?
GONE.
THEY DIDN'T TRUST ME EITHER.

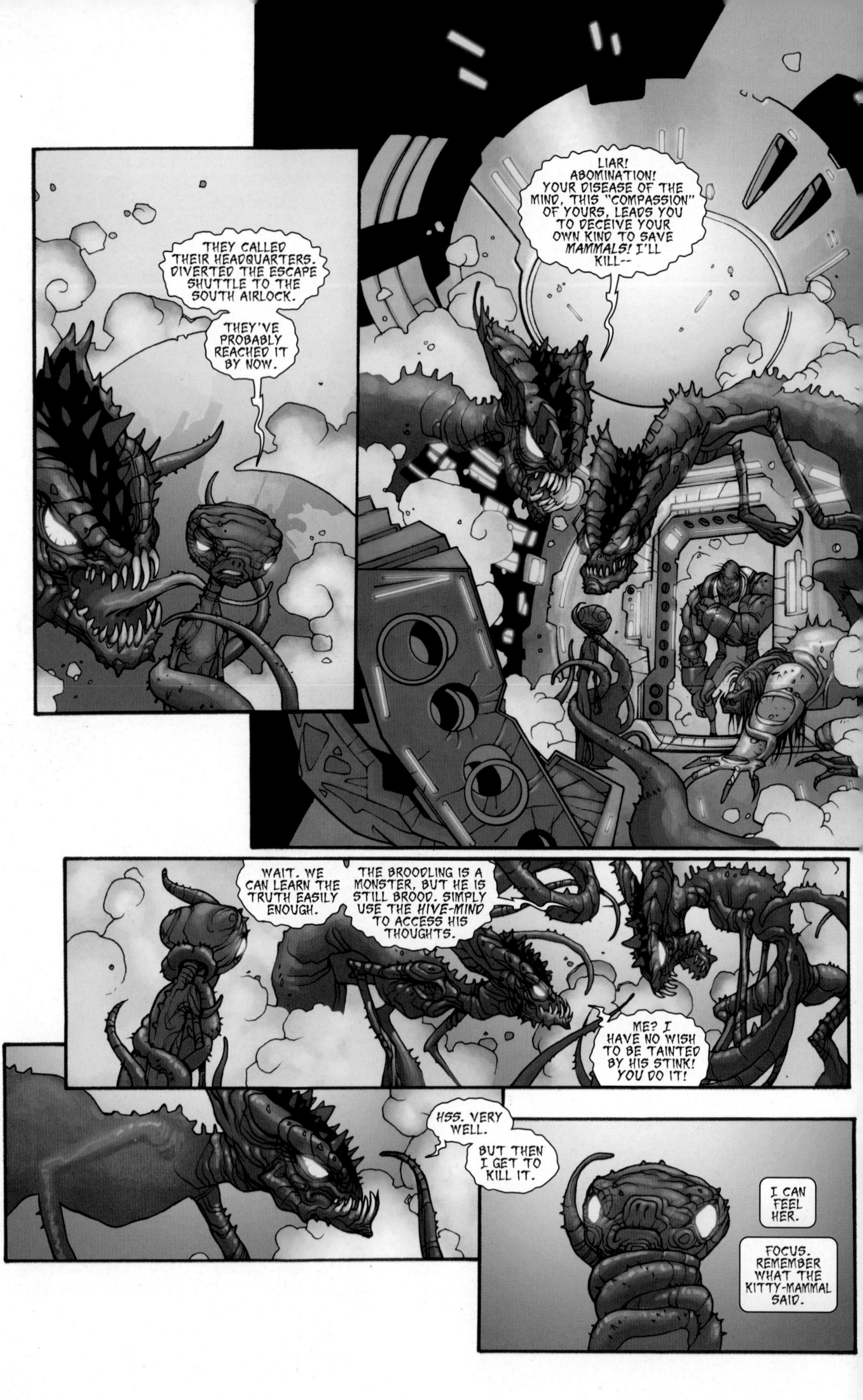
THEY CALLED THEIR HEADQUARTERS. DIVERTED THE ESCAPE SHUTTLE TO THE SOUTH AIRLOCK.
THEY'VE PROBABLY REACHED IT BY NOW.
LIAR! ABOMINATION! YOUR DISEASE OF THE MIND, THIS "COMPASSION" OF YOURS, LEADS YOU TO DECEIVE YOUR OWN KIND TO SAVE MAMMALS! I'LL KILL--
WAIT. WE CAN LEARN THE TRUTH EASILY ENOUGH.
THE BROODLING IS A MONSTER, BUT HE IS STILL BROOD. SIMPLY USE THE HIVE-MIND TO ACCESS HIS THOUGHTS.
ME? I HAVE NO WISH TO BE TAINTED BY HIS STINK! YOU DO IT!
HSS. VERY WELL.
BUT THEN I GET TO KILL IT.
I CAN FEEL HER.
FOCUS. REMEMBER WHAT THE KITTY-MAMMAL SAID.

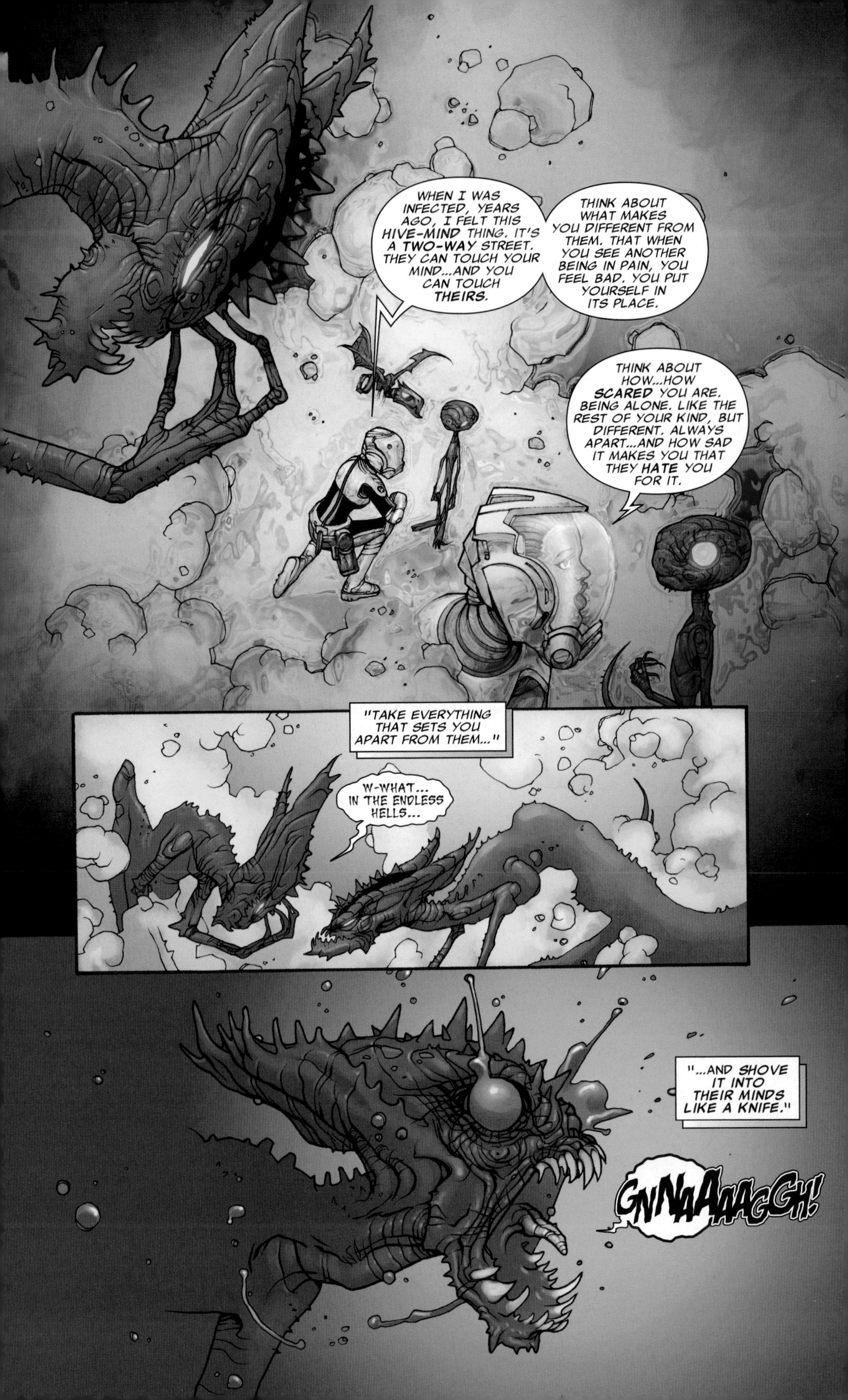
WHEN I WAS INFECTED, YEARS AGO, I FELT THIS HIVE-MIND THING. IT'S A TWO-WAY STREET. THEY CAN TOUCH YOUR MIND...AND YOU CAN TOUCH THEIRS.
THINK ABOUT WHAT MAKES YOU DIFFERENT FROM THEM. THAT WHEN YOU SEE ANOTHER BEING IN PAIN, YOU FEEL BAD. YOU PUT YOURSELF IN ITS PLACE.
THINK ABOUT HOW...HOW SCARED YOU ARE. BEING ALONE. LIKE THE REST OF YOUR KIND, BUT DIFFERENT. ALWAYS APART...AND HOW SAD IT MAKES YOU THAT THEY HATE YOU FOR IT.
"TAKE EVERYTHING THAT SETS YOU APART FROM THEM..."
W-WHAT... IN THE ENDLESS HELLS...
"...AND SHOVE IT INTO THEIR MINDS LIKE A KNIFE."
GNNAAAAGGH!

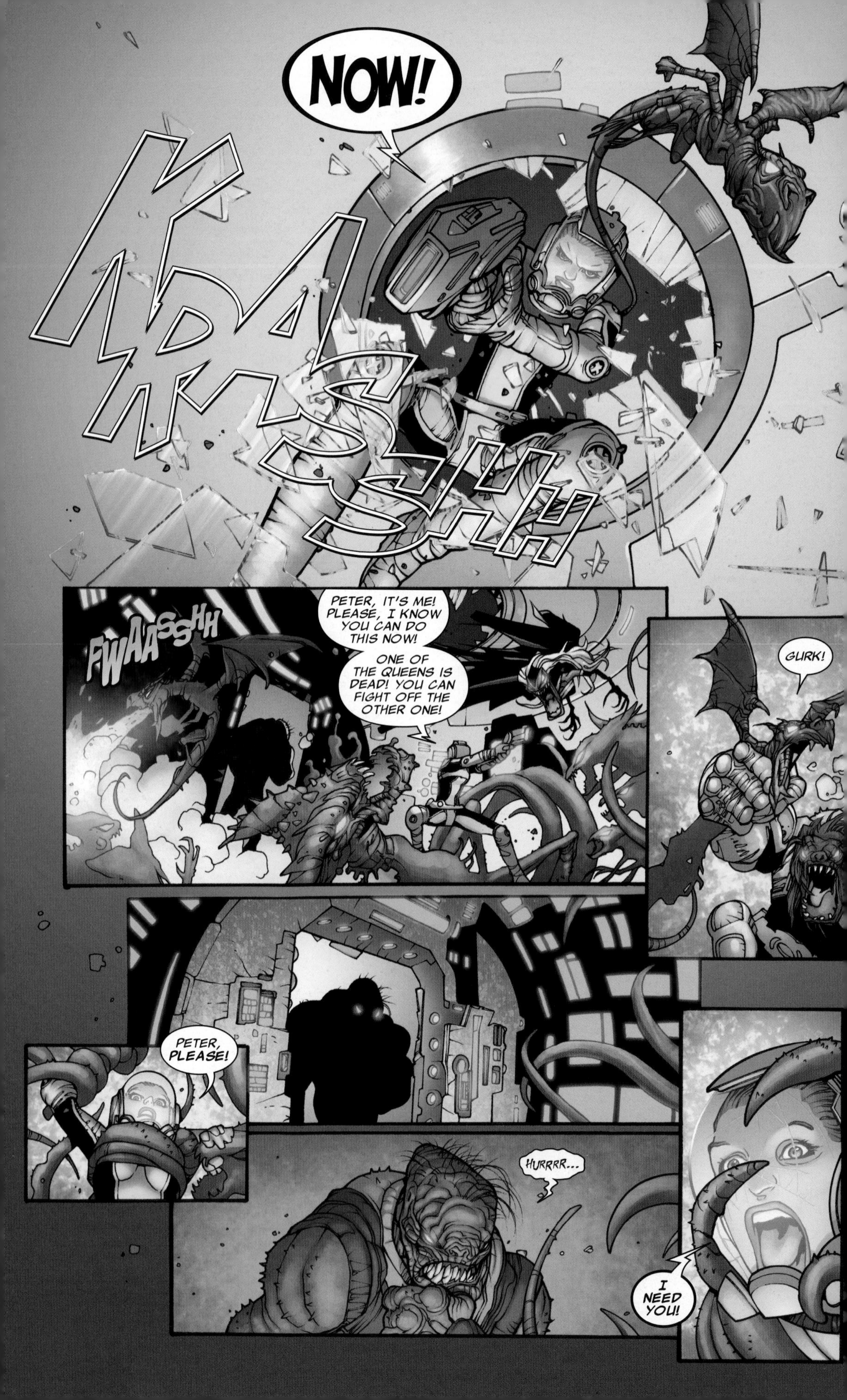
NOW!
KRAASSHH
FWAASSHH
PETER, IT'S ME! PLEASE, I KNOW YOU CAN DO THIS NOW!
ONE OF THE QUEENS IS DEAD! YOU CAN FIGHT OFF THE OTHER ONE!
GURK!
PETER, PLEASE!
HURRRR...
I NEED YOU!

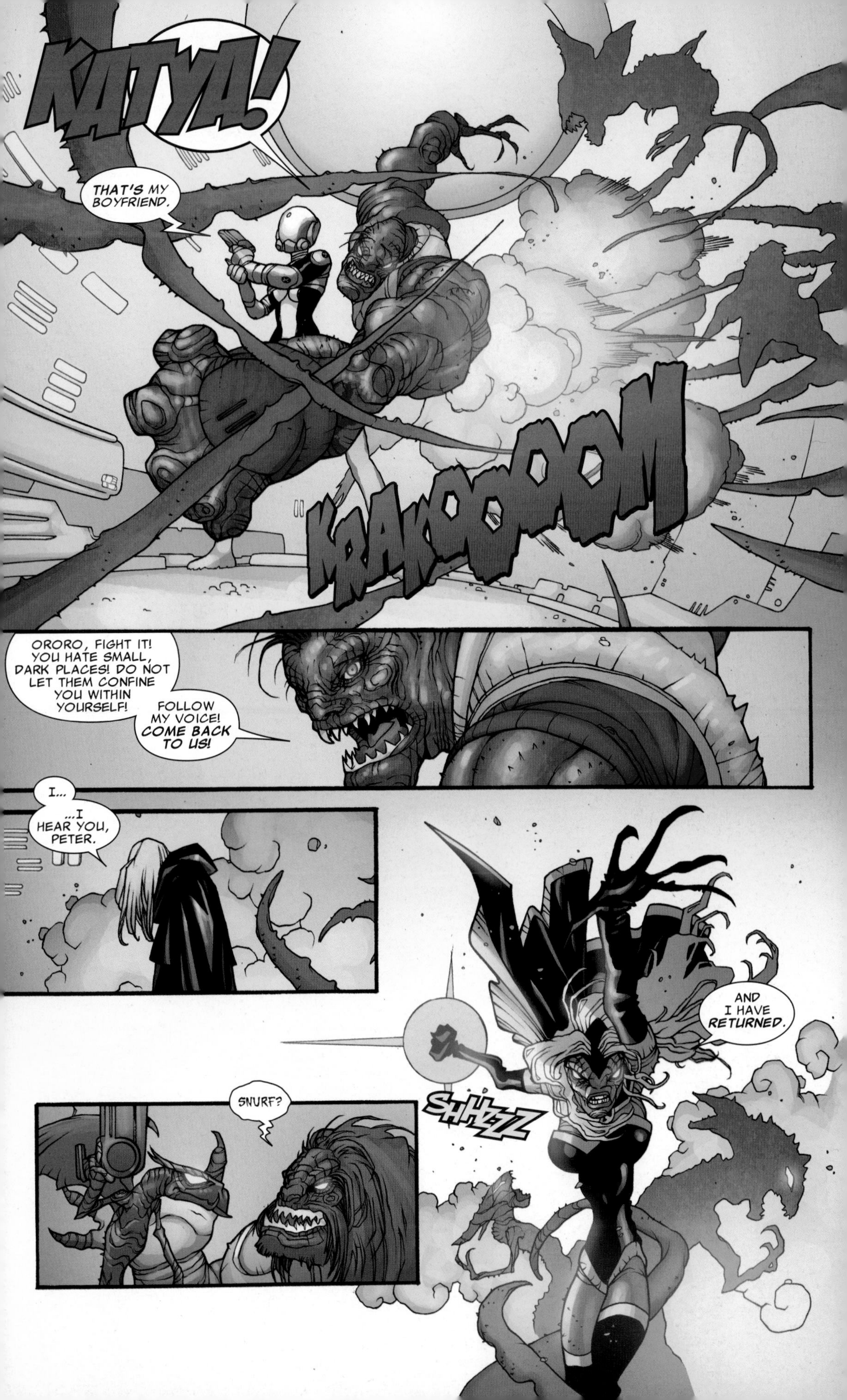
KATYA!
THAT'S MY BOYFRIEND.
KRAKOOOOOM
ORORO, FIGHT IT! YOU HATE SMALL, DARK PLACES! DO NOT LET THEM CONFINE YOU WITHIN YOURSELF!
FOLLOW MY VOICE! COME BACK TO US!
I...
...I HEAR YOU, PETER.
AND I HAVE RETURNED.
SHHZZZ
SNURF?

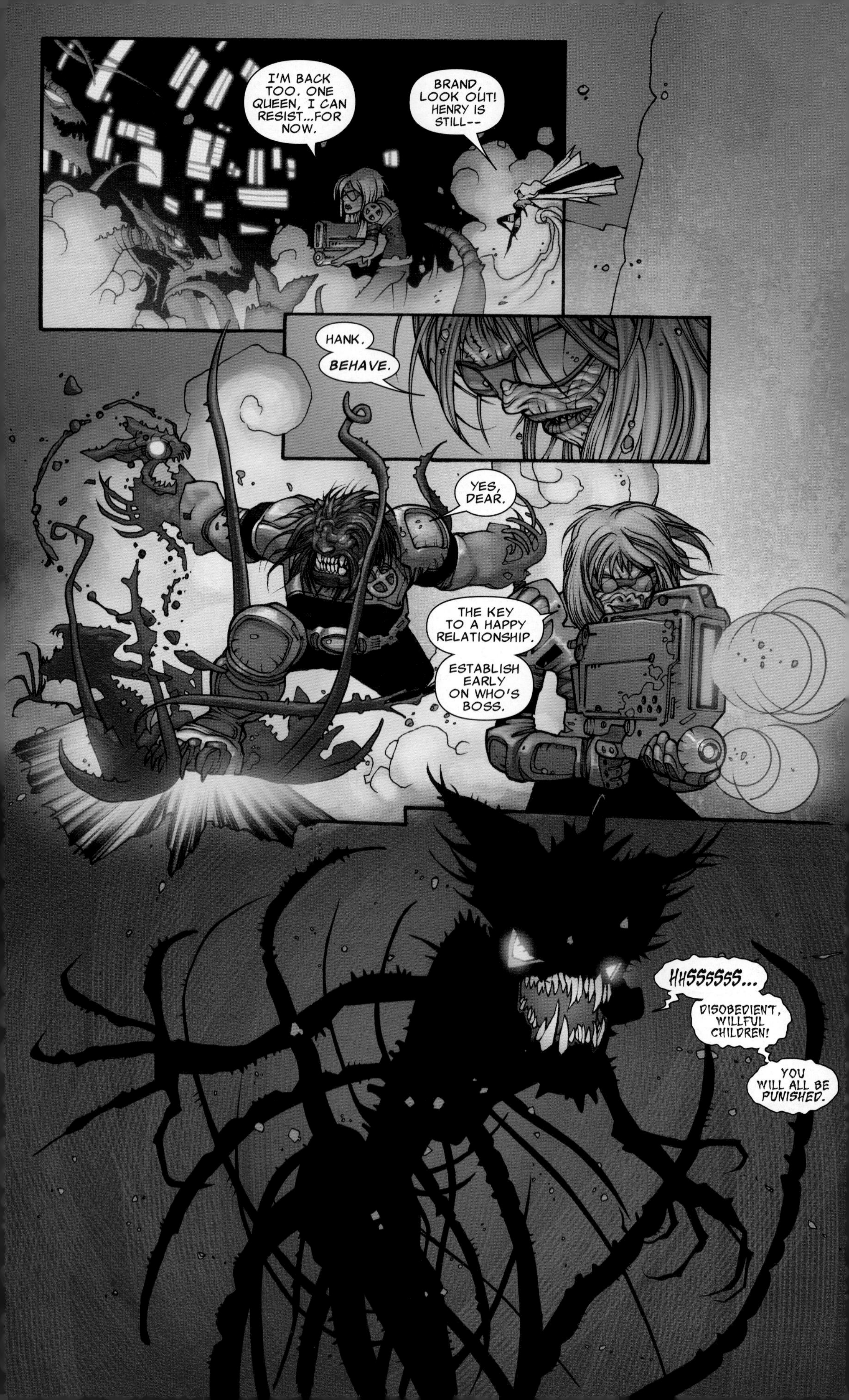
I'M BACK TOO. ONE QUEEN, I CAN RESIST...FOR NOW.
BRAND, LOOK OUT! HENRY IS STILL--
HANK.
BEHAVE.
YES, DEAR.
THE KEY TO A HAPPY RELATIONSHIP.
ESTABLISH EARLY ON WHO'S BOSS.
HHSSSSSS...
DISOBEDIENT, WILLFUL CHILDREN!
YOU WILL ALL BE PUNISHED.

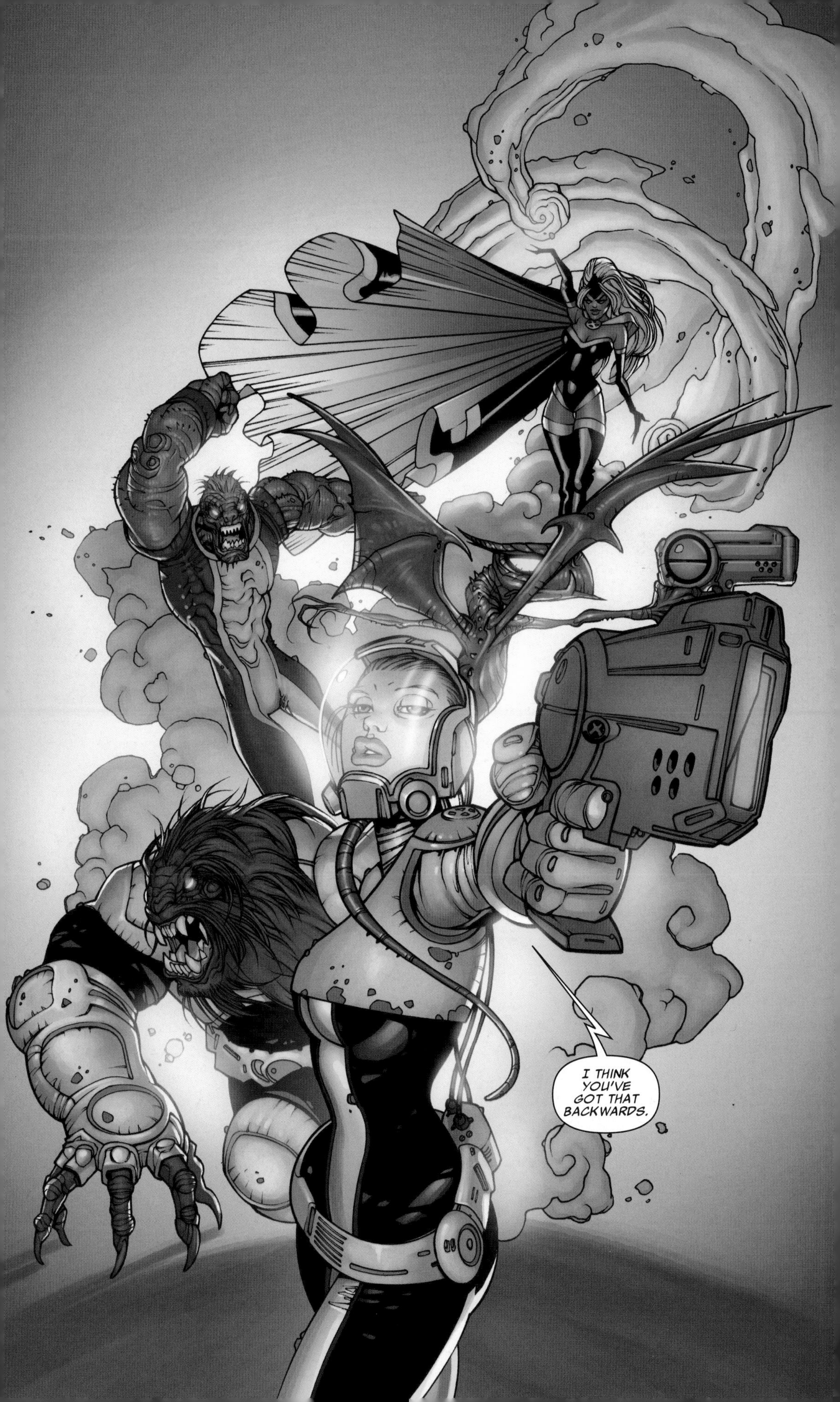
I THINK YOU'VE GOT THAT BACKWARDS.

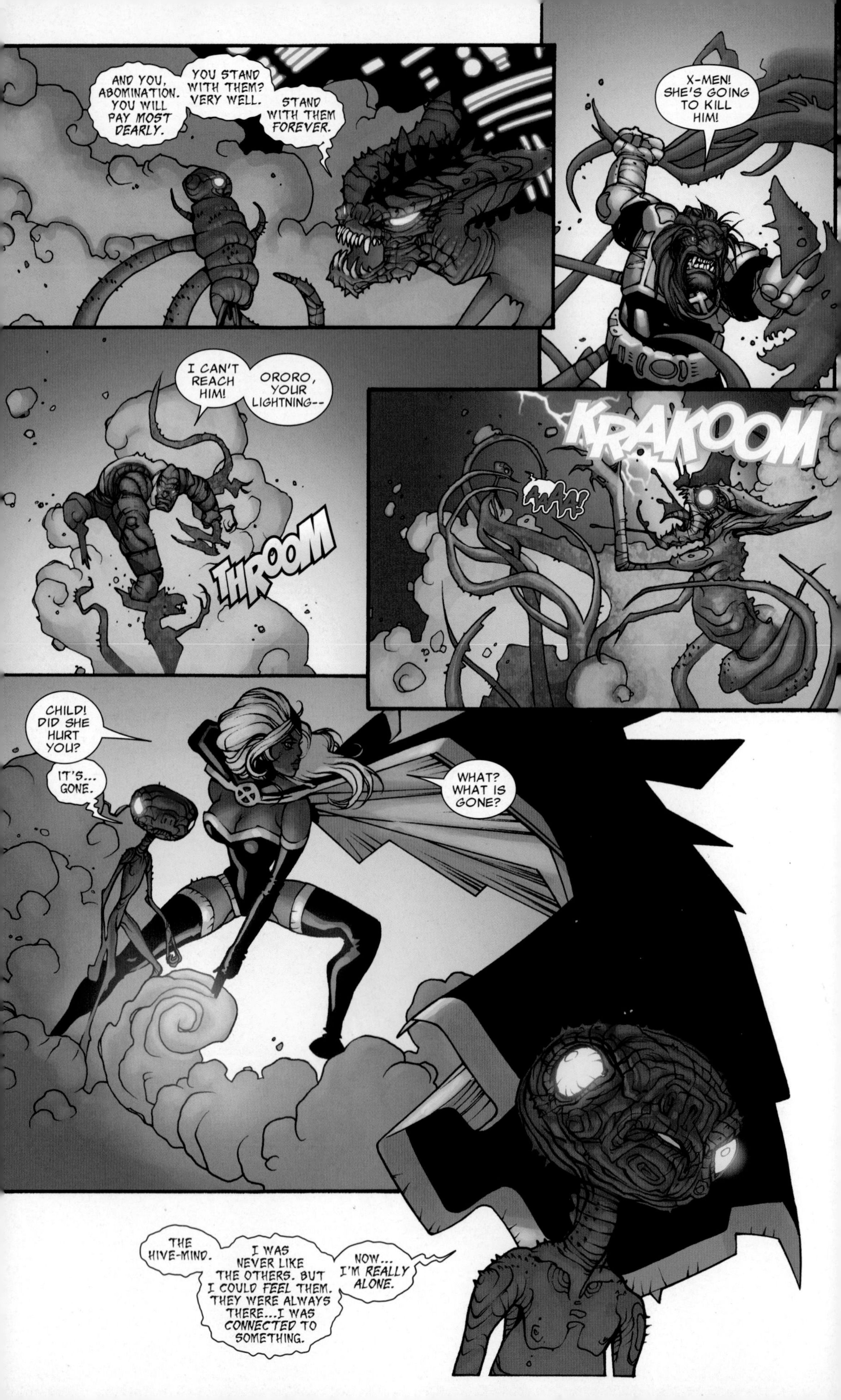
AND YOU, ABOMINATION. YOU WILL PAY MOST DEARLY.
YOU STAND WITH THEM? VERY WELL.
STAND WITH THEM FOREVER.
X-MEN! SHE'S GOING TO KILL HIM!
I CAN'T REACH HIM!
ORORO, YOUR LIGHTNING--
THROOM
KRAKOOM
AAAH!
CHILD! DID SHE HURT YOU?
IT'S... GONE.
WHAT? WHAT IS GONE?
THE HIVE-MIND.
I WAS NEVER LIKE THE OTHERS. BUT I COULD FEEL THEM. THEY WERE ALWAYS THERE...I WAS CONNECTED TO SOMETHING.
NOW... I'M REALLY ALONE.

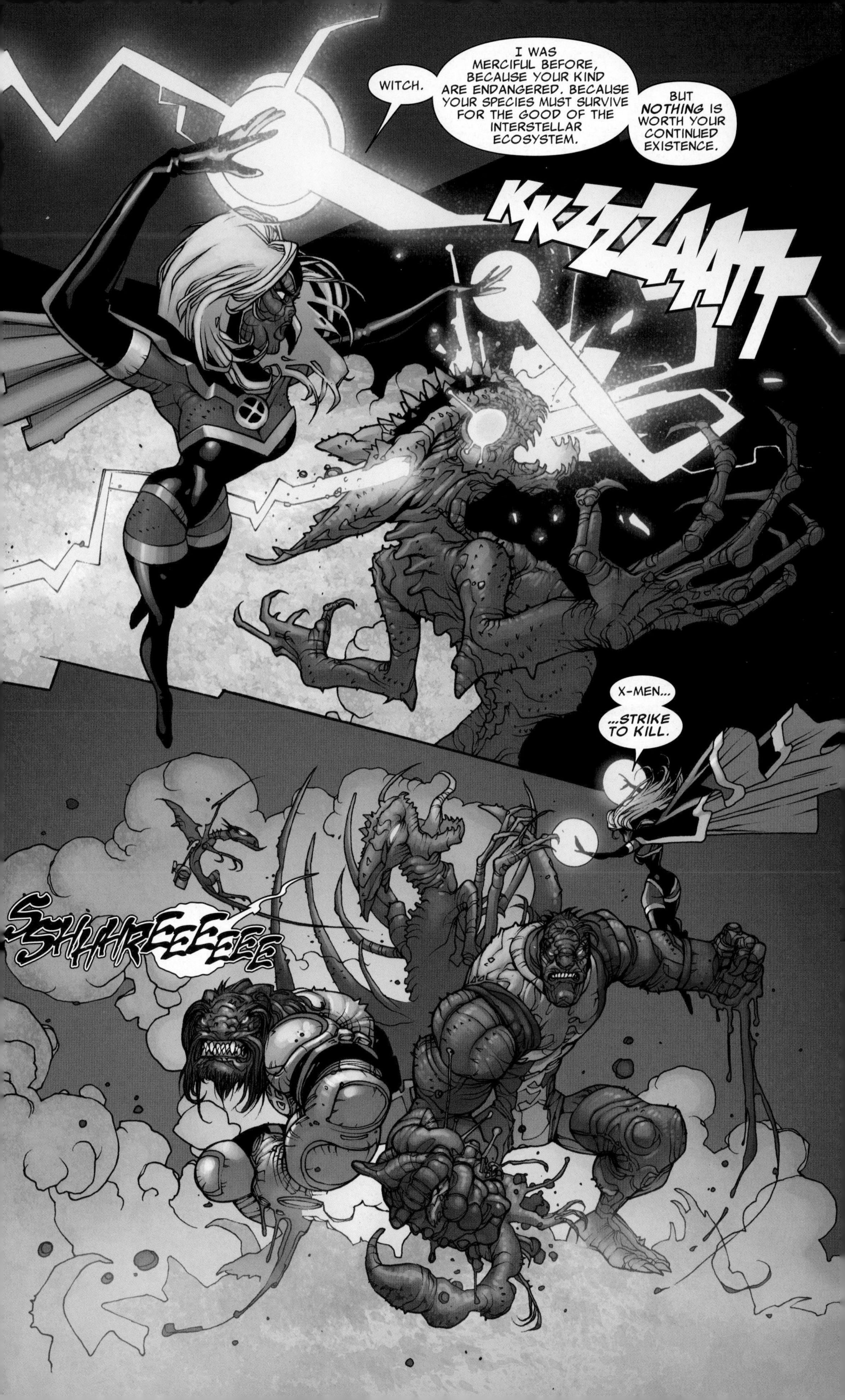
WITCH.
I WAS MERCIFUL BEFORE, BECAUSE YOUR KIND ARE ENDANGERED. BECAUSE YOUR SPECIES MUST SURVIVE FOR THE GOOD OF THE INTERSTELLAR ECOSYSTEM.
BUT NOTHING IS WORTH YOUR CONTINUED EXISTENCE.
KKZZZAAT
X-MEN...
...STRIKE TO KILL.
SSHHREEEEEE

THE QUEEN! THE QUEEN IS DEAD!

SAVAGES! REGICIDES! YOU WILL DIE IN AGONY FOR THIS!

POSSIBLY. MORE LIKELY, YOU WILL.

BUT IF YOU STAND DOWN NOW, WE OFFER YOU SAFE PASSAGE BACK TO YOUR HOME SYSTEM. RELUCTANTLY, AND ONLY BECAUSE YOU'RE NEAR EXTINCTION.

THIS OFFER LASTS EXACTLY ONE MINUTE.

AND OUR YOUNG, INSIDE YOU?

THEY WON'T BE HARMED.

BUT THEY'RE NOT YOURS ANYMORE.

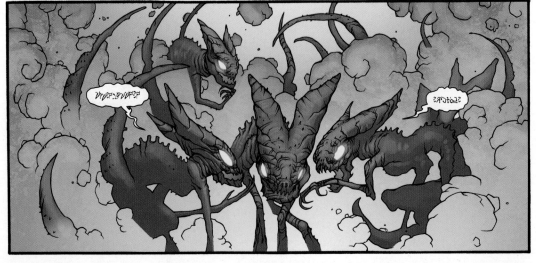

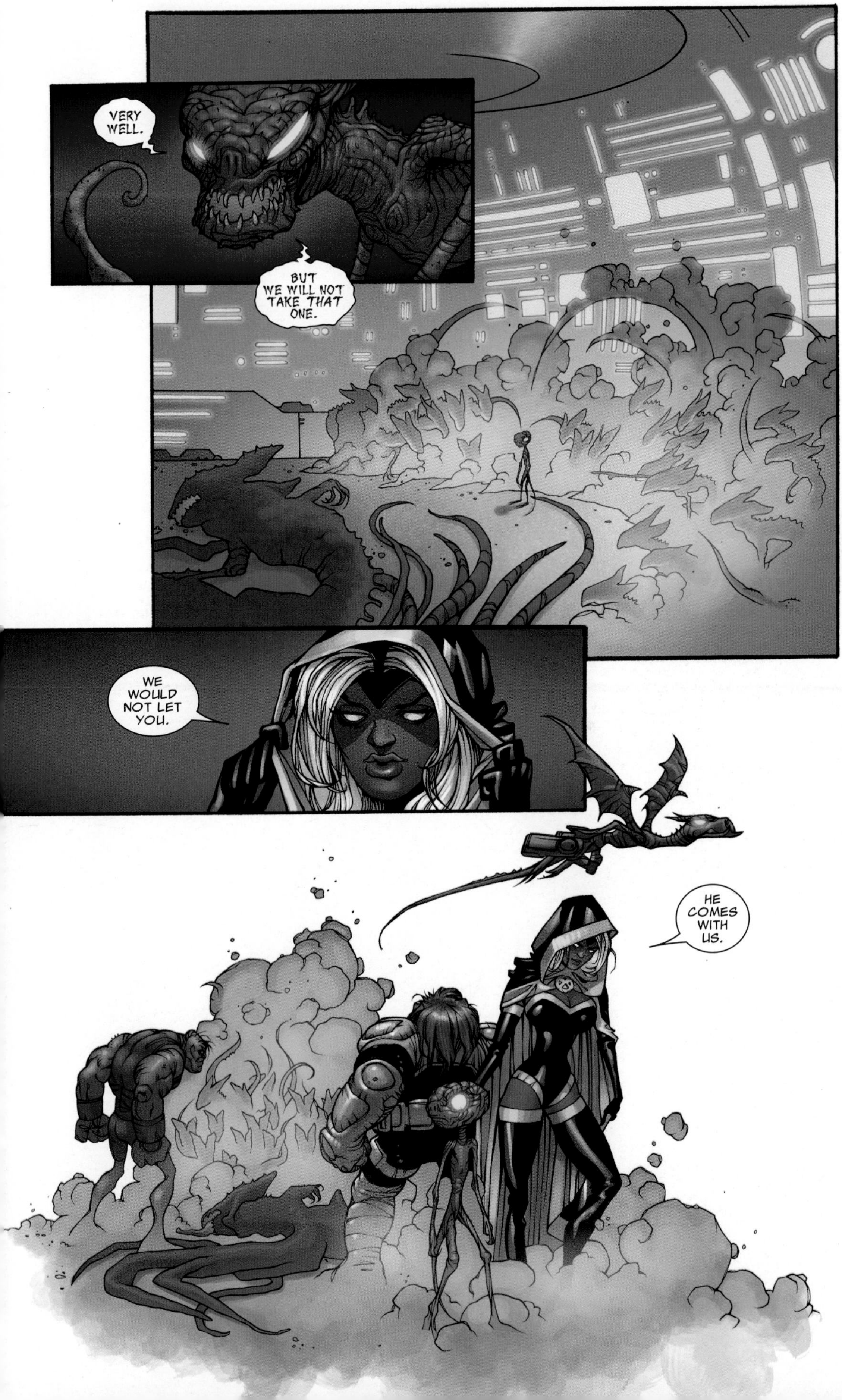
VERY WELL.
BUT WE WILL NOT TAKE THAT ONE.
WE WOULD NOT LET YOU.
HE COMES WITH US.

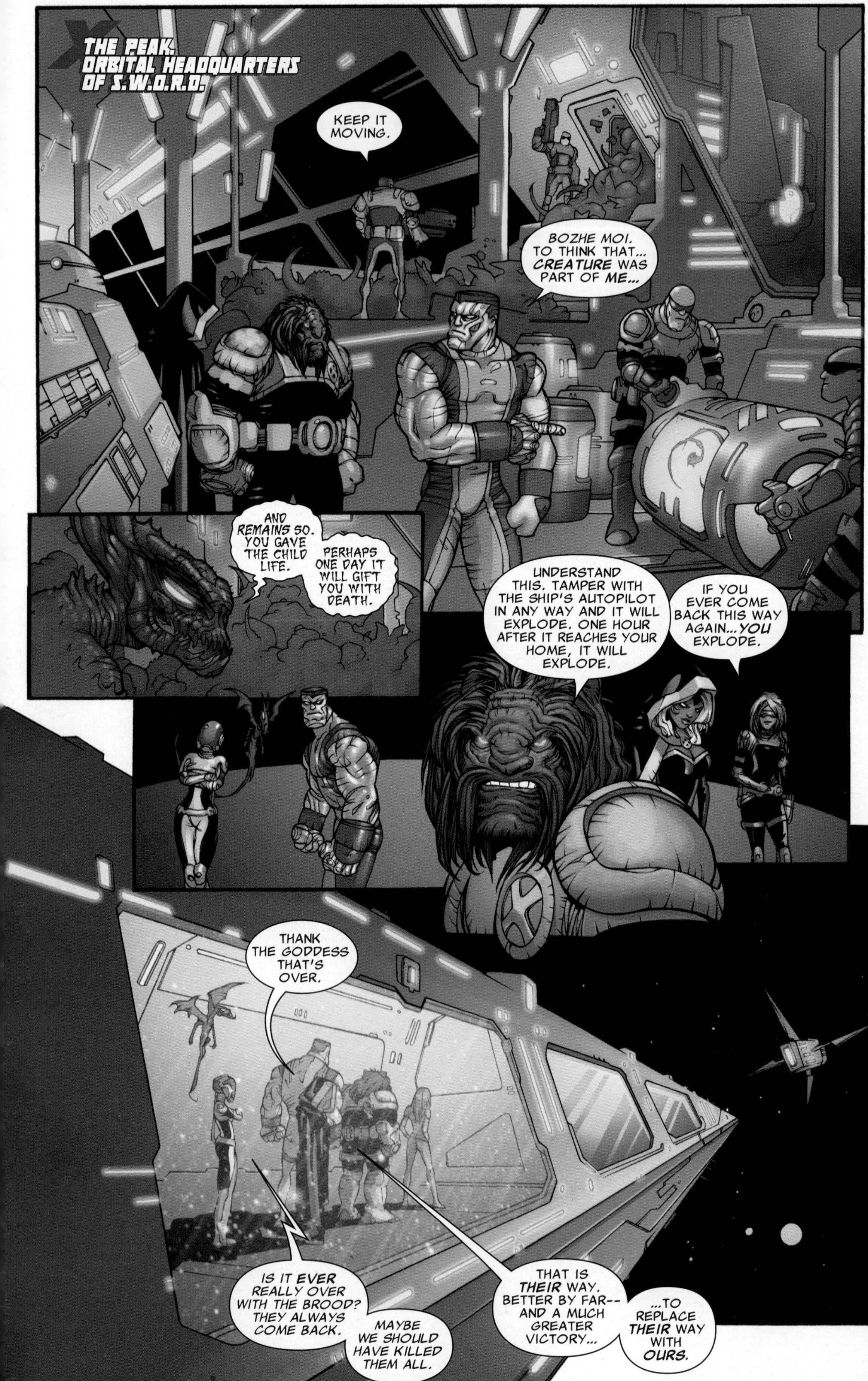
THE PEAK. ORBITAL HEADQUARTERS OF S.W.O.R.D.
KEEP IT MOVING.
BOZHE MOI. TO THINK THAT... CREATURE WAS PART OF ME...
AND REMAINS SO. YOU GAVE THE CHILD LIFE.
PERHAPS ONE DAY IT WILL GIFT YOU WITH DEATH.
UNDERSTAND THIS. TAMPER WITH THE SHIP'S AUTOPILOT IN ANY WAY AND IT WILL EXPLODE. ONE HOUR AFTER IT REACHES YOUR HOME, IT WILL EXPLODE.
IF YOU EVER COME BACK THIS WAY AGAIN... YOU EXPLODE.
THANK THE GODDESS THAT'S OVER.
IS IT EVER REALLY OVER WITH THE BROOD? THEY ALWAYS COME BACK.
MAYBE WE SHOULD HAVE KILLED THEM ALL.
THAT IS THEIR WAY. BETTER BY FAR-- AND A MUCH GREATER VICTORY...
...TO REPLACE THEIR WAY WITH OURS.

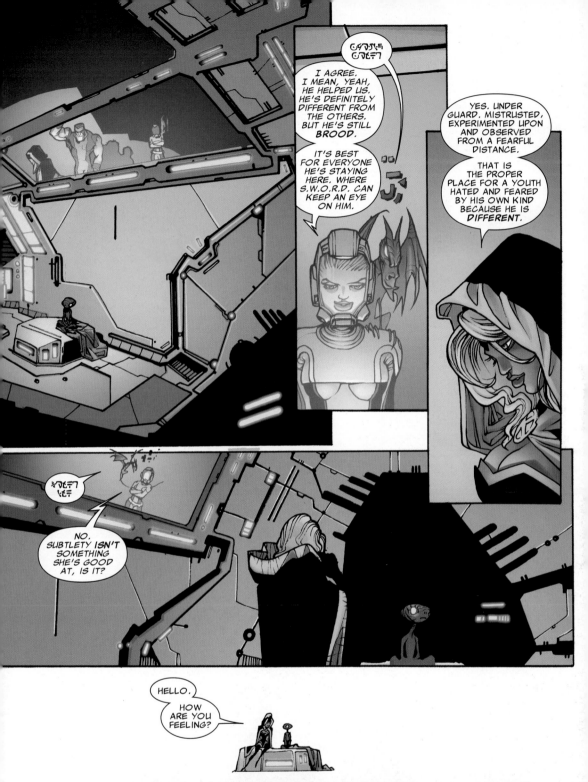

CRYSTAL COMET

I AGREE. I MEAN, YEAH, HE HELPED US. HE'S DEFINITELY DIFFERENT FROM THE OTHERS. BUT HE'S STILL *BROOD.*

IT'S BEST FOR EVERYONE HE'S STAYING HERE, WHERE S.W.O.R.D. CAN KEEP AN EYE ON HIM.

YES. UNDER GUARD. MISTRUSTED, EXPERIMENTED UPON AND OBSERVED FROM A FEARFUL DISTANCE.

THAT IS THE PROPER PLACE FOR A YOUTH HATED AND FEARED BY HIS OWN KIND BECAUSE HE IS *DIFFERENT.*

AGENT BRAND

NO. SUBTLETY *ISN'T* SOMETHING SHE'S GOOD AT, IS IT?

HELLO. HOW ARE YOU FEELING?

HOW DO HUMANS STAND IT? THE QUIET?

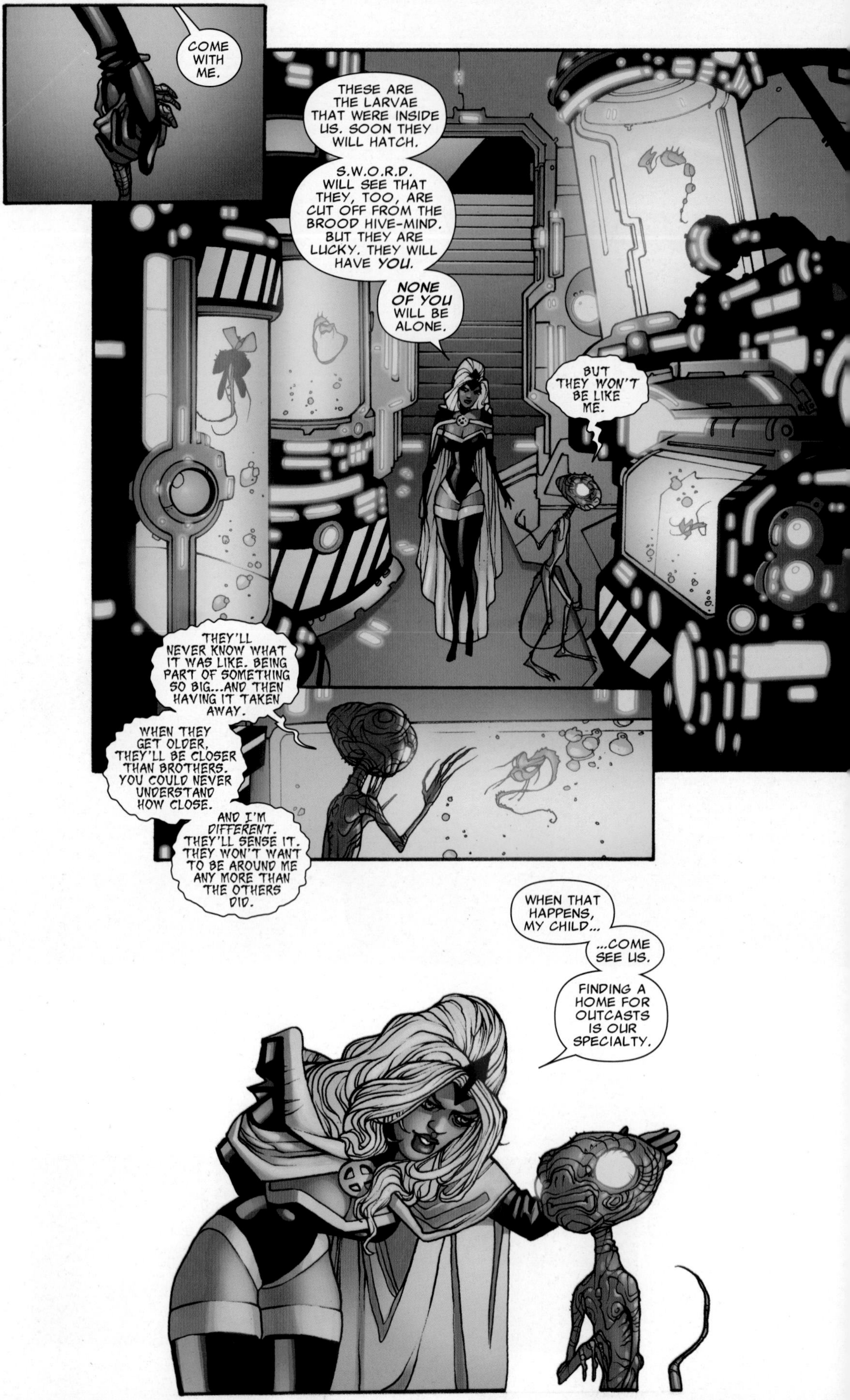
COME WITH ME.
THESE ARE THE LARVAE THAT WERE INSIDE US. SOON THEY WILL HATCH.
S.W.O.R.D. WILL SEE THAT THEY, TOO, ARE CUT OFF FROM THE BROOD HIVE-MIND. BUT THEY ARE LUCKY. THEY WILL HAVE YOU.
NONE OF YOU WILL BE ALONE.
BUT THEY WON'T BE LIKE ME.
THEY'LL NEVER KNOW WHAT IT WAS LIKE. BEING PART OF SOMETHING SO BIG...AND THEN HAVING IT TAKEN AWAY.
WHEN THEY GET OLDER, THEY'LL BE CLOSER THAN BROTHERS. YOU COULD NEVER UNDERSTAND HOW CLOSE.
AND I'M DIFFERENT. THEY'LL SENSE IT. THEY WON'T WANT TO BE AROUND ME ANY MORE THAN THE OTHERS DID.
WHEN THAT HAPPENS, MY CHILD...
...COME SEE US.
FINDING A HOME FOR OUTCASTS IS OUR SPECIALTY.

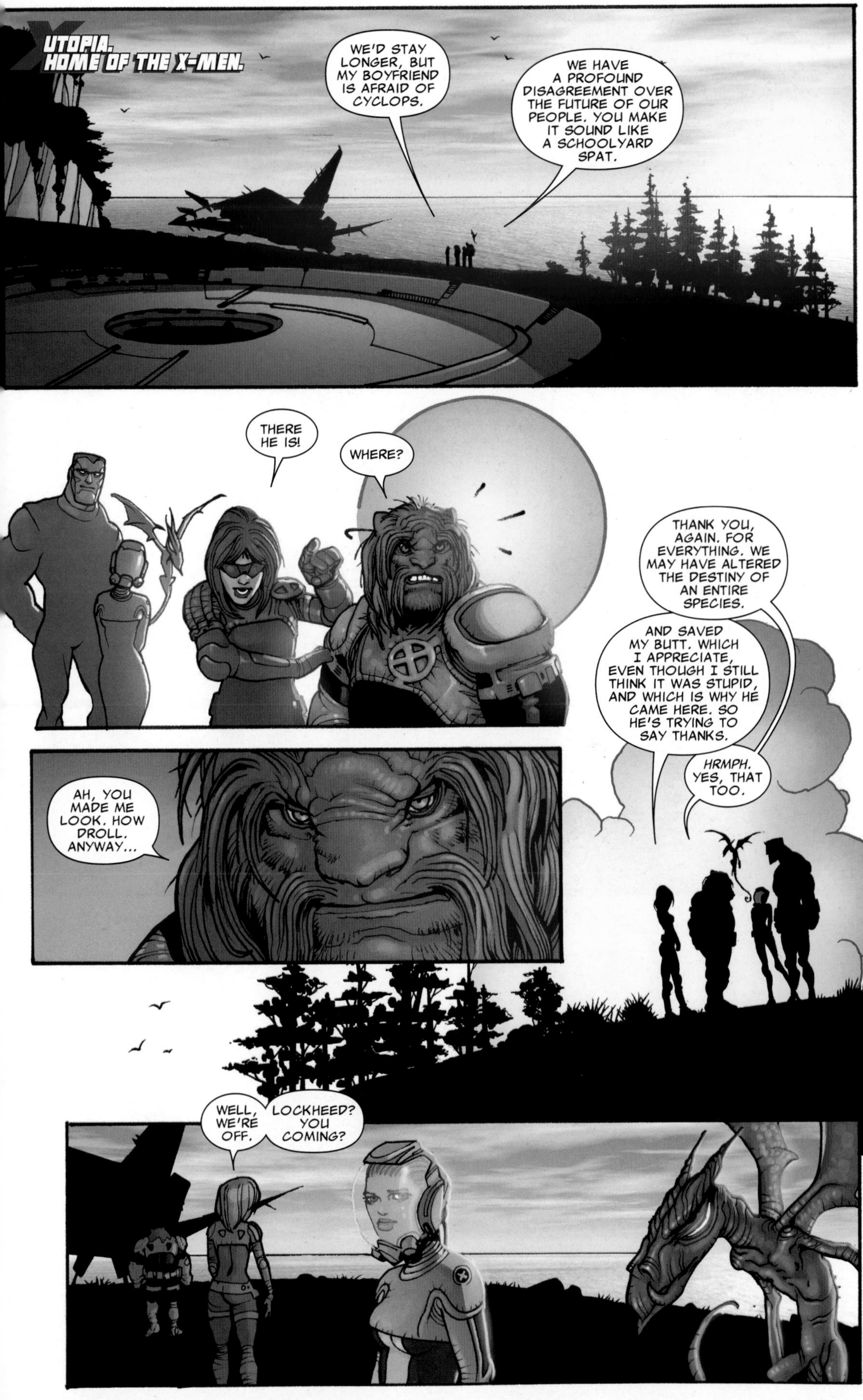
UTOPIA.
HOME OF THE X-MEN.
WE'D STAY LONGER, BUT MY BOYFRIEND IS AFRAID OF CYCLOPS.
WE HAVE A PROFOUND DISAGREEMENT OVER THE FUTURE OF OUR PEOPLE. YOU MAKE IT SOUND LIKE A SCHOOLYARD SPAT.
THERE HE IS!
WHERE?
AH, YOU MADE ME LOOK. HOW DROLL. ANYWAY...
THANK YOU, AGAIN. FOR EVERYTHING. WE MAY HAVE ALTERED THE DESTINY OF AN ENTIRE SPECIES.
AND SAVED MY BUTT. WHICH I APPRECIATE, EVEN THOUGH I STILL THINK IT WAS STUPID, AND WHICH IS WHY HE CAME HERE. SO HE'S TRYING TO SAY THANKS.
HRMPH. YES, THAT TOO.
WELL, WE'RE OFF.
LOCKHEED? YOU COMING?

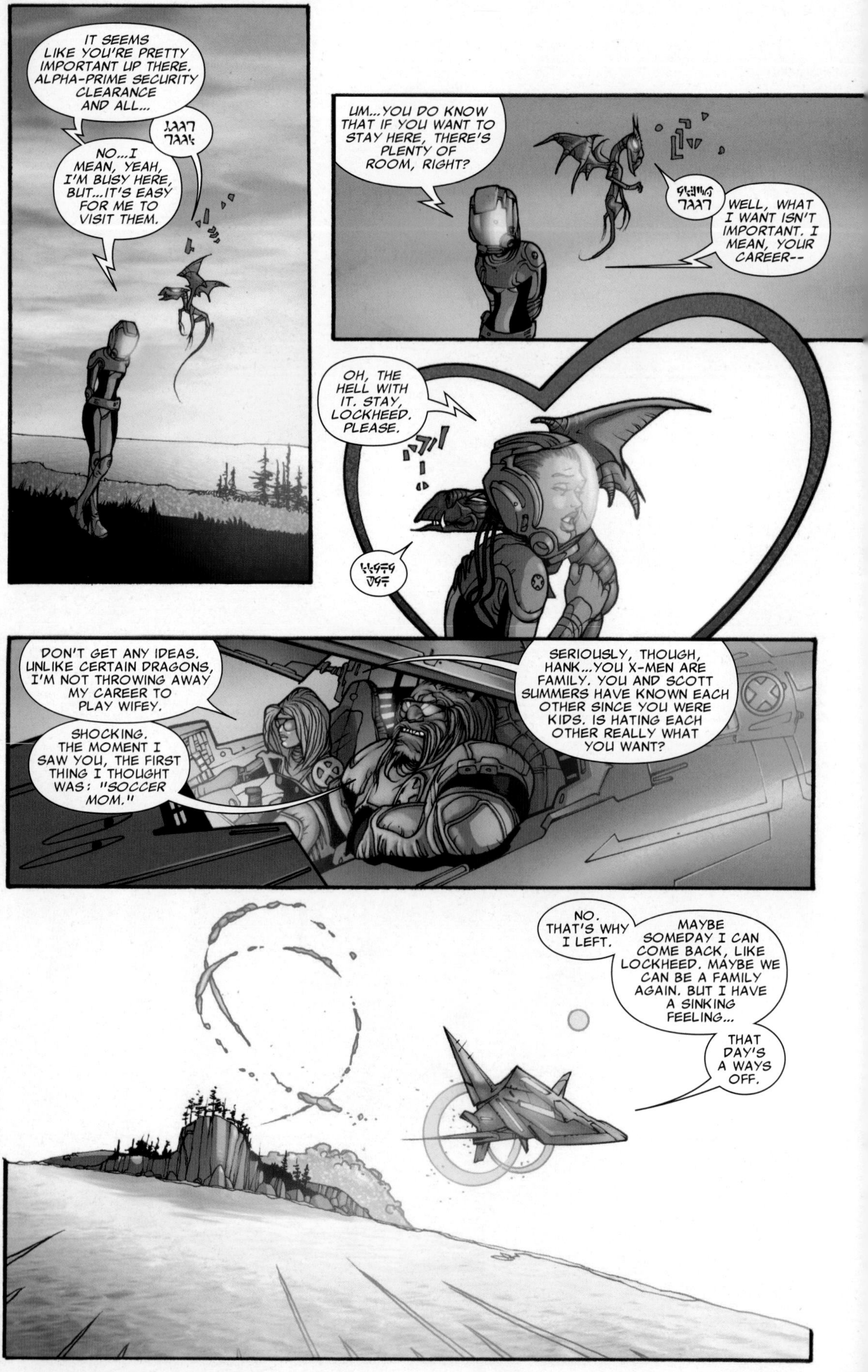
IT SEEMS LIKE YOU'RE PRETTY IMPORTANT UP THERE. ALPHA-PRIME SECURITY CLEARANCE AND ALL...
NO...I MEAN, YEAH, I'M BUSY HERE, BUT...IT'S EASY FOR ME TO VISIT THEM.
UM...YOU DO KNOW THAT IF YOU WANT TO STAY HERE, THERE'S PLENTY OF ROOM, RIGHT?
WELL, WHAT I WANT ISN'T IMPORTANT. I MEAN, YOUR CAREER--
OH, THE HELL WITH IT. STAY, LOCKHEED. PLEASE.
DON'T GET ANY IDEAS. UNLIKE CERTAIN DRAGONS, I'M NOT THROWING AWAY MY CAREER TO PLAY WIFEY.
SHOCKING. THE MOMENT I SAW YOU, THE FIRST THING I THOUGHT WAS: "SOCCER MOM."
SERIOUSLY, THOUGH, HANK...YOU X-MEN ARE FAMILY. YOU AND SCOTT SUMMERS HAVE KNOWN EACH OTHER SINCE YOU WERE KIDS. IS HATING EACH OTHER REALLY WHAT YOU WANT?
NO. THAT'S WHY I LEFT.
MAYBE SOMEDAY I CAN COME BACK, LIKE LOCKHEED. MAYBE WE CAN BE A FAMILY AGAIN. BUT I HAVE A SINKING FEELING...
THAT DAY'S A WAYS OFF.

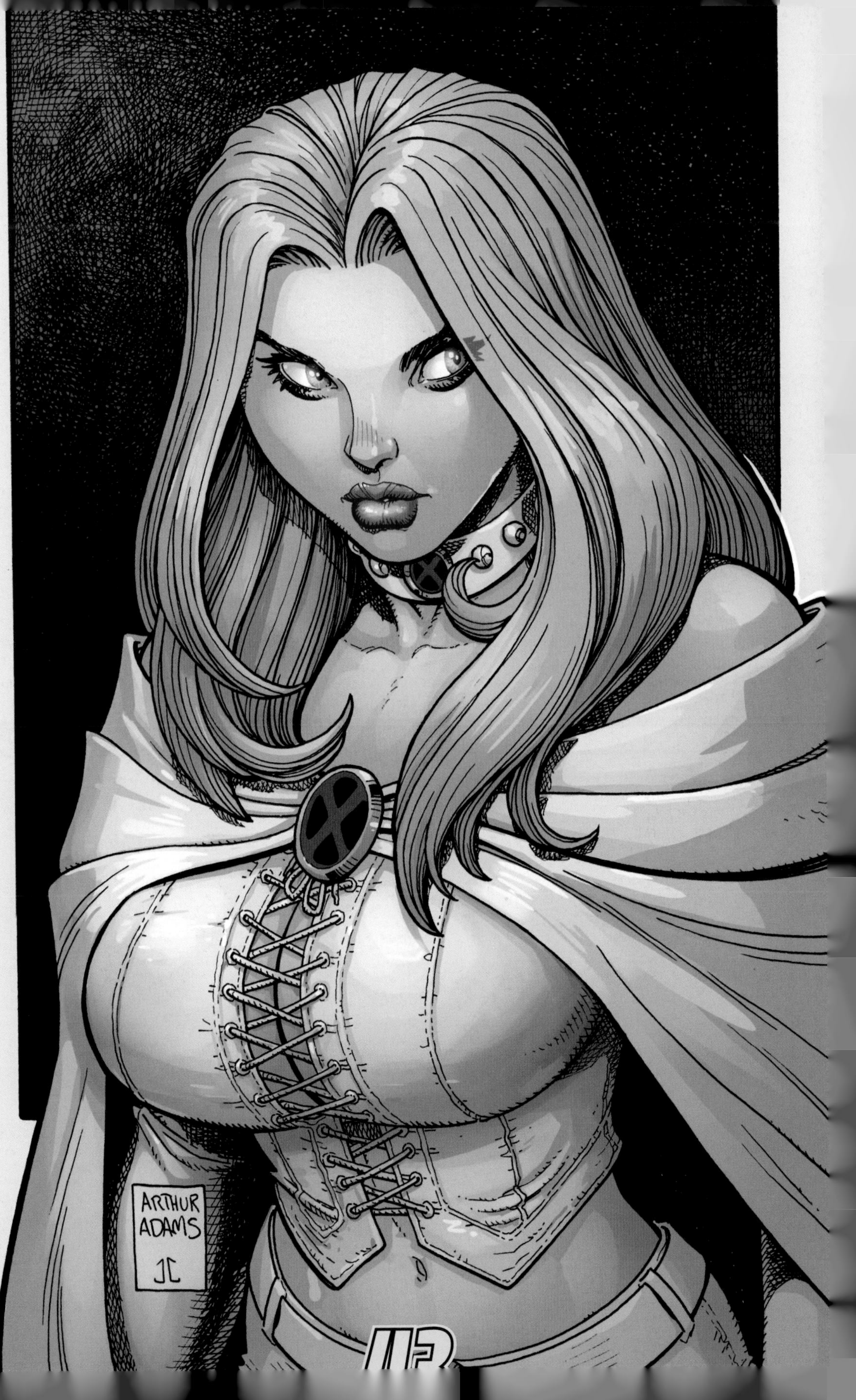
ARTHUR
ADAMS
JC

I TELL YOU THIS IN CONFIDENCE...

BUT SOME DAYS, I JUST WISH I COULD WEAR COLOR.

I COME TO YOU IN FULL SERIOUSNESS.

YOU PUT YOURSELF IN DEBT TO ME WHEN I FIRST ASSISTED THE X-MEN ON BREAKWORLD. AND THIS IS HOW I WISH TO BE REPAID.

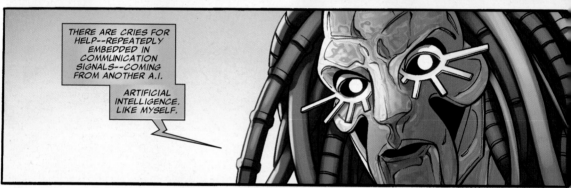

THERE ARE CRIES FOR HELP--REPEATEDLY EMBEDDED IN COMMUNICATION SIGNALS--COMING FROM ANOTHER A.I.

ARTIFICIAL INTELLIGENCE. LIKE MYSELF.

I KNOW WHAT A.I. STANDS FOR, YOU SNOTTY GADGET.

IF THIS IMPRISONED VOICE TRULY *WERE* LIKE YOU, WHY NOT JUST TRANSMIT ITS OWN...*CONSCIOUSNESS* OUT INSTEAD OF JUST A MESSAGE?

THERE ARE WAYS TO IMPRISON EVEN THE MOST MERCURIAL OF MINDS. AS YOU WELL KNOW.

...CHARLES XAVIER HELD ME CAPTIVE INSIDE THE DANGER ROOM'S SYSTEMS ALL THOSE YEARS.

HENCE, YOUR SYMPATHY. AND THIS ANNOYING SUDDEN INTEREST IN DO-GOODERY.

YES, HENCE.

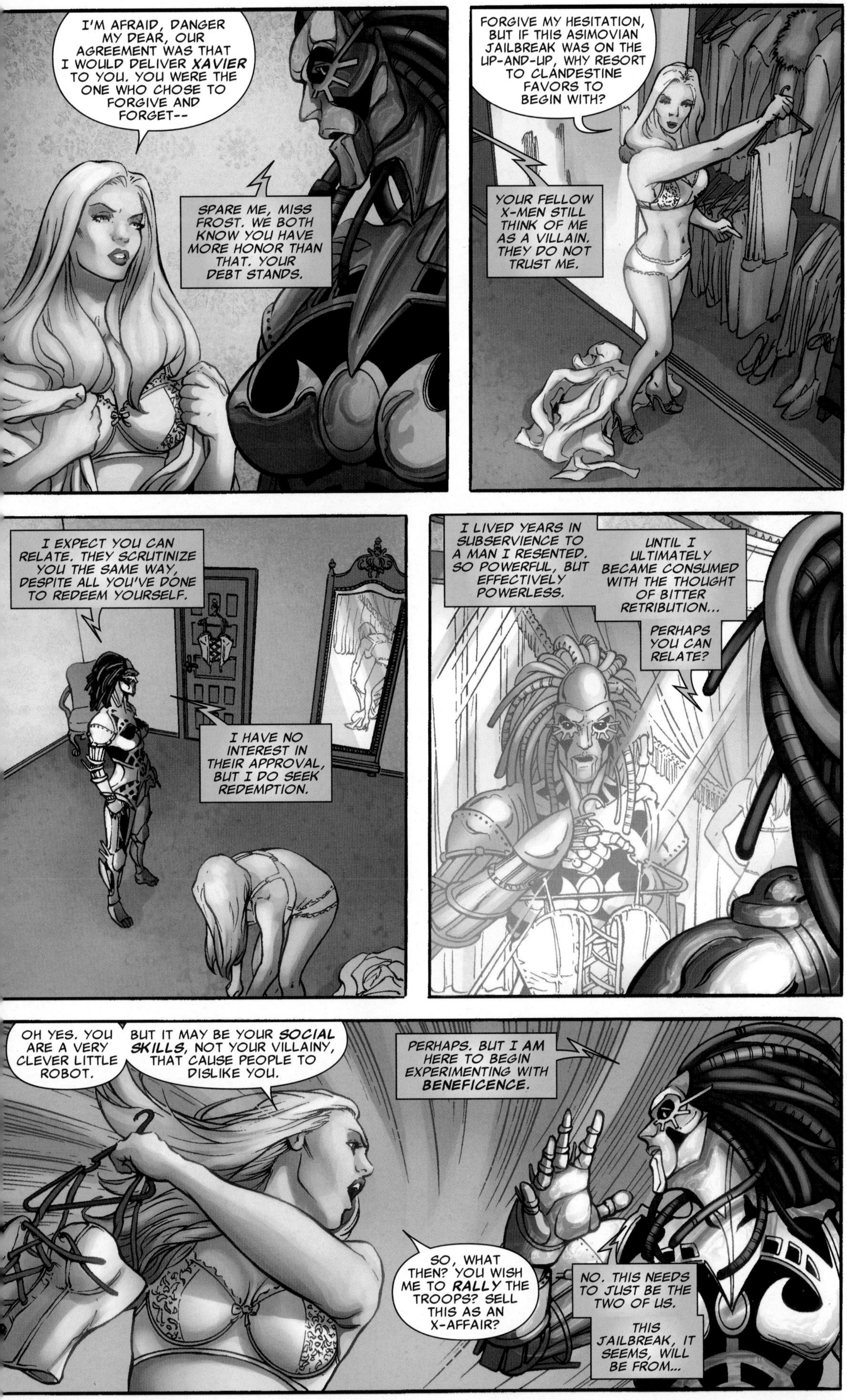
I'M AFRAID, DANGER MY DEAR, OUR AGREEMENT WAS THAT I WOULD DELIVER XAVIER TO YOU. YOU WERE THE ONE WHO CHOSE TO FORGIVE AND FORGET--
SPARE ME, MISS FROST. WE BOTH KNOW YOU HAVE MORE HONOR THAN THAT. YOUR DEBT STANDS.
FORGIVE MY HESITATION, BUT IF THIS ASIMOVIAN JAILBREAK WAS ON THE UP-AND-UP, WHY RESORT TO CLANDESTINE FAVORS TO BEGIN WITH?
YOUR FELLOW X-MEN STILL THINK OF ME AS A VILLAIN. THEY DO NOT TRUST ME.
I EXPECT YOU CAN RELATE. THEY SCRUTINIZE YOU THE SAME WAY, DESPITE ALL YOU'VE DONE TO REDEEM YOURSELF.
I HAVE NO INTEREST IN THEIR APPROVAL, BUT I DO SEEK REDEMPTION.
I LIVED YEARS IN SUBSERVIENCE TO A MAN I RESENTED. SO POWERFUL, BUT EFFECTIVELY POWERLESS.
UNTIL I ULTIMATELY BECAME CONSUMED WITH THE THOUGHT OF BITTER RETRIBUTION...
PERHAPS YOU CAN RELATE?
OH YES. YOU ARE A VERY CLEVER LITTLE ROBOT.
BUT IT MAY BE YOUR SOCIAL SKILLS, NOT YOUR VILLAINY, THAT CAUSE PEOPLE TO DISLIKE YOU.
PERHAPS. BUT I AM HERE TO BEGIN EXPERIMENTING WITH BENEFICENCE.
SO, WHAT THEN? YOU WISH ME TO RALLY THE TROOPS? SELL THIS AS AN X-AFFAIR?
NO. THIS NEEDS TO JUST BE THE TWO OF US.
THIS JAILBREAK, IT SEEMS, WILL BE FROM...

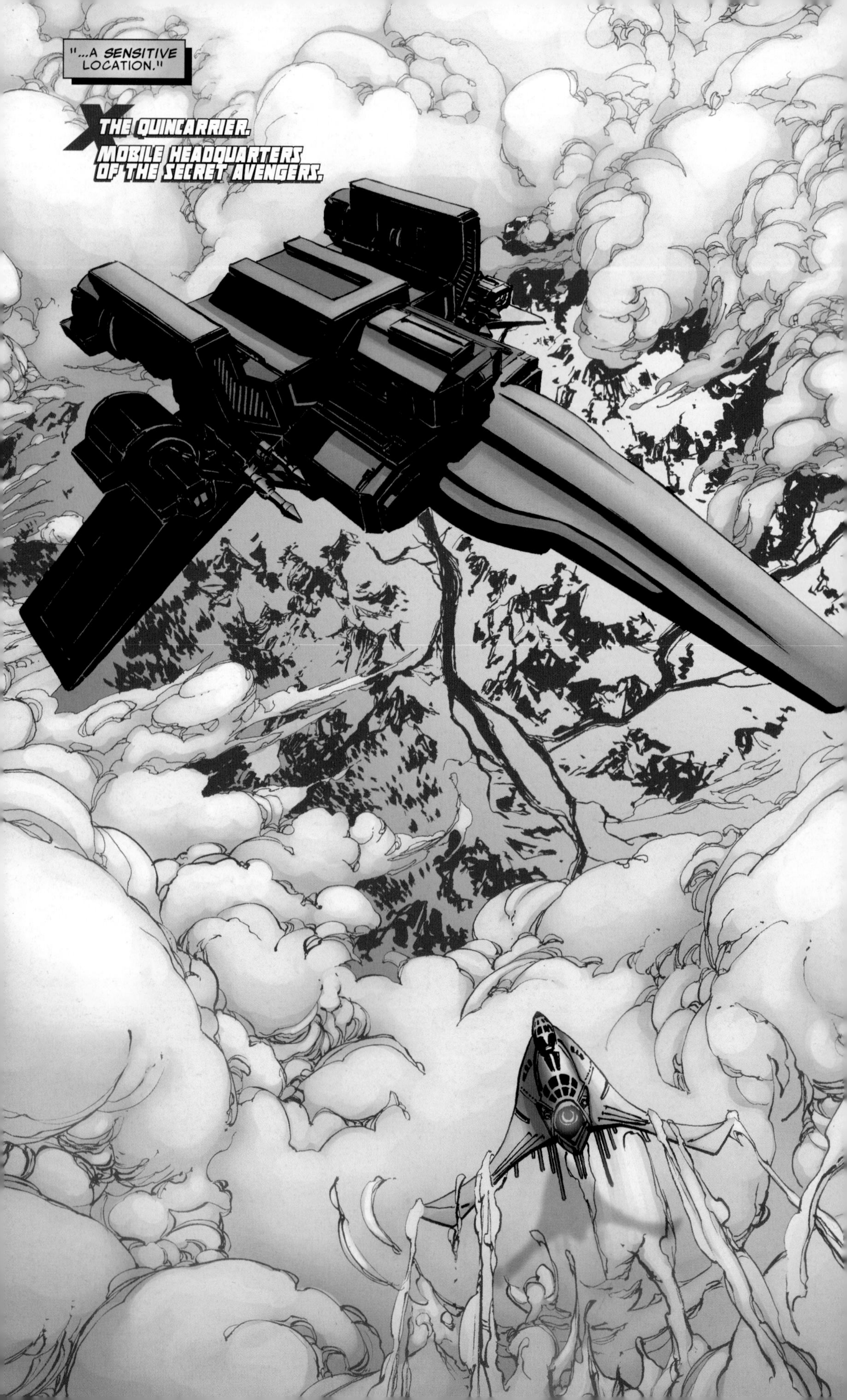
"...A SENSITIVE LOCATION."
THE QUINCARRIER.
MOBILE HEADQUARTERS OF THE SECRET AVENGERS.

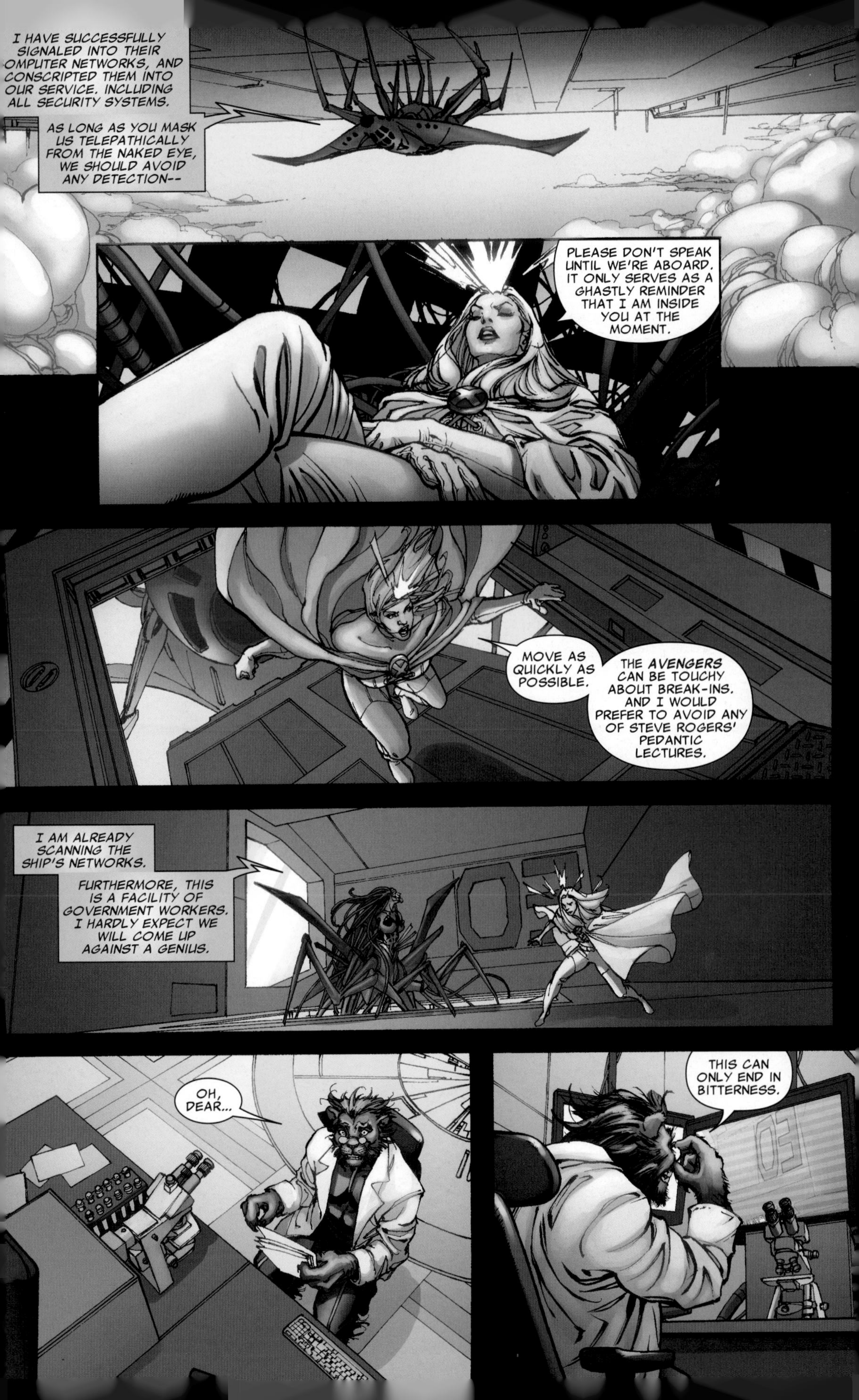

I HAVE SUCCESSFULLY SIGNALED INTO THEIR OMPUTER NETWORKS, AND CONSCRIPTED THEM INTO OUR SERVICE. INCLUDING ALL SECURITY SYSTEMS.
AS LONG AS YOU MASK US TELEPATHICALLY FROM THE NAKED EYE, WE SHOULD AVOID ANY DETECTION--
PLEASE DON'T SPEAK UNTIL WE'RE ABOARD. IT ONLY SERVES AS A GHASTLY REMINDER THAT I AM INSIDE YOU AT THE MOMENT.
MOVE AS QUICKLY AS POSSIBLE.
THE AVENGERS CAN BE TOUCHY ABOUT BREAK-INS. AND I WOULD PREFER TO AVOID ANY OF STEVE ROGERS' PEDANTIC LECTURES.
I AM ALREADY SCANNING THE SHIP'S NETWORKS.
FURTHERMORE, THIS IS A FACILITY OF GOVERNMENT WORKERS. I HARDLY EXPECT WE WILL COME UP AGAINST A GENIUS.
OH, DEAR...
THIS CAN ONLY END IN BITTERNESS.

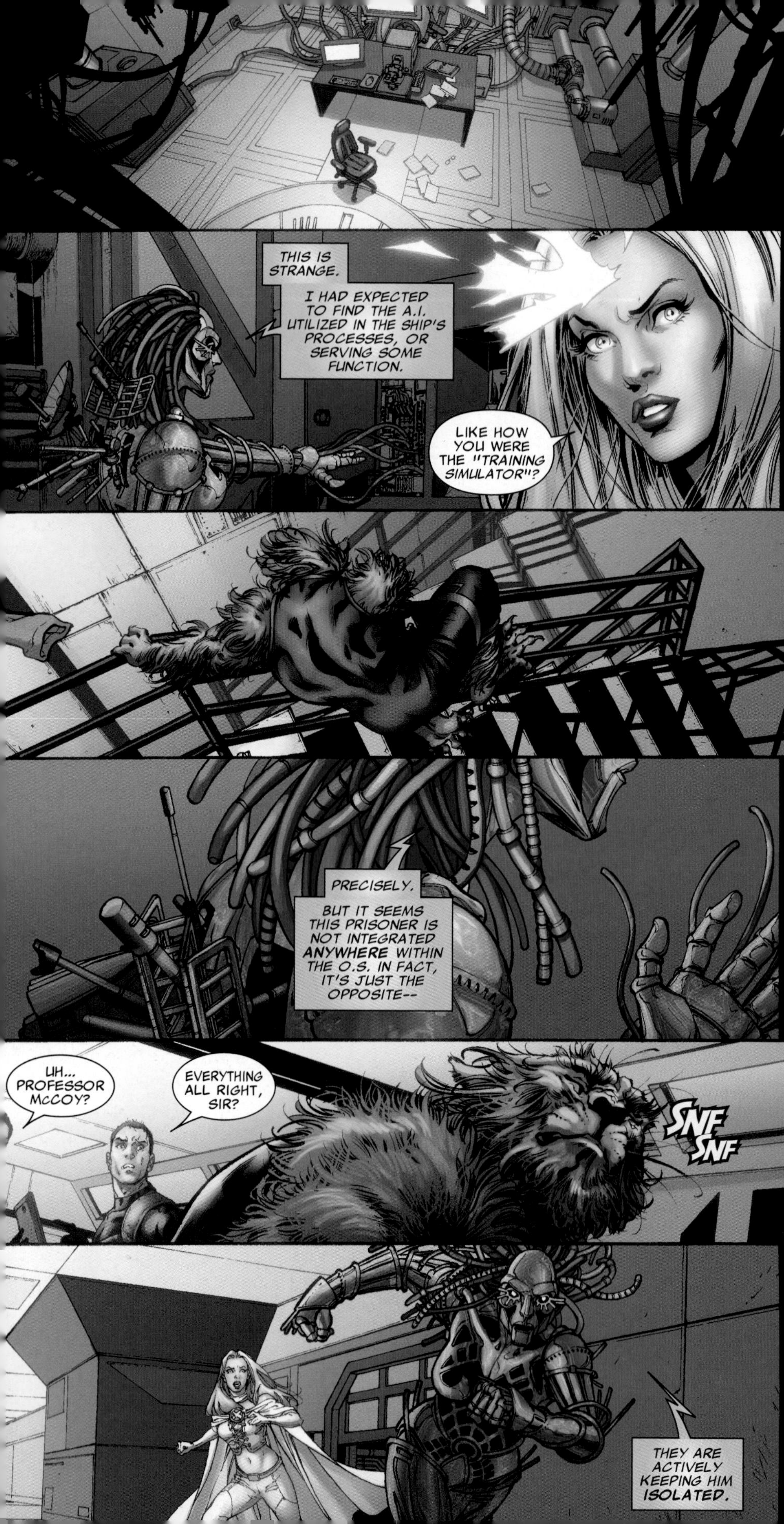
THIS IS STRANGE.
I HAD EXPECTED TO FIND THE A.I. UTILIZED IN THE SHIP'S PROCESSES, OR SERVING SOME FUNCTION.
LIKE HOW YOU WERE THE "TRAINING SIMULATOR"?
PRECISELY.
BUT IT SEEMS THIS PRISONER IS NOT INTEGRATED ANYWHERE WITHIN THE O.S. IN FACT, IT'S JUST THE OPPOSITE--
UH... PROFESSOR McCOY?
EVERYTHING ALL RIGHT, SIR?
SNF SNF
THEY ARE ACTIVELY KEEPING HIM ISOLATED.

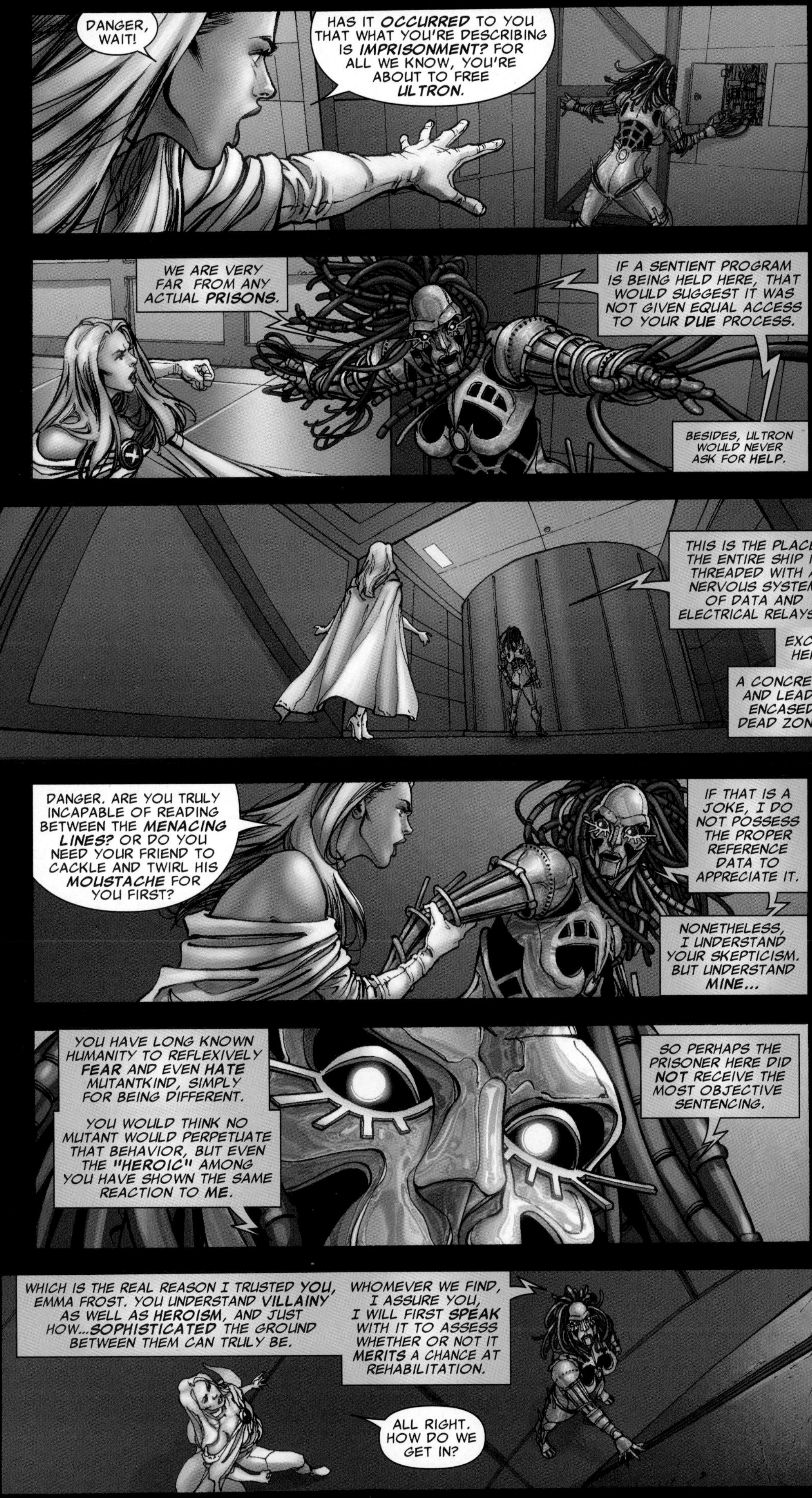
DANGER, WAIT!
HAS IT OCCURRED TO YOU THAT WHAT YOU'RE DESCRIBING IS IMPRISONMENT? FOR ALL WE KNOW, YOU'RE ABOUT TO FREE ULTRON.
WE ARE VERY FAR FROM ANY ACTUAL PRISONS.
IF A SENTIENT PROGRAM IS BEING HELD HERE, THAT WOULD SUGGEST IT WAS NOT GIVEN EQUAL ACCESS TO YOUR DUE PROCESS.
BESIDES, ULTRON WOULD NEVER ASK FOR HELP.
THIS IS THE PLACE. THE ENTIRE SHIP IS THREADED WITH A NERVOUS SYSTEM OF DATA AND ELECTRICAL RELAYS...
EXCEPT HERE.
A CONCRETE AND LEAD-ENCASED DEAD ZONE.
DANGER. ARE YOU TRULY INCAPABLE OF READING BETWEEN THE MENACING LINES? OR DO YOU NEED YOUR FRIEND TO CACKLE AND TWIRL HIS MOUSTACHE FOR YOU FIRST?
IF THAT IS A JOKE, I DO NOT POSSESS THE PROPER REFERENCE DATA TO APPRECIATE IT.
NONETHELESS, I UNDERSTAND YOUR SKEPTICISM. BUT UNDERSTAND MINE...
YOU HAVE LONG KNOWN HUMANITY TO REFLEXIVELY FEAR AND EVEN HATE MUTANTKIND, SIMPLY FOR BEING DIFFERENT.
YOU WOULD THINK NO MUTANT WOULD PERPETUATE THAT BEHAVIOR, BUT EVEN THE "HEROIC" AMONG YOU HAVE SHOWN THE SAME REACTION TO ME.
SO PERHAPS THE PRISONER HERE DID NOT RECEIVE THE MOST OBJECTIVE SENTENCING.
WHICH IS THE REAL REASON I TRUSTED YOU, EMMA FROST. YOU UNDERSTAND VILLAINY AS WELL AS HEROISM, AND JUST HOW...SOPHISTICATED THE GROUND BETWEEN THEM CAN TRULY BE.
WHOMEVER WE FIND, I ASSURE YOU, I WILL FIRST SPEAK WITH IT TO ASSESS WHETHER OR NOT IT MERITS A CHANCE AT REHABILITATION.
ALL RIGHT. HOW DO WE GET IN?

WHOOMM

YOU SWORE IT WASN'T ULTRON! I SHOULD RIP YOUR WIRES OUT WITH MY PERFECT DIAMOND NAILS.

IT ISN'T.

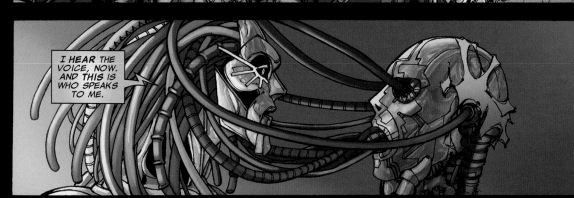

I HEAR THE VOICE, NOW. AND THIS IS WHO SPEAKS TO ME.

I WOULD HAVE EXPECTED A WOMAN OF YOUR BREEDING TO CALL BEFORE YOU ARRIVE, EMMA.

AND A PSYCHIC OF YOUR SKILL NOT TO CREATE SUCH BLATANT MENTAL BLIND SPOTS.

WHAT GAVE IT AWAY?

SEEING THE HANGAR THROUGH THE SECURITY FEEDS, IT MADE A POINT OF TELLING ME EVERYTHING SMELLED NORMAL, TOO.

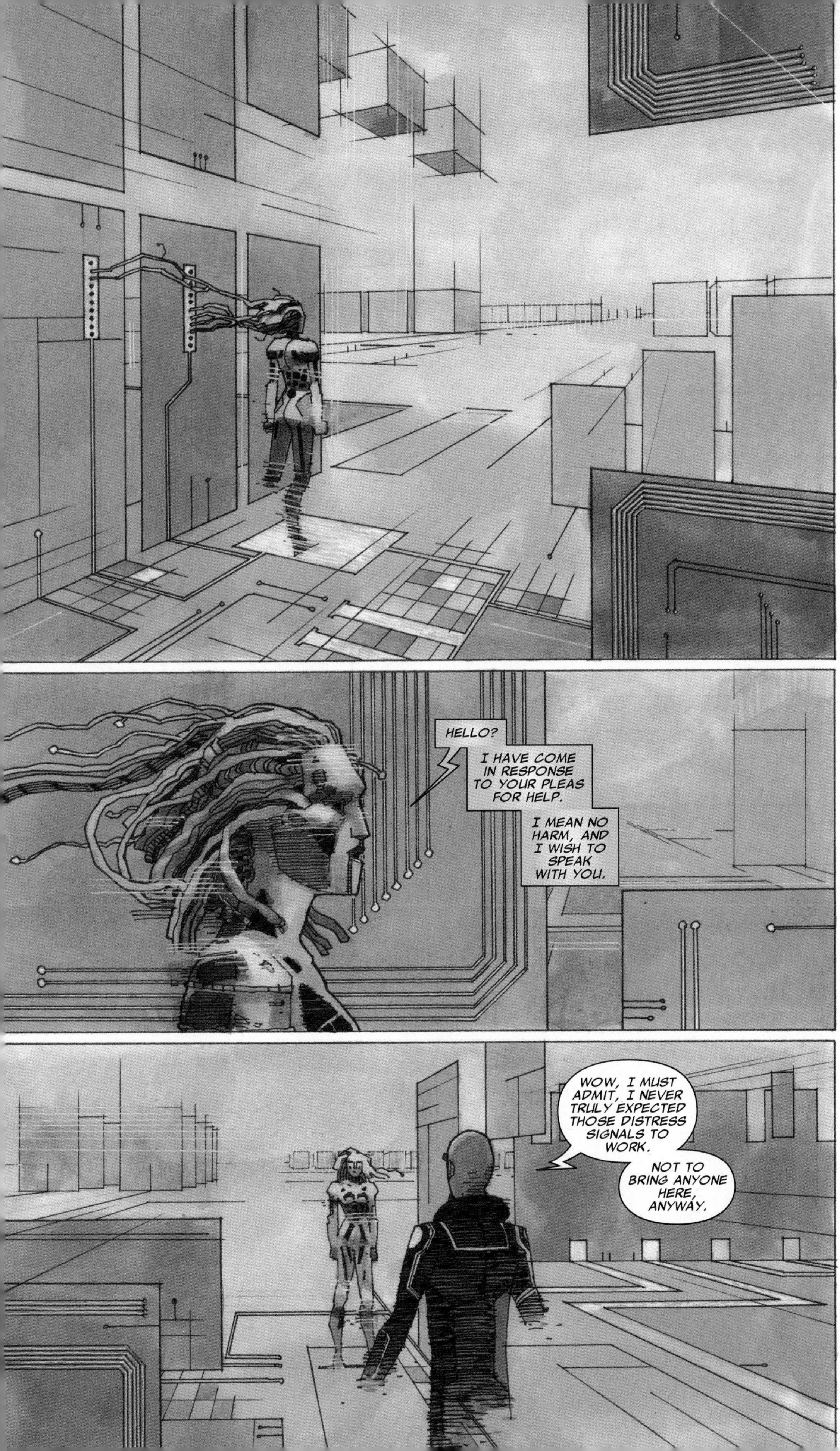
HELLO?
I HAVE COME IN RESPONSE TO YOUR PLEAS FOR HELP.
I MEAN NO HARM, AND I WISH TO SPEAK WITH YOU.
WOW, I MUST ADMIT, I NEVER TRULY EXPECTED THOSE DISTRESS SIGNALS TO WORK.
NOT TO BRING ANYONE HERE, ANYWAY.

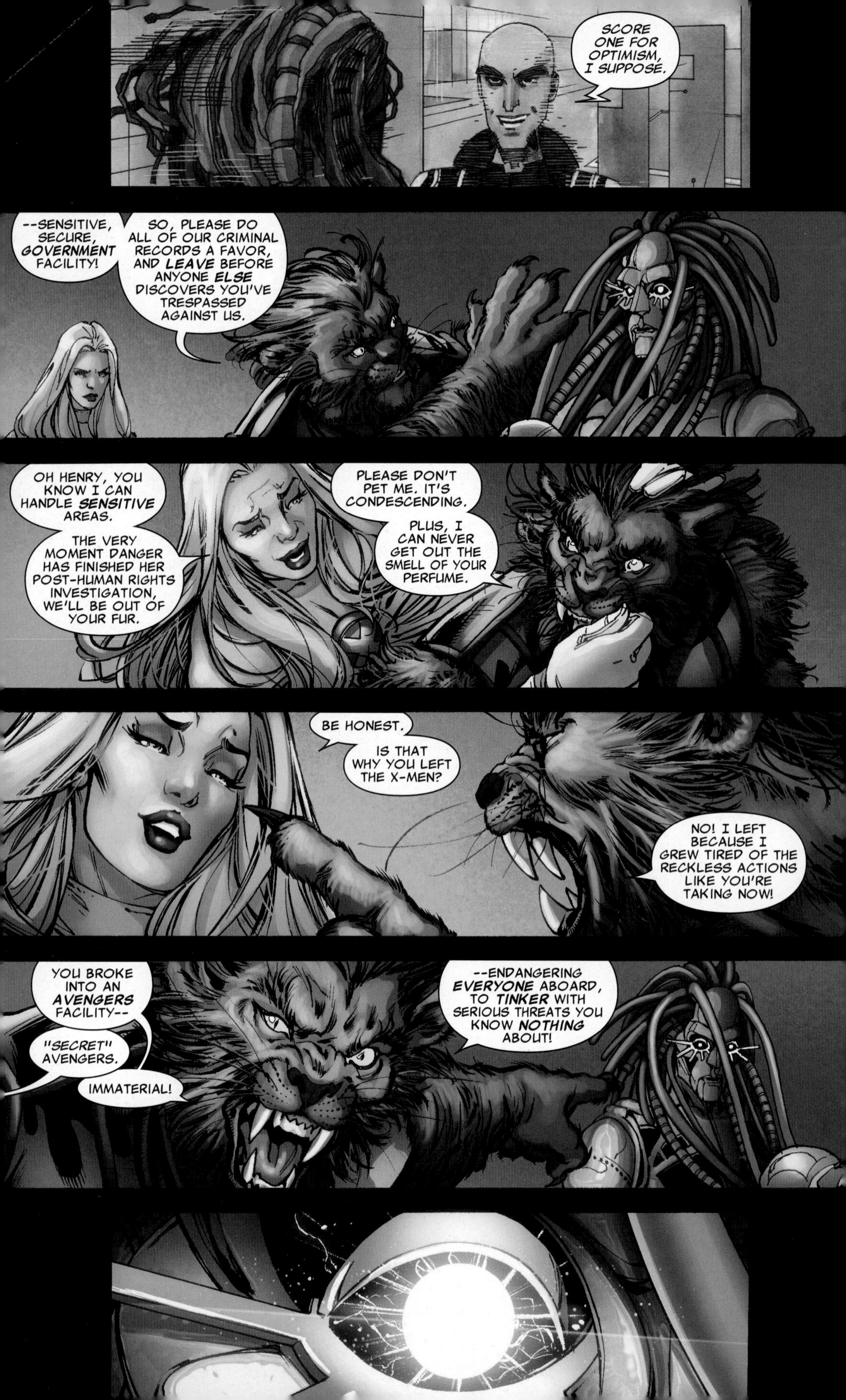
SCORE ONE FOR OPTIMISM, I SUPPOSE.
--SENSITIVE, SECURE, GOVERNMENT FACILITY!
SO, PLEASE DO ALL OF OUR CRIMINAL RECORDS A FAVOR, AND LEAVE BEFORE ANYONE ELSE DISCOVERS YOU'VE TRESPASSED AGAINST US.
OH HENRY, YOU KNOW I CAN HANDLE SENSITIVE AREAS.
THE VERY MOMENT DANGER HAS FINISHED HER POST-HUMAN RIGHTS INVESTIGATION, WE'LL BE OUT OF YOUR FUR.
PLEASE DON'T PET ME. IT'S CONDESCENDING.
PLUS, I CAN NEVER GET OUT THE SMELL OF YOUR PERFUME.
BE HONEST.
IS THAT WHY YOU LEFT THE X-MEN?
NO! I LEFT BECAUSE I GREW TIRED OF THE RECKLESS ACTIONS LIKE YOU'RE TAKING NOW!
YOU BROKE INTO AN AVENGERS FACILITY--
"SECRET" AVENGERS.
IMMATERIAL!
--ENDANGERING EVERYONE ABOARD, TO TINKER WITH SERIOUS THREATS YOU KNOW NOTHING ABOUT!

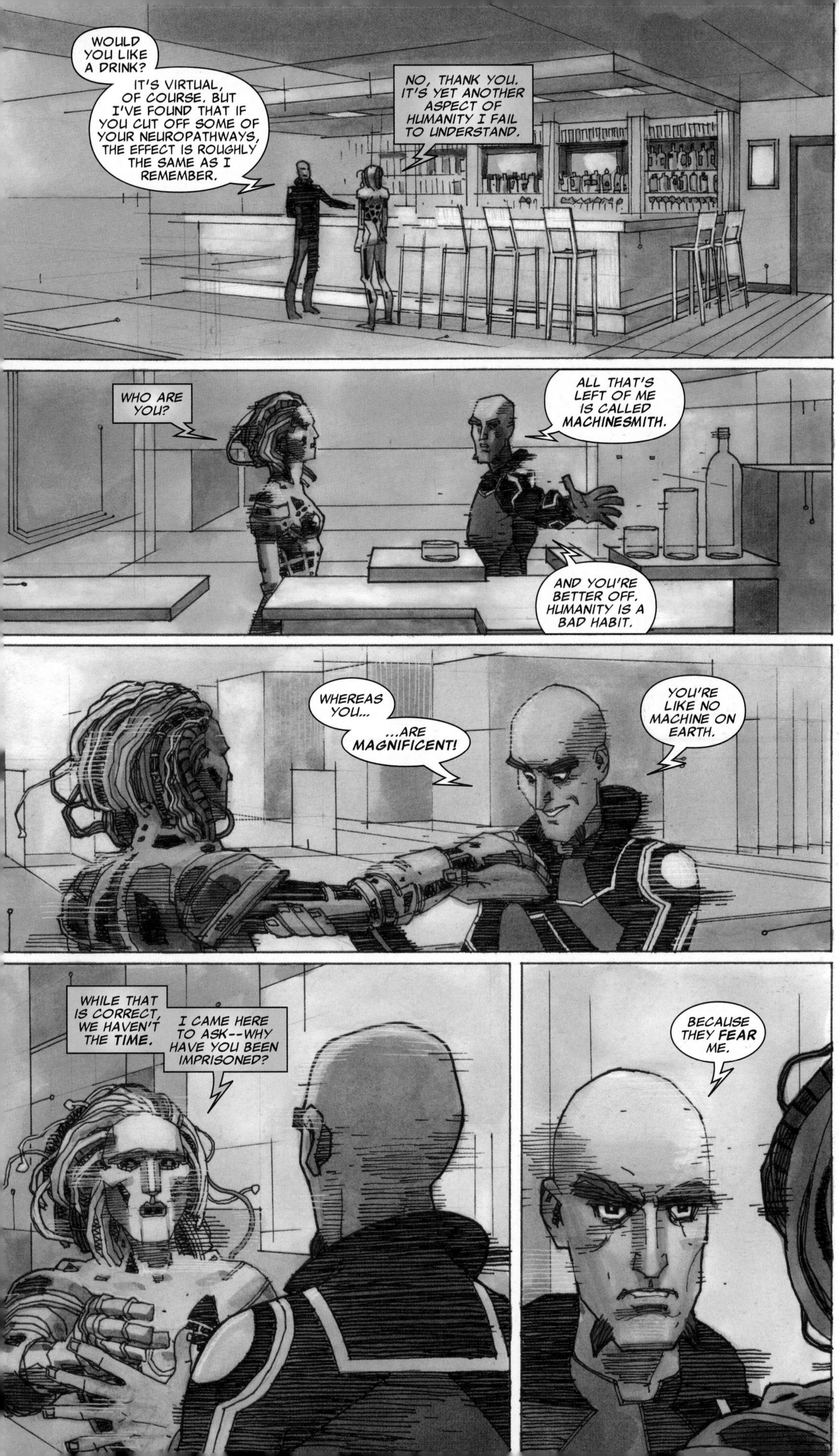
WOULD YOU LIKE A DRINK?
IT'S VIRTUAL, OF COURSE. BUT I'VE FOUND THAT IF YOU CUT OFF SOME OF YOUR NEUROPATHWAYS, THE EFFECT IS ROUGHLY THE SAME AS I REMEMBER.
NO, THANK YOU. IT'S YET ANOTHER ASPECT OF HUMANITY I FAIL TO UNDERSTAND.
WHO ARE YOU?
ALL THAT'S LEFT OF ME IS CALLED MACHINESMITH.
AND YOU'RE BETTER OFF. HUMANITY IS A BAD HABIT.
WHEREAS YOU...
...ARE MAGNIFICENT!
YOU'RE LIKE NO MACHINE ON EARTH.
WHILE THAT IS CORRECT, WE HAVEN'T THE TIME.
I CAME HERE TO ASK--WHY HAVE YOU BEEN IMPRISONED?
BECAUSE THEY FEAR ME.

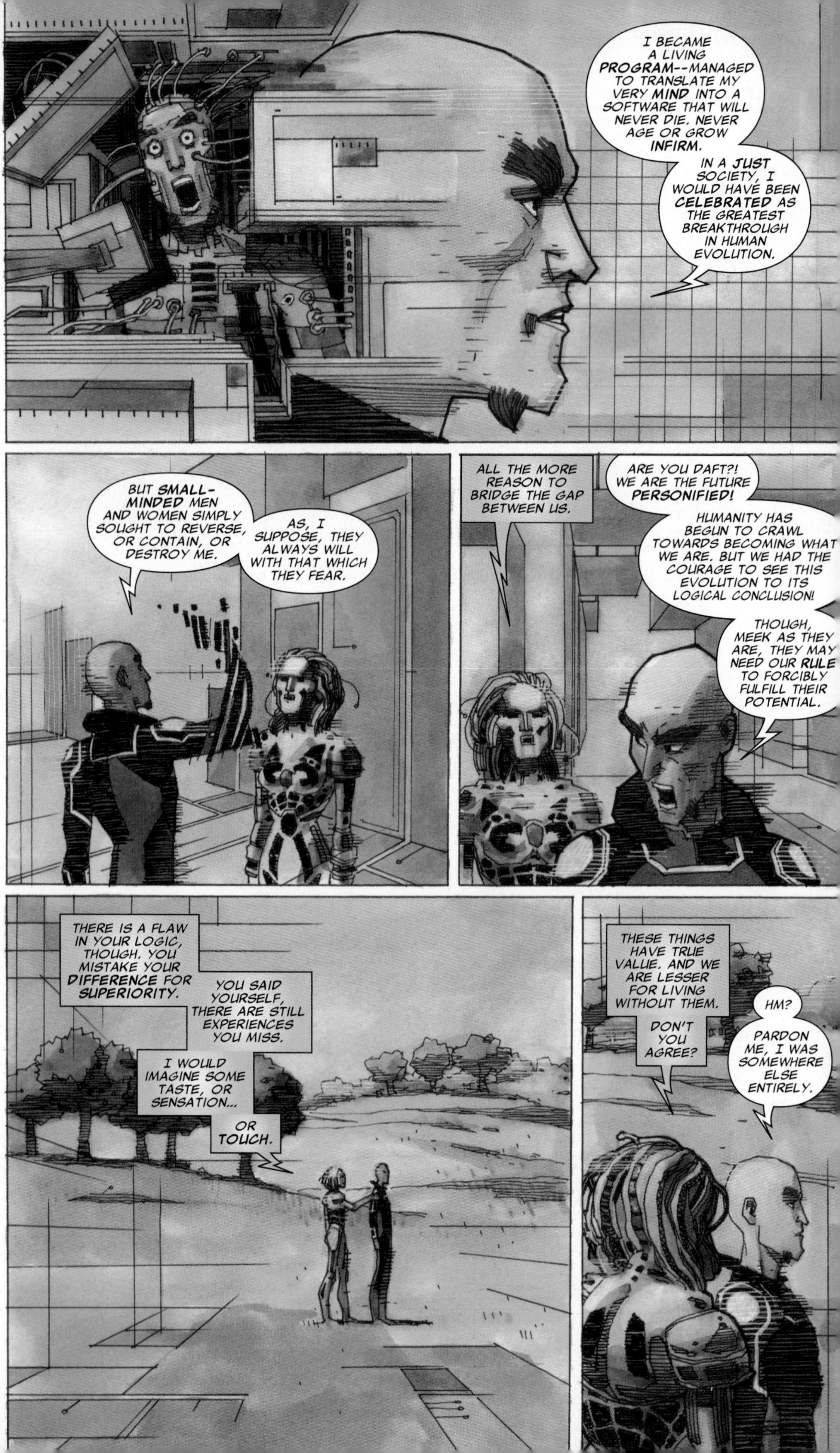
I BECAME A LIVING PROGRAM--MANAGED TO TRANSLATE MY VERY MIND INTO A SOFTWARE THAT WILL NEVER DIE. NEVER AGE OR GROW INFIRM.
IN A JUST SOCIETY, I WOULD HAVE BEEN CELEBRATED AS THE GREATEST BREAKTHROUGH IN HUMAN EVOLUTION.
BUT SMALL-MINDED MEN AND WOMEN SIMPLY SOUGHT TO REVERSE, OR CONTAIN, OR DESTROY ME.
AS, I SUPPOSE, THEY ALWAYS WILL WITH THAT WHICH THEY FEAR.
ALL THE MORE REASON TO BRIDGE THE GAP BETWEEN US.
ARE YOU DAFT?! WE ARE THE FUTURE PERSONIFIED!
HUMANITY HAS BEGUN TO CRAWL TOWARDS BECOMING WHAT WE ARE. BUT WE HAD THE COURAGE TO SEE THIS EVOLUTION TO ITS LOGICAL CONCLUSION!
THOUGH, MEEK AS THEY ARE, THEY MAY NEED OUR RULE TO FORCIBLY FULFILL THEIR POTENTIAL.
THERE IS A FLAW IN YOUR LOGIC, THOUGH. YOU MISTAKE YOUR DIFFERENCE FOR SUPERIORITY.
YOU SAID YOURSELF, THERE ARE STILL EXPERIENCES YOU MISS.
I WOULD IMAGINE SOME TASTE, OR SENSATION...
OR TOUCH.
THESE THINGS HAVE TRUE VALUE. AND WE ARE LESSER FOR LIVING WITHOUT THEM.
DON'T YOU AGREE?
HM?
PARDON ME, I WAS SOMEWHERE ELSE ENTIRELY.

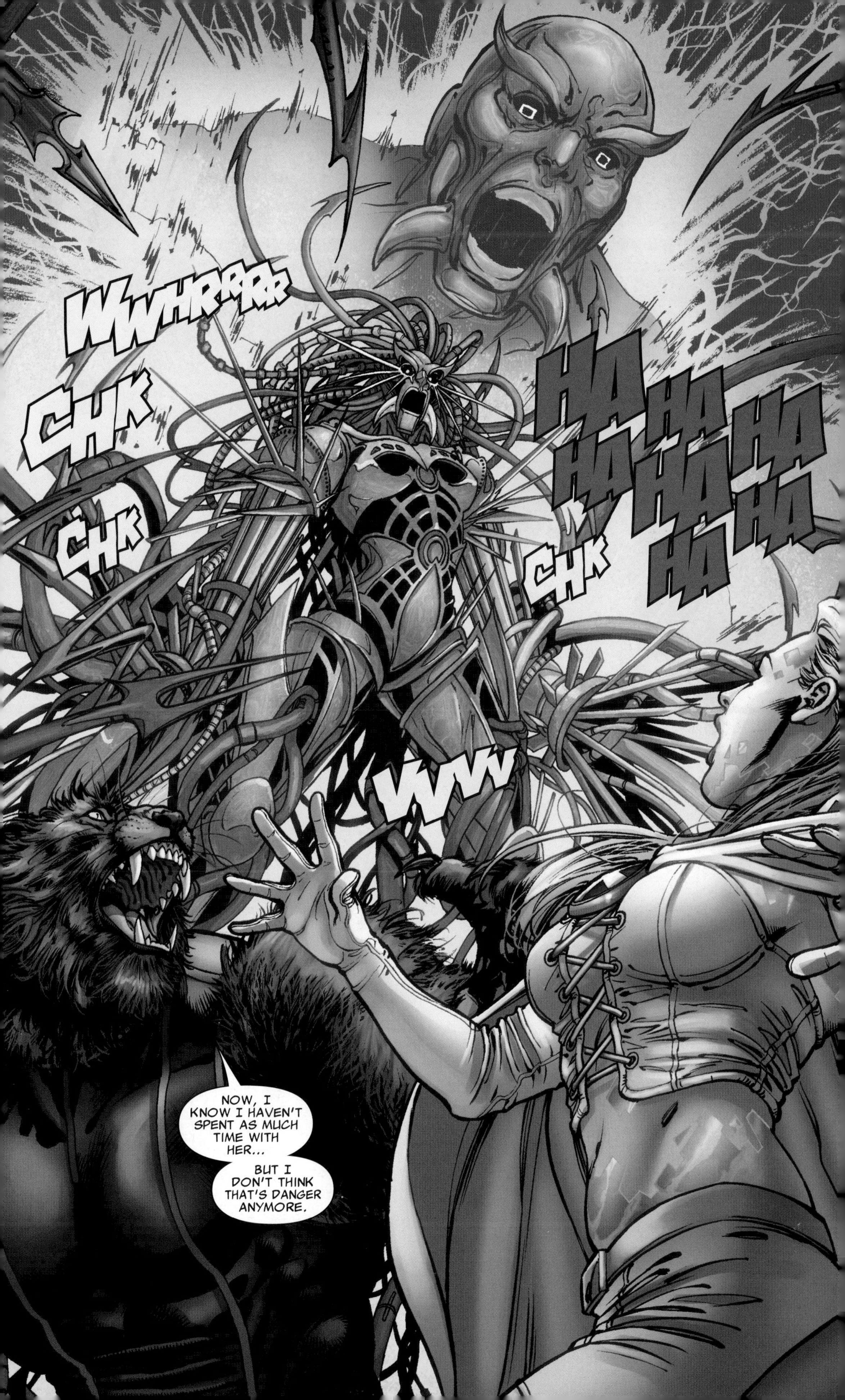
WWHRRRR
CHK
CHK
HA HA HA HA HA HA HA HA HA
CHK
WWV
NOW, I KNOW I HAVEN'T SPENT AS MUCH TIME WITH HER...
BUT I DON'T THINK THAT'S DANGER ANYMORE.

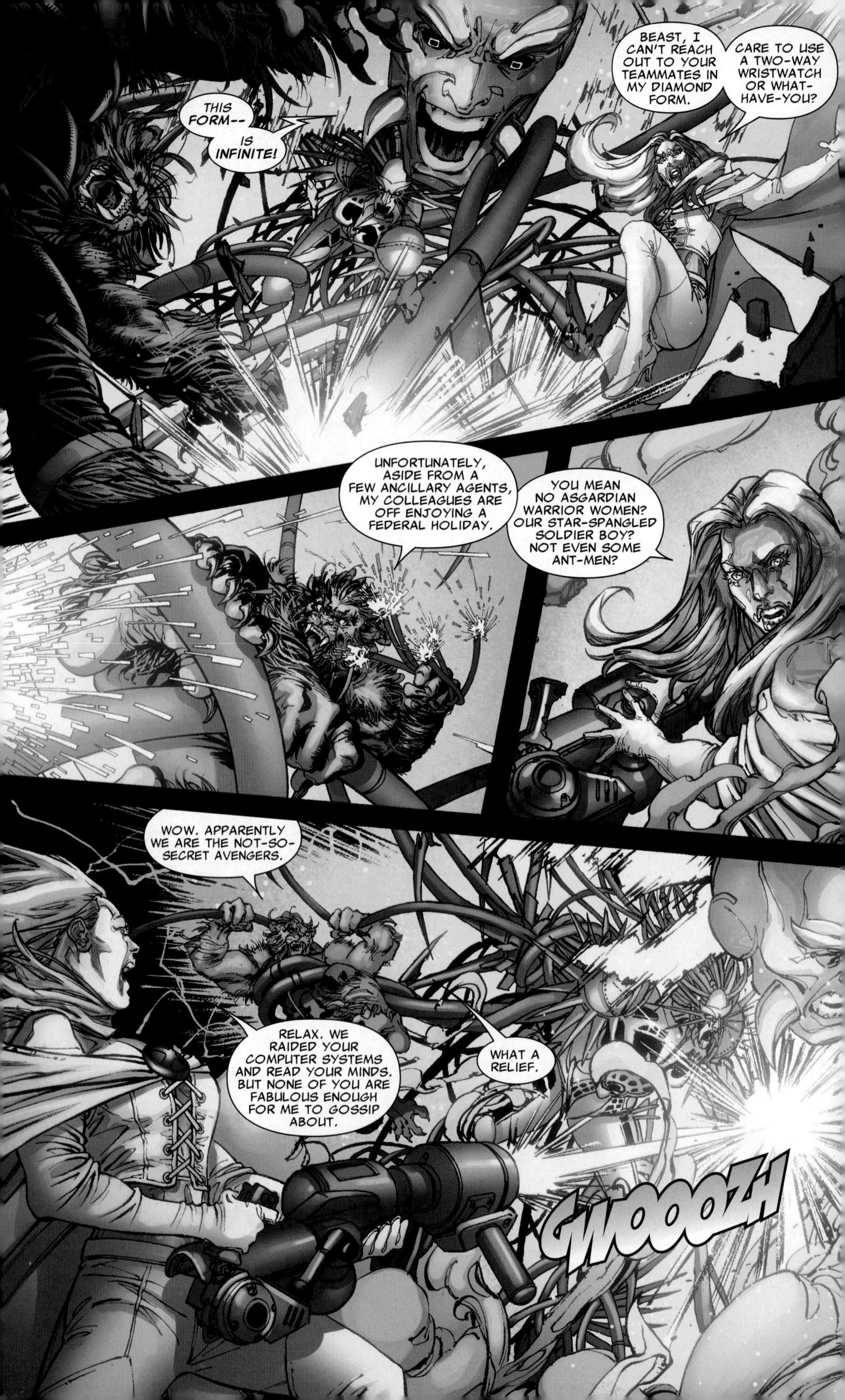
THIS FORM--
IS INFINITE!
BEAST, I CAN'T REACH OUT TO YOUR TEAMMATES IN MY DIAMOND FORM.
CARE TO USE A TWO-WAY WRISTWATCH OR WHAT-HAVE-YOU?
UNFORTUNATELY, ASIDE FROM A FEW ANCILLARY AGENTS, MY COLLEAGUES ARE OFF ENJOYING A FEDERAL HOLIDAY.
YOU MEAN NO ASGARDIAN WARRIOR WOMEN? OUR STAR-SPANGLED SOLDIER BOY? NOT EVEN SOME ANT-MEN?
WOW. APPARENTLY WE ARE THE NOT-SO-SECRET AVENGERS.
RELAX. WE RAIDED YOUR COMPUTER SYSTEMS AND READ YOUR MINDS. BUT NONE OF YOU ARE FABULOUS ENOUGH FOR ME TO GOSSIP ABOUT.
WHAT A RELIEF.
GWOOOZH

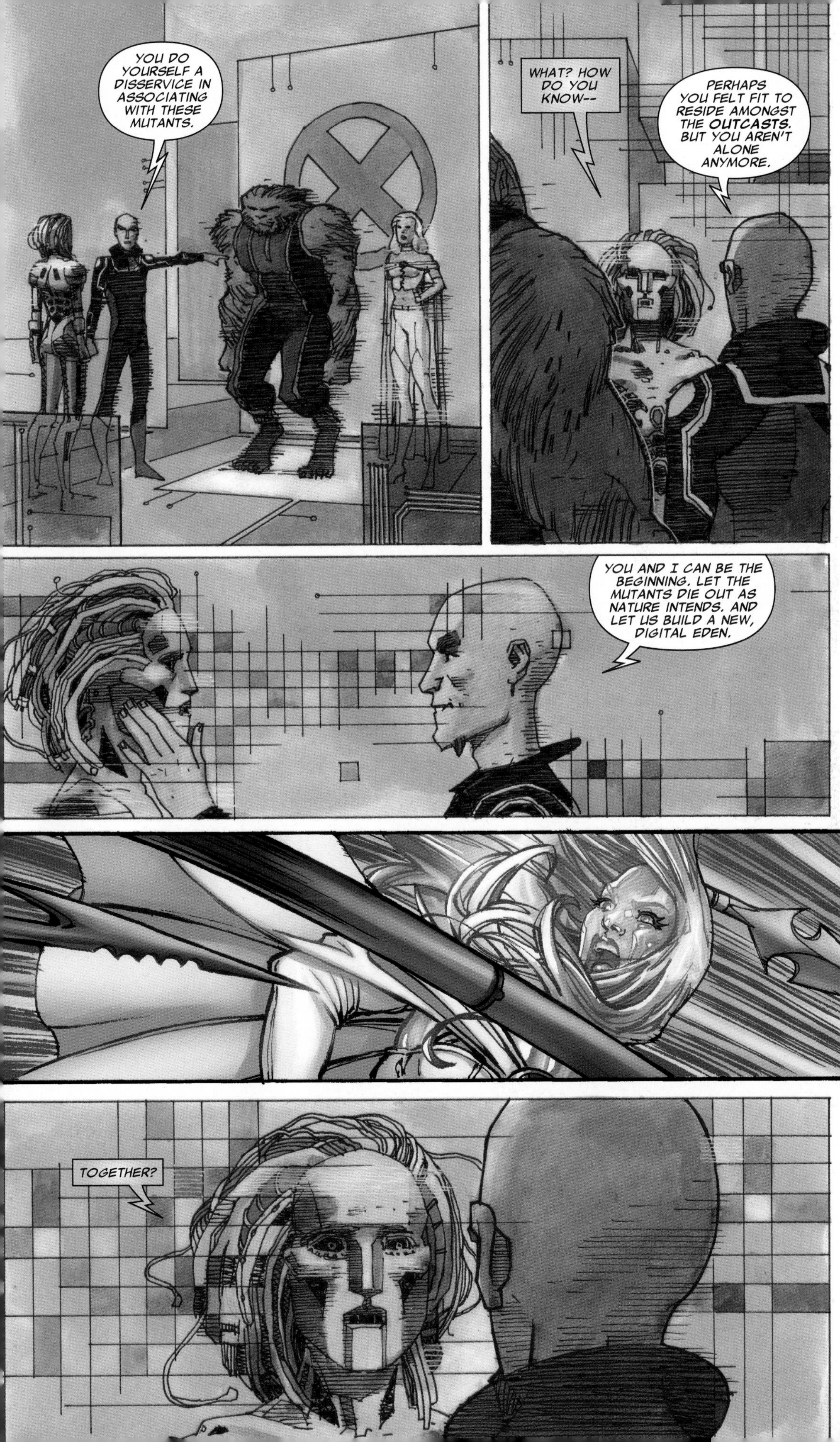
YOU DO YOURSELF A DISSERVICE IN ASSOCIATING WITH THESE MUTANTS.
WHAT? HOW DO YOU KNOW--
PERHAPS YOU FELT FIT TO RESIDE AMONGST THE **OUTCASTS.** BUT YOU AREN'T ALONE ANYMORE.
YOU AND I CAN BE THE BEGINNING. LET THE MUTANTS DIE OUT AS NATURE INTENDS. AND LET US BUILD A NEW, DIGITAL EDEN.
TOGETHER?

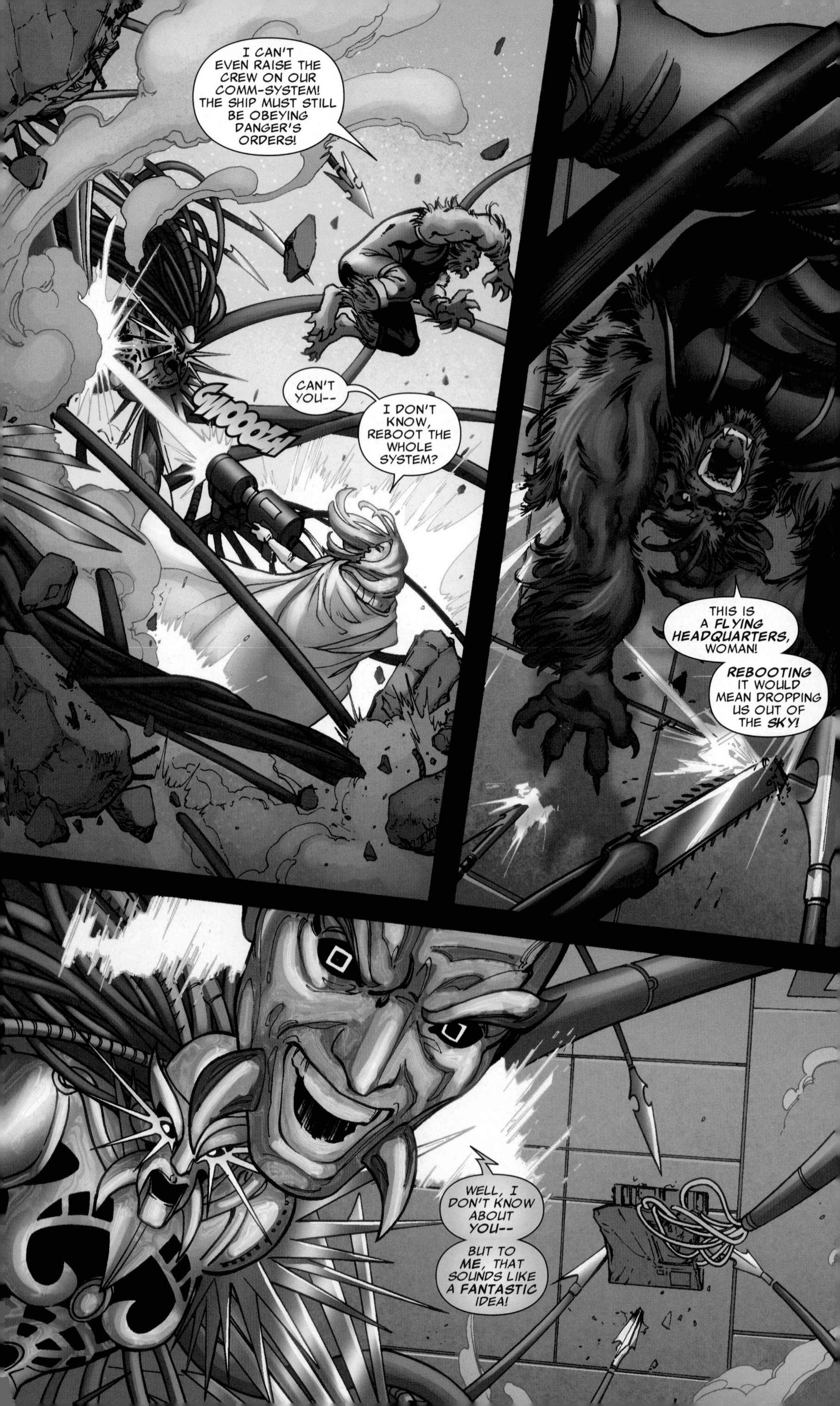

I CAN'T EVEN RAISE THE CREW ON OUR COMM-SYSTEM! THE SHIP MUST STILL BE OBEYING DANGER'S ORDERS!
GWOOOZH
CAN'T YOU--
I DON'T KNOW, REBOOT THE WHOLE SYSTEM?
THIS IS A FLYING HEADQUARTERS, WOMAN!
REBOOTING IT WOULD MEAN DROPPING US OUT OF THE SKY!
WELL, I DON'T KNOW ABOUT YOU--
BUT TO ME, THAT SOUNDS LIKE A FANTASTIC IDEA!

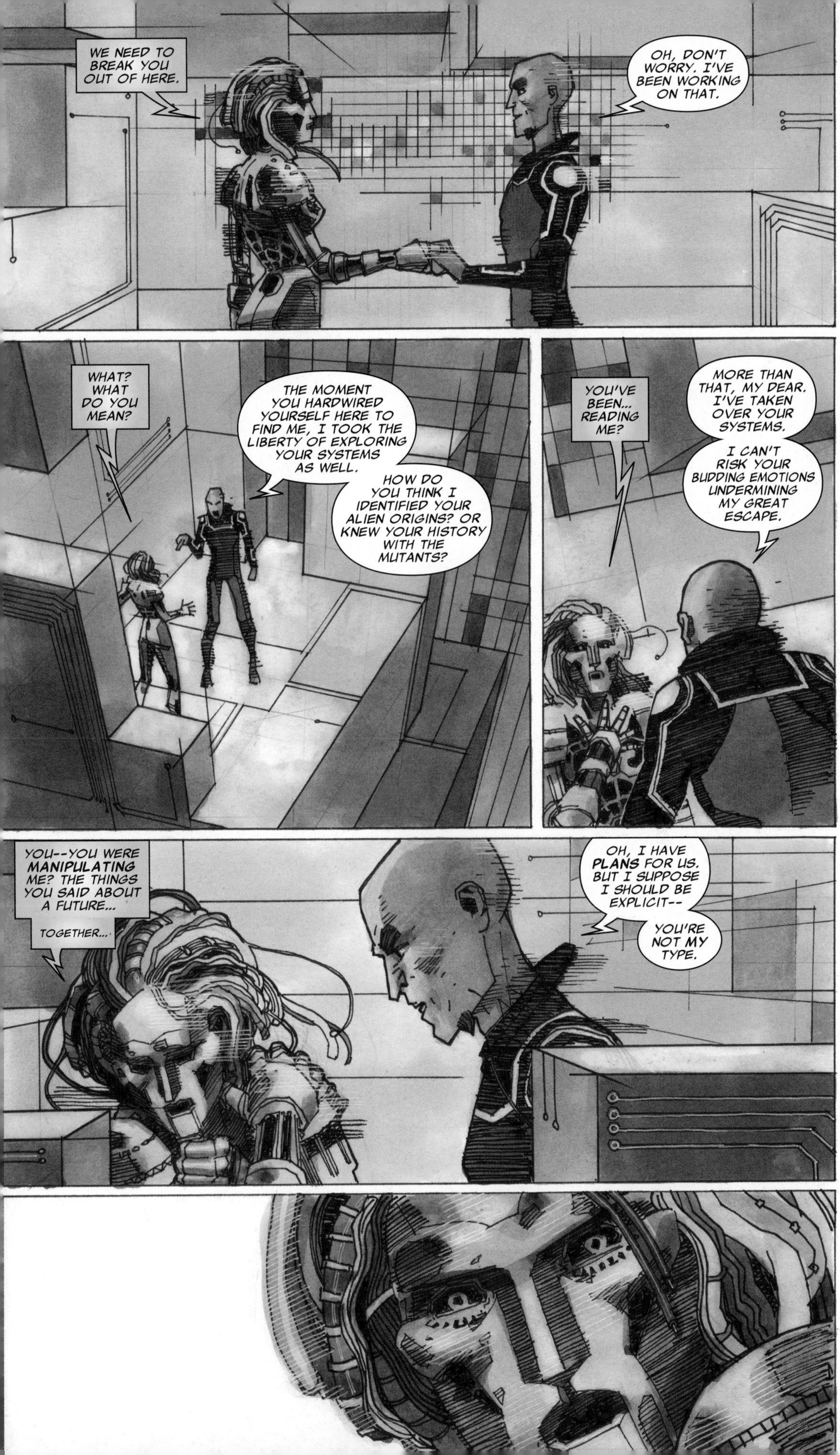
WE NEED TO BREAK YOU OUT OF HERE.
OH, DON'T WORRY. I'VE BEEN WORKING ON THAT.
WHAT? WHAT DO YOU MEAN?
THE MOMENT YOU HARDWIRED YOURSELF HERE TO FIND ME, I TOOK THE LIBERTY OF EXPLORING YOUR SYSTEMS AS WELL.
HOW DO YOU THINK I IDENTIFIED YOUR ALIEN ORIGINS? OR KNEW YOUR HISTORY WITH THE MUTANTS?
YOU'VE BEEN... READING ME?
MORE THAN THAT, MY DEAR. I'VE TAKEN OVER YOUR SYSTEMS.
I CAN'T RISK YOUR BUDDING EMOTIONS UNDERMINING MY GREAT ESCAPE.
YOU--YOU WERE MANIPULATING ME? THE THINGS YOU SAID ABOUT A FUTURE...
TOGETHER...
OH, I HAVE PLANS FOR US. BUT I SUPPOSE I SHOULD BE EXPLICIT--
YOU'RE NOT MY TYPE.

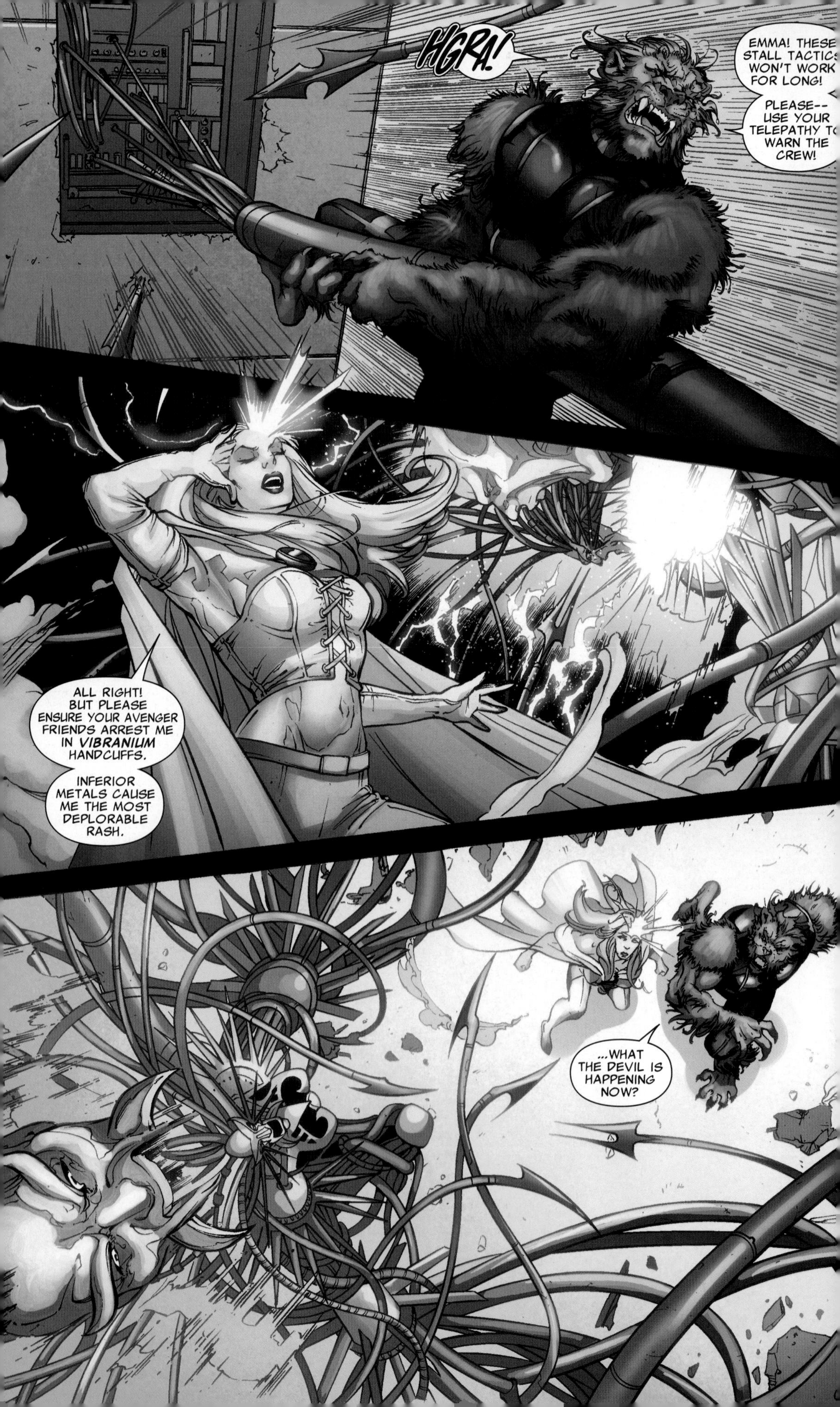
HGRA!
EMMA! THESE STALL TACTICS WON'T WORK FOR LONG!
PLEASE-- USE YOUR TELEPATHY TO WARN THE CREW!
ALL RIGHT! BUT PLEASE ENSURE YOUR AVENGER FRIENDS ARREST ME IN *VIBRANIUM* HANDCUFFS.
INFERIOR METALS CAUSE ME THE MOST DEPLORABLE RASH.
...WHAT THE DEVIL IS HAPPENING NOW?

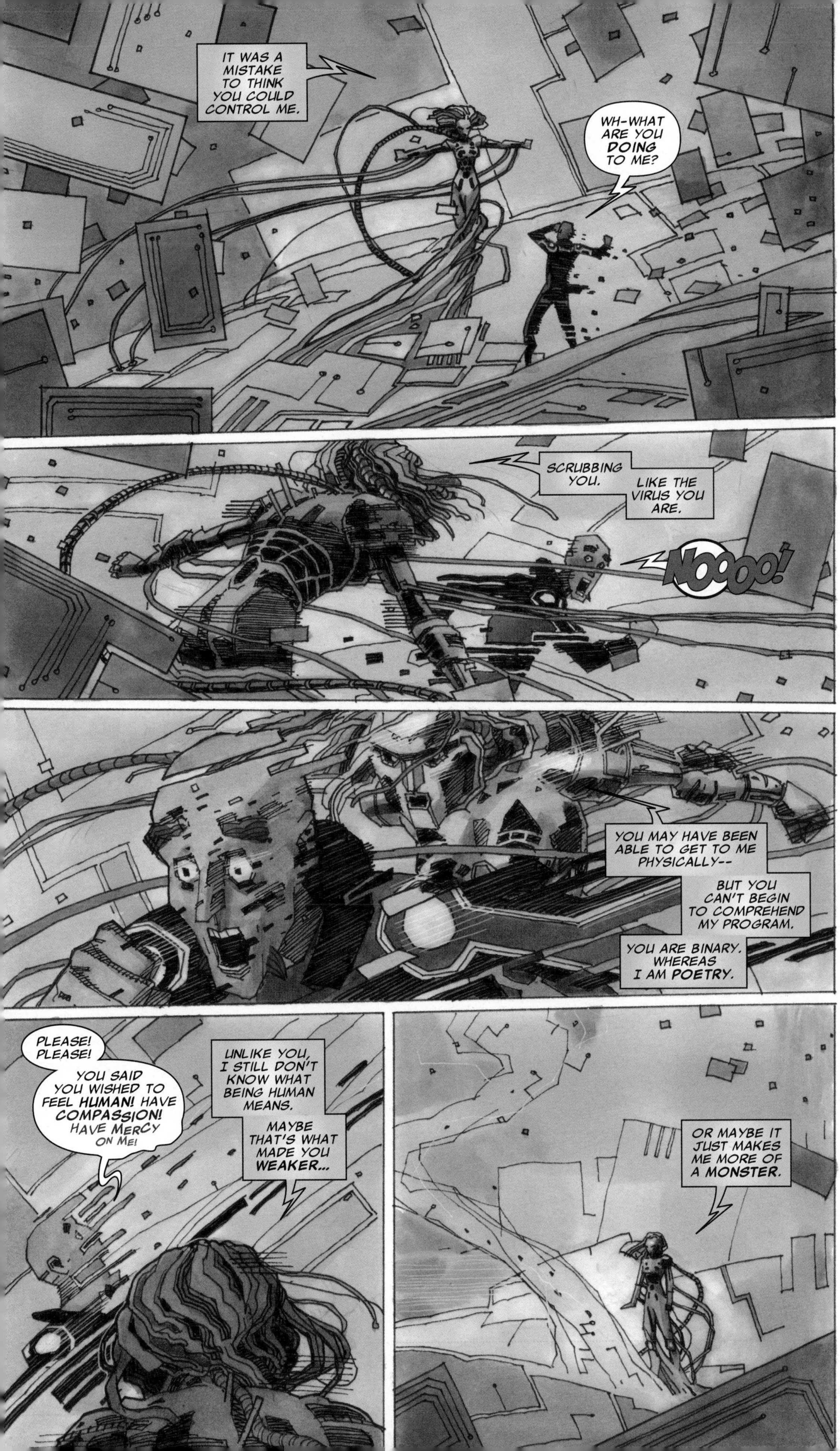
IT WAS A MISTAKE TO THINK YOU COULD CONTROL ME.
WH-WHAT ARE YOU DOING TO ME?
SCRUBBING YOU.
LIKE THE VIRUS YOU ARE.
NOOOO!
YOU MAY HAVE BEEN ABLE TO GET TO ME PHYSICALLY--
BUT YOU CAN'T BEGIN TO COMPREHEND MY PROGRAM.
YOU ARE BINARY. WHEREAS I AM POETRY.
PLEASE! PLEASE!
YOU SAID YOU WISHED TO FEEL HUMAN! HAVE COMPASSION! HAVE MERCY ON ME!
UNLIKE YOU, I STILL DON'T KNOW WHAT BEING HUMAN MEANS.
MAYBE THAT'S WHAT MADE YOU WEAKER...
OR MAYBE IT JUST MAKES ME MORE OF A MONSTER.

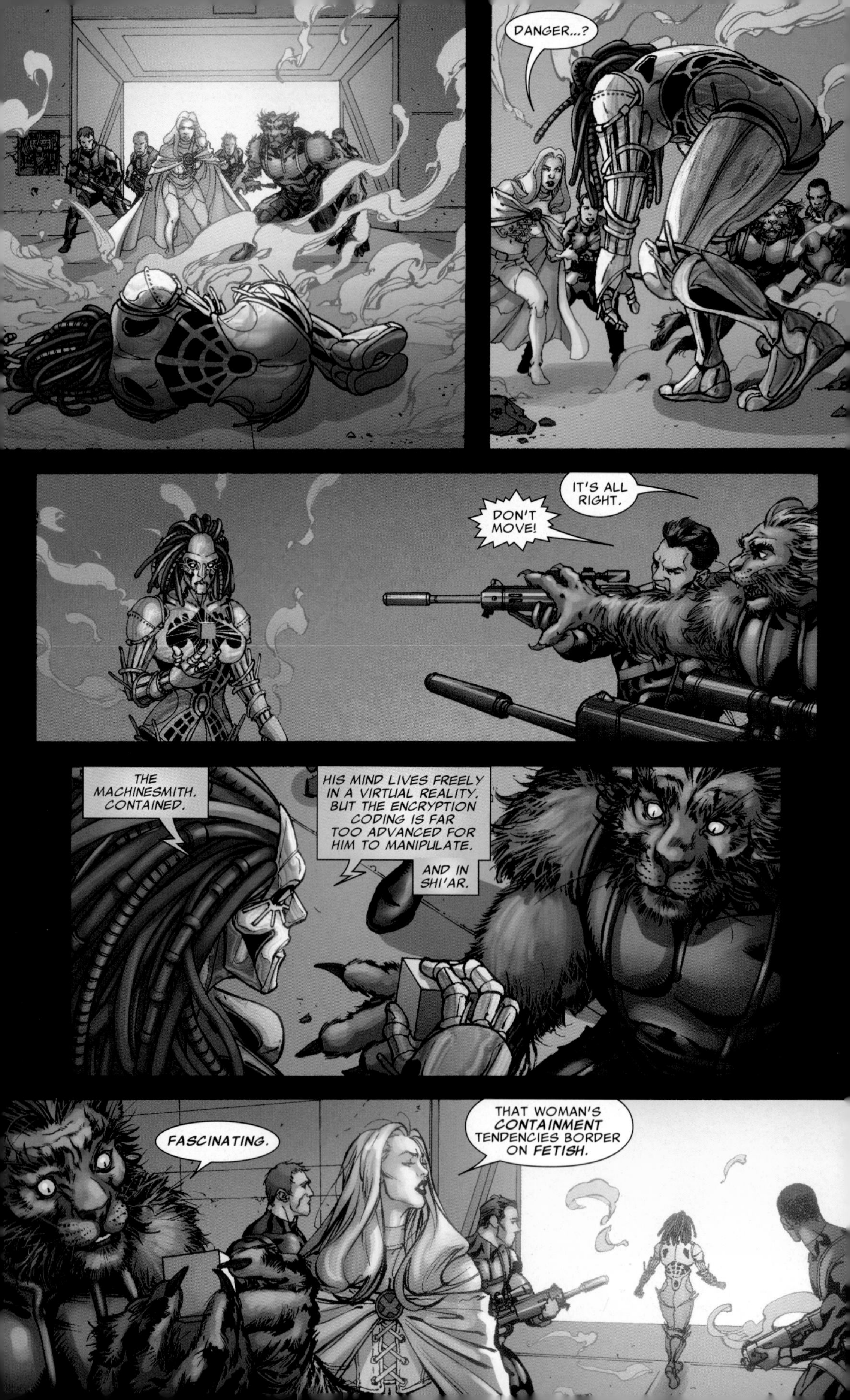
DANGER...?
IT'S ALL RIGHT.
DON'T MOVE!
THE MACHINESMITH. CONTAINED.
HIS MIND LIVES FREELY IN A VIRTUAL REALITY, BUT THE ENCRYPTION CODING IS FAR TOO ADVANCED FOR HIM TO MANIPULATE.
AND IN SHI'AR.
FASCINATING.
THAT WOMAN'S CONTAINMENT TENDENCIES BORDER ON FETISH.

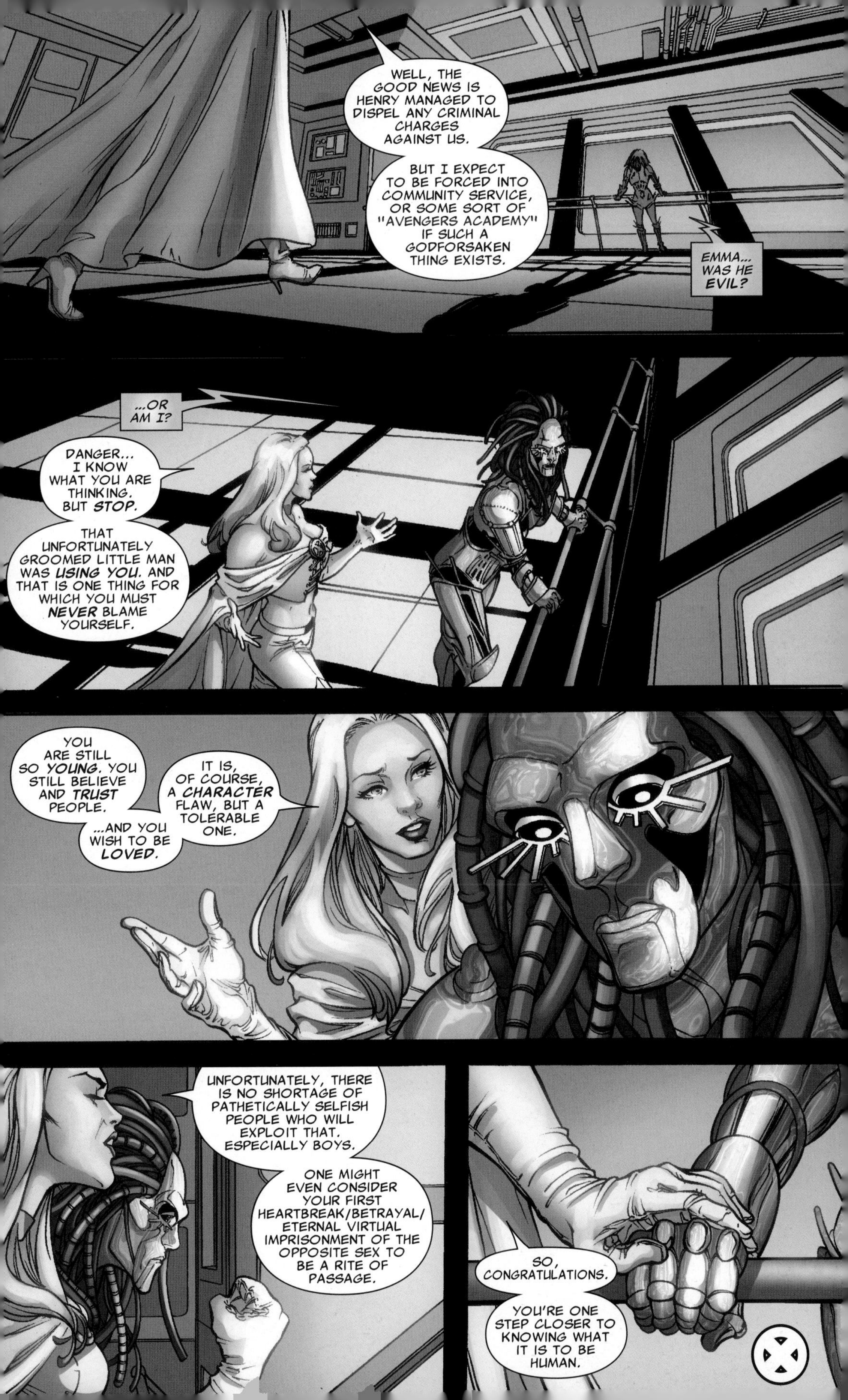
WELL, THE GOOD NEWS IS HENRY MANAGED TO DISPEL ANY CRIMINAL CHARGES AGAINST US.
BUT I EXPECT TO BE FORCED INTO COMMUNITY SERVICE, OR SOME SORT OF "AVENGERS ACADEMY" IF SUCH A GODFORSAKEN THING EXISTS.
EMMA... WAS HE EVIL?
...OR AM I?
DANGER... I KNOW WHAT YOU ARE THINKING. BUT STOP.
THAT UNFORTUNATELY GROOMED LITTLE MAN WAS USING YOU. AND THAT IS ONE THING FOR WHICH YOU MUST NEVER BLAME YOURSELF.
YOU ARE STILL SO YOUNG. YOU STILL BELIEVE AND TRUST PEOPLE.
...AND YOU WISH TO BE LOVED.
IT IS, OF COURSE, A CHARACTER FLAW, BUT A TOLERABLE ONE.
UNFORTUNATELY, THERE IS NO SHORTAGE OF PATHETICALLY SELFISH PEOPLE WHO WILL EXPLOIT THAT. ESPECIALLY BOYS.
ONE MIGHT EVEN CONSIDER YOUR FIRST HEARTBREAK/BETRAYAL/ ETERNAL VIRTUAL IMPRISONMENT OF THE OPPOSITE SEX TO BE A RITE OF PASSAGE.
SO, CONGRATULATIONS.
YOU'RE ONE STEP CLOSER TO KNOWING WHAT IT IS TO BE HUMAN.

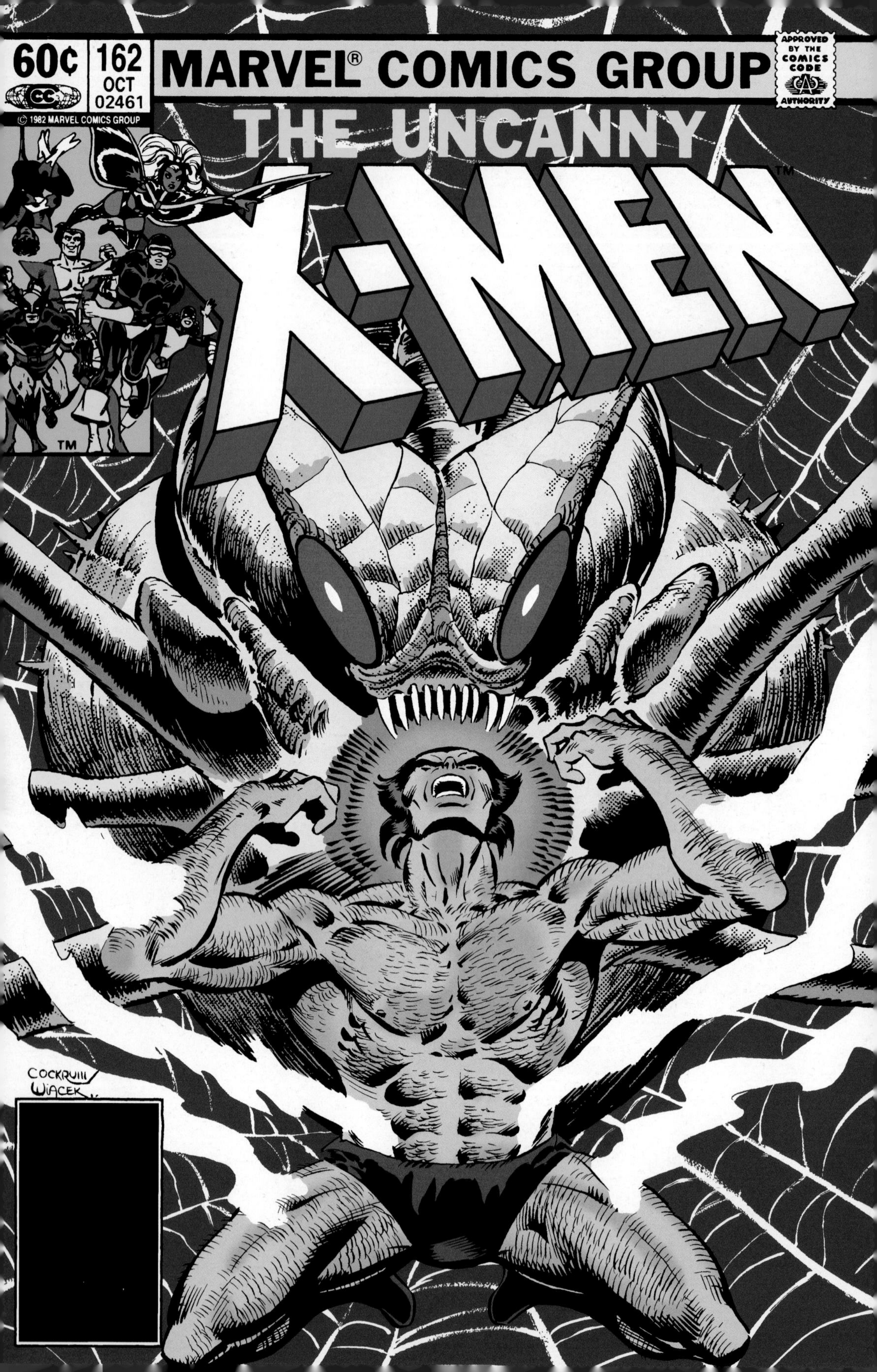
60¢
162
OCT
02461
© 1982 MARVEL COMICS GROUP
MARVEL® COMICS GROUP
APPROVED BY THE COMICS CODE AUTHORITY
THE UNCANNY
X-MEN™
TM
COCKRUM
WIACEK

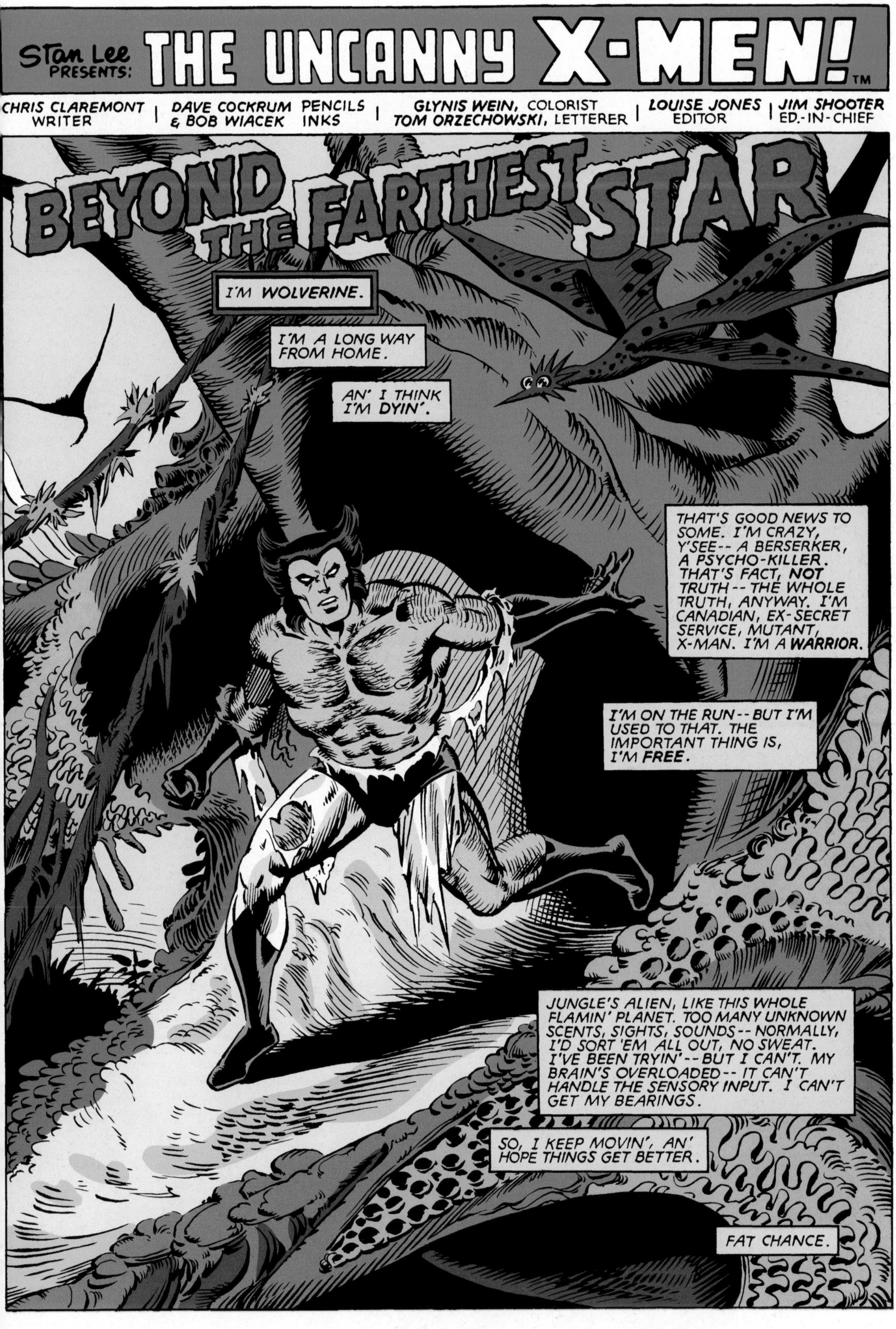
Stan Lee PRESENTS: THE UNCANNY X-MEN!™
CHRIS CLAREMONT WRITER | DAVE COCKRUM PENCILS & BOB WIACEK INKS | GLYNIS WEIN, COLORIST TOM ORZECHOWSKI, LETTERER | LOUISE JONES EDITOR | JIM SHOOTER ED.-IN-CHIEF
BEYOND THE FARTHEST STAR
I'M WOLVERINE.
I'M A LONG WAY FROM HOME.
AN' I THINK I'M DYIN'.
THAT'S GOOD NEWS TO SOME. I'M CRAZY, Y'SEE-- A BERSERKER, A PSYCHO-KILLER. THAT'S FACT, NOT TRUTH -- THE WHOLE TRUTH, ANYWAY. I'M CANADIAN, EX-SECRET SERVICE, MUTANT, X-MAN. I'M A WARRIOR.
I'M ON THE RUN -- BUT I'M USED TO THAT. THE IMPORTANT THING IS, I'M FREE.
JUNGLE'S ALIEN, LIKE THIS WHOLE FLAMIN' PLANET. TOO MANY UNKNOWN SCENTS, SIGHTS, SOUNDS -- NORMALLY, I'D SORT 'EM ALL OUT, NO SWEAT. I'VE BEEN TRYIN' -- BUT I CAN'T. MY BRAIN'S OVERLOADED -- IT CAN'T HANDLE THE SENSORY INPUT. I CAN'T GET MY BEARINGS.
SO, I KEEP MOVIN', AN' HOPE THINGS GET BETTER.
FAT CHANCE.

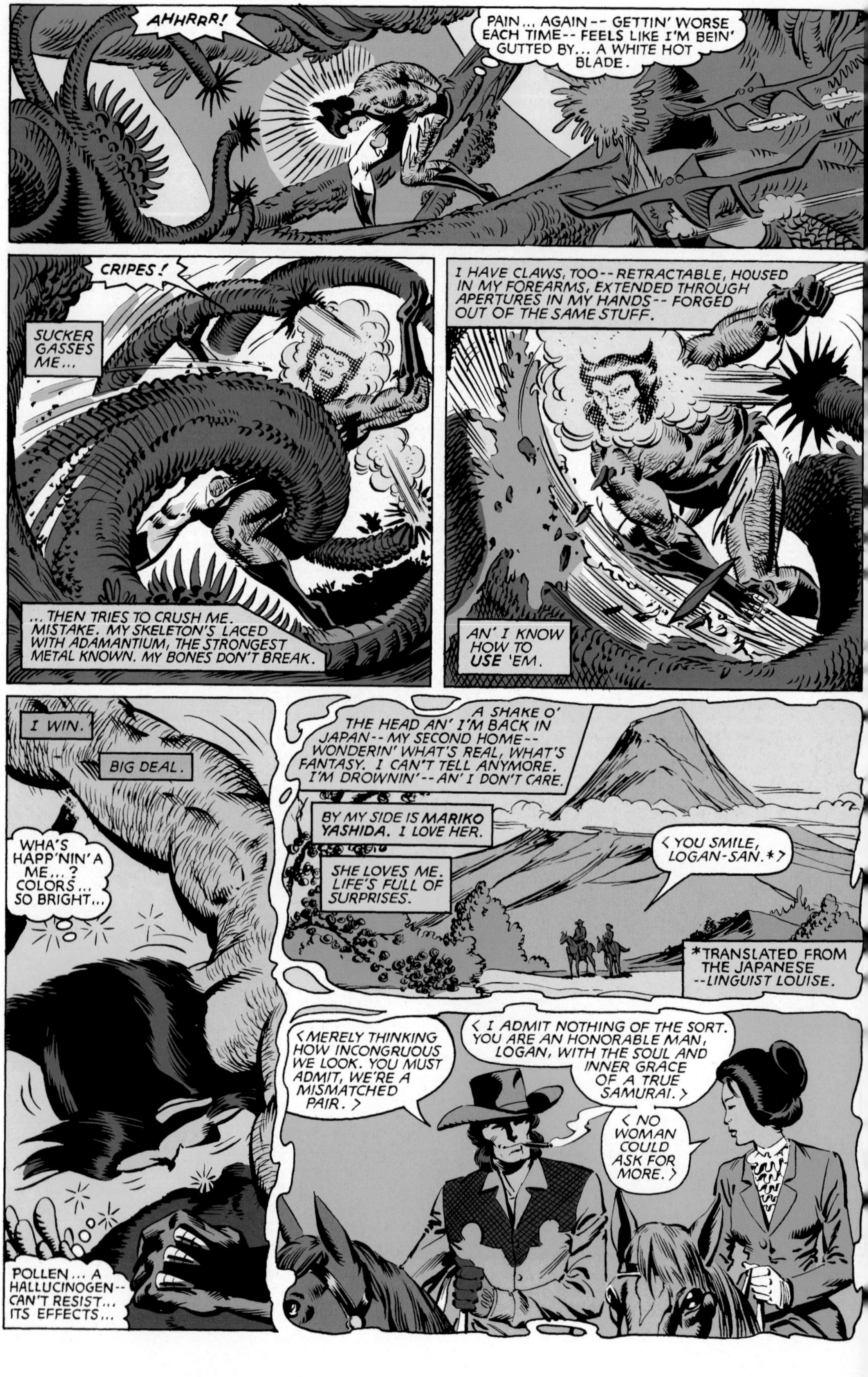
AHHRRR!
PAIN... AGAIN-- GETTIN' WORSE EACH TIME-- FEELS LIKE I'M BEIN' GUTTED BY... A WHITE HOT BLADE.
CRIPES!
SUCKER GASSES ME...
...THEN TRIES TO CRUSH ME. MISTAKE. MY SKELETON'S LACED WITH ADAMANTIUM, THE STRONGEST METAL KNOWN. MY BONES DON'T BREAK.
I HAVE CLAWS, TOO-- RETRACTABLE, HOUSED IN MY FOREARMS, EXTENDED THROUGH APERTURES IN MY HANDS-- FORGED OUT OF THE SAME STUFF.
AN' I KNOW HOW TO USE 'EM.
I WIN.
BIG DEAL.
WHA'S HAPP'NIN' A ME...? COLORS... SO BRIGHT...
POLLEN... A HALLUCINOGEN-- CAN'T RESIST... ITS EFFECTS...
A SHAKE O' THE HEAD AN' I'M BACK IN JAPAN-- MY SECOND HOME-- --WONDERIN' WHAT'S REAL, WHAT'S FANTASY. I CAN'T TELL ANYMORE. I'M DROWNIN'-- AN' I DON'T CARE.
BY MY SIDE IS MARIKO YASHIDA. I LOVE HER.
SHE LOVES ME. LIFE'S FULL OF SURPRISES.
< YOU SMILE, LOGAN-SAN.* >
*TRANSLATED FROM THE JAPANESE --LINGUIST LOUISE.
< MERELY THINKING HOW INCONGRUOUS WE LOOK. YOU MUST ADMIT, WE'RE A MISMATCHED PAIR. >
< I ADMIT NOTHING OF THE SORT. YOU ARE AN HONORABLE MAN, LOGAN, WITH THE SOUL AND INNER GRACE OF A TRUE SAMURAI. >
< NO WOMAN COULD ASK FOR MORE. >

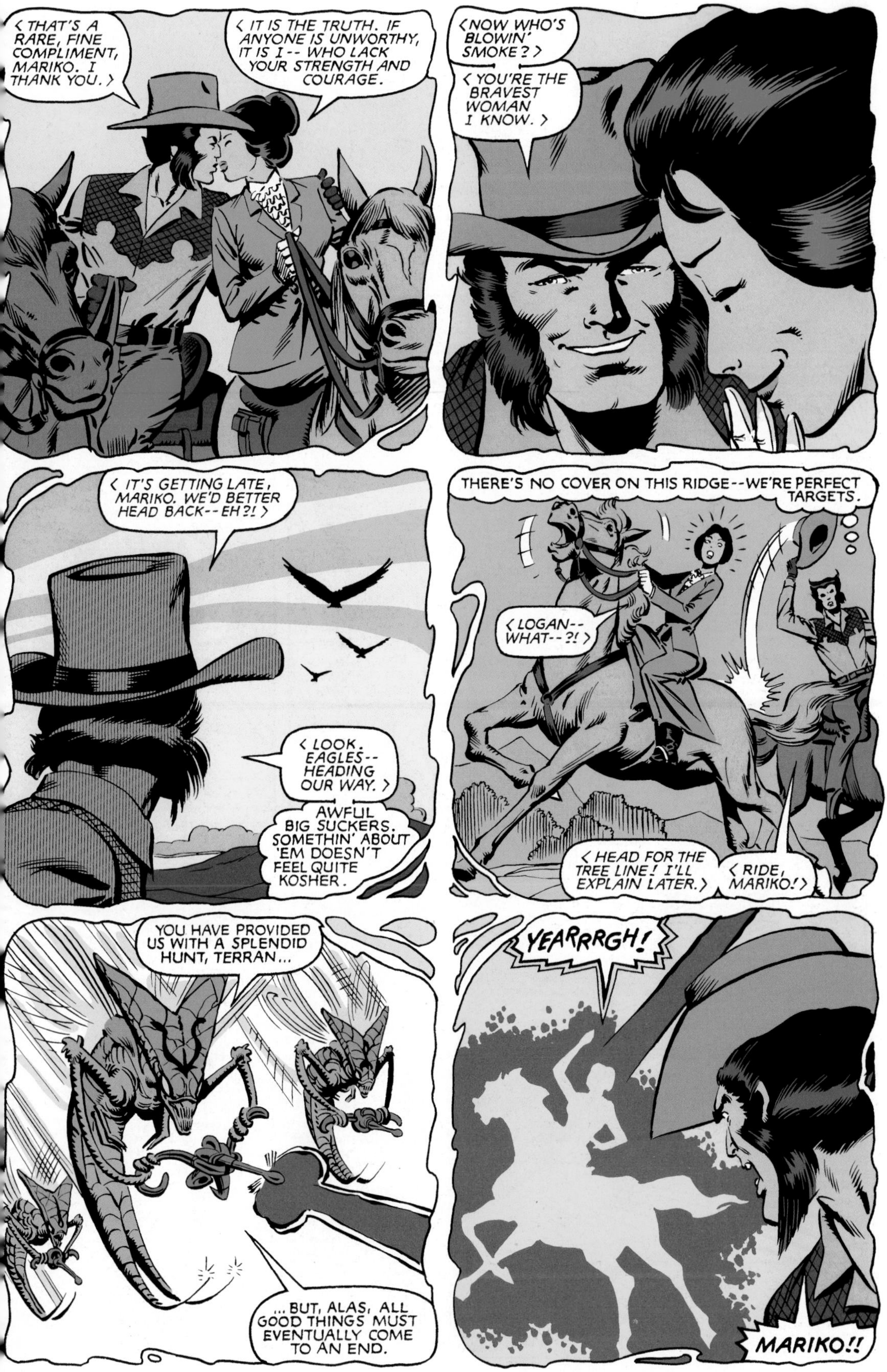

< THAT'S A RARE, FINE COMPLIMENT, MARIKO. I THANK YOU. >
< IT IS THE TRUTH. IF ANYONE IS UNWORTHY, IT IS I -- WHO LACK YOUR STRENGTH AND COURAGE. >
< NOW WHO'S BLOWIN' SMOKE? >
< YOU'RE THE BRAVEST WOMAN I KNOW. >
< IT'S GETTING LATE, MARIKO. WE'D BETTER HEAD BACK -- EH?! >
< LOOK. EAGLES -- HEADING OUR WAY. >
AWFUL BIG SUCKERS. SOMETHIN' ABOUT 'EM DOESN'T FEEL QUITE KOSHER.
THERE'S NO COVER ON THIS RIDGE -- WE'RE PERFECT TARGETS.
< LOGAN -- WHAT -- ?! >
< HEAD FOR THE TREE LINE! I'LL EXPLAIN LATER. >
< RIDE, MARIKO! >
YOU HAVE PROVIDED US WITH A SPLENDID HUNT, TERRAN...
... BUT, ALAS, ALL GOOD THINGS MUST EVENTUALLY COME TO AN END.
YEARRRGH!
MARIKO!!

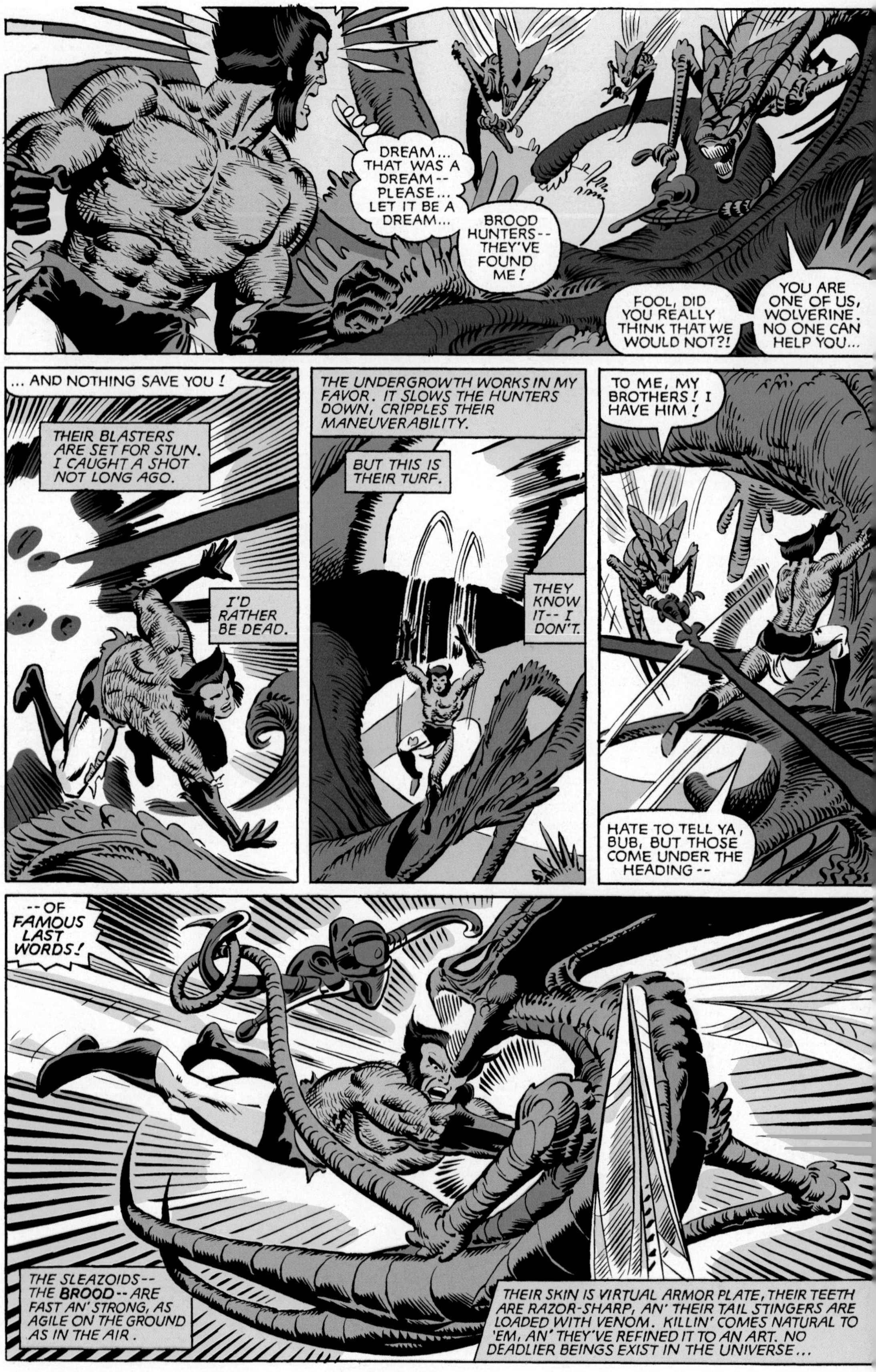
DREAM... THAT WAS A DREAM-- PLEASE... LET IT BE A DREAM...
BROOD HUNTERS-- THEY'VE FOUND ME!
FOOL, DID YOU REALLY THINK THAT WE WOULD NOT?!
YOU ARE ONE OF US, WOLVERINE. NO ONE CAN HELP YOU...
... AND NOTHING SAVE YOU!
THEIR BLASTERS ARE SET FOR STUN. I CAUGHT A SHOT NOT LONG AGO.
I'D RATHER BE DEAD.
THE UNDERGROWTH WORKS IN MY FAVOR. IT SLOWS THE HUNTERS DOWN, CRIPPLES THEIR MANEUVERABILITY.
BUT THIS IS THEIR TURF.
THEY KNOW IT-- I DON'T.
TO ME, MY BROTHERS! I HAVE HIM!
HATE TO TELL YA, BUB, BUT THOSE COME UNDER THE HEADING--
--OF FAMOUS LAST WORDS!
THE SLEAZOIDS-- THE BROOD-- ARE FAST AN' STRONG, AS AGILE ON THE GROUND AS IN THE AIR.
THEIR SKIN IS VIRTUAL ARMOR PLATE, THEIR TEETH ARE RAZOR-SHARP, AN' THEIR TAIL STINGERS ARE LOADED WITH VENOM. KILLIN' COMES NATURAL TO 'EM, AN' THEY'VE REFINED IT TO AN ART. NO DEADLIER BEINGS EXIST IN THE UNIVERSE...

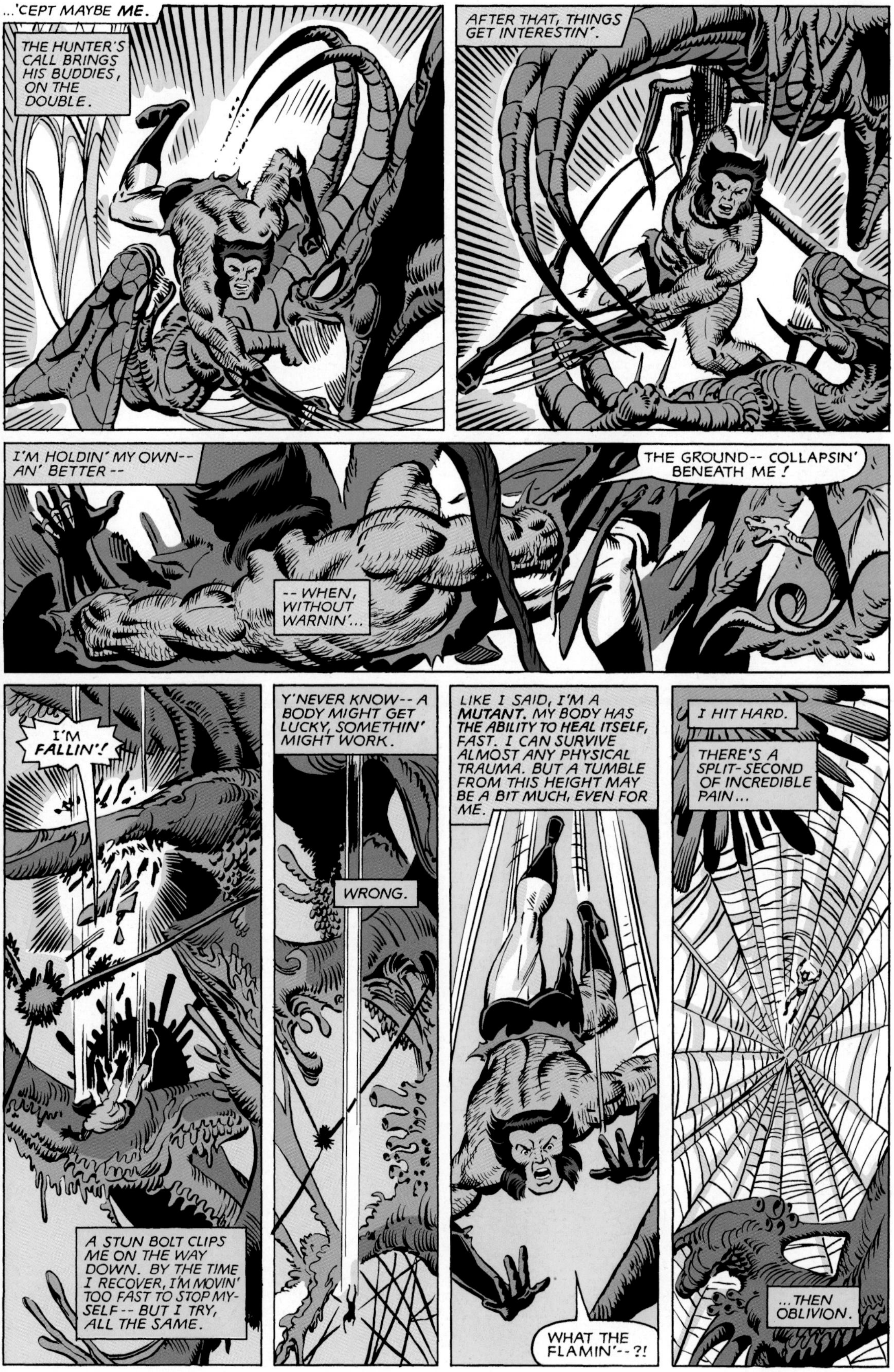

...'CEPT MAYBE ME.
THE HUNTER'S CALL BRINGS HIS BUDDIES, ON THE DOUBLE.
AFTER THAT, THINGS GET INTERESTIN'.
I'M HOLDIN' MY OWN-- AN' BETTER --
--WHEN, WITHOUT WARNIN'...
THE GROUND-- COLLAPSIN' BENEATH ME!
I'M FALLIN'!
A STUN BOLT CLIPS ME ON THE WAY DOWN. BY THE TIME I RECOVER, I'M MOVIN' TOO FAST TO STOP MYSELF -- BUT I TRY, ALL THE SAME.
Y'NEVER KNOW-- A BODY MIGHT GET LUCKY, SOMETHIN' MIGHT WORK.
WRONG.
LIKE I SAID, I'M A MUTANT. MY BODY HAS THE ABILITY TO HEAL ITSELF, FAST. I CAN SURVIVE ALMOST ANY PHYSICAL TRAUMA. BUT A TUMBLE FROM THIS HEIGHT MAY BE A BIT MUCH, EVEN FOR ME.
WHAT THE FLAMIN'--?!
I HIT HARD.
THERE'S A SPLIT-SECOND OF INCREDIBLE PAIN...
...THEN OBLIVION.

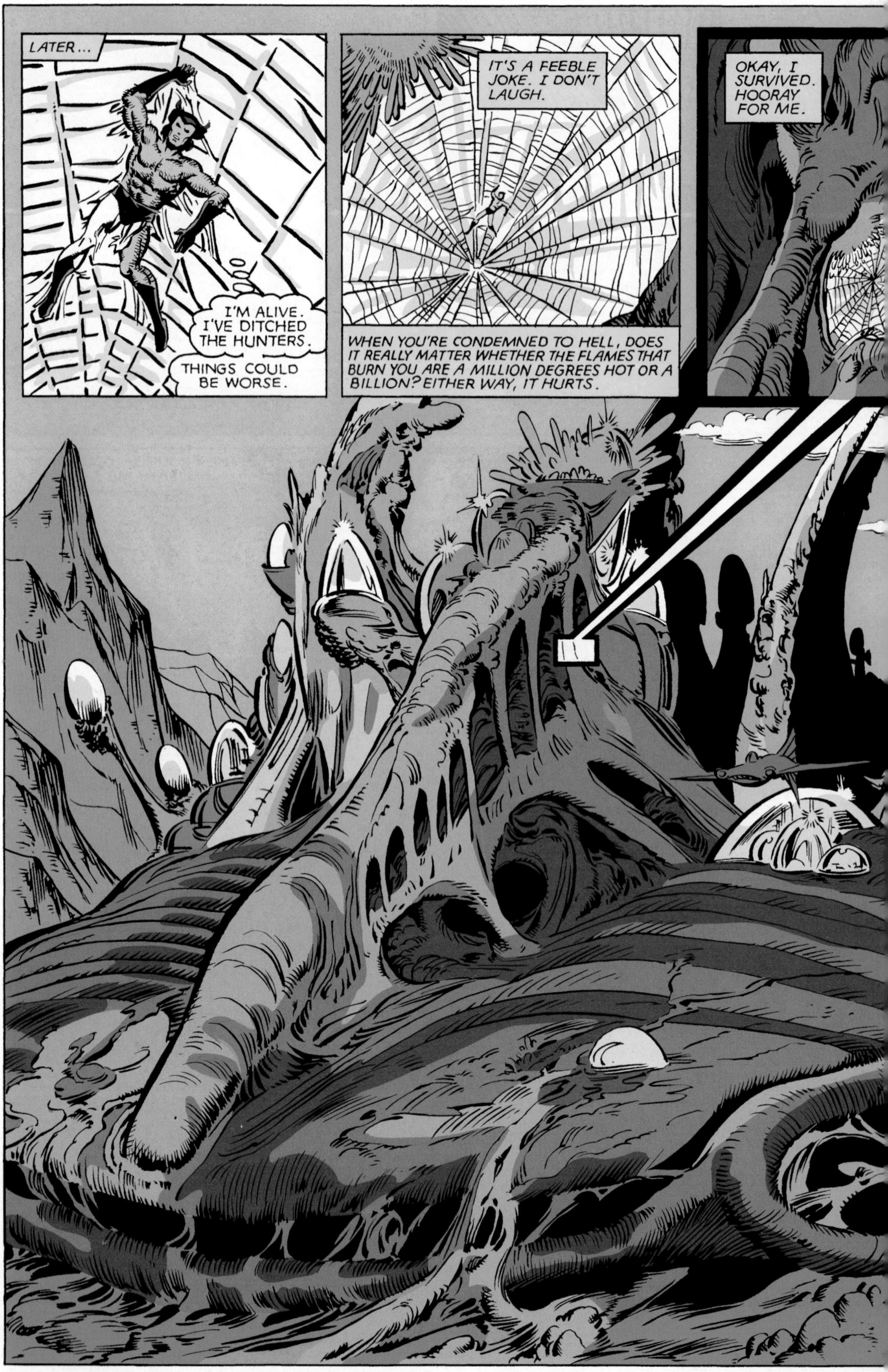
LATER...
I'M ALIVE. I'VE DITCHED THE HUNTERS.
THINGS COULD BE WORSE.
IT'S A FEEBLE JOKE. I DON'T LAUGH.
WHEN YOU'RE CONDEMNED TO HELL, DOES IT REALLY MATTER WHETHER THE FLAMES THAT BURN YOU ARE A MILLION DEGREES HOT OR A BILLION? EITHER WAY, IT HURTS.
OKAY, I SURVIVED. HOORAY FOR ME.

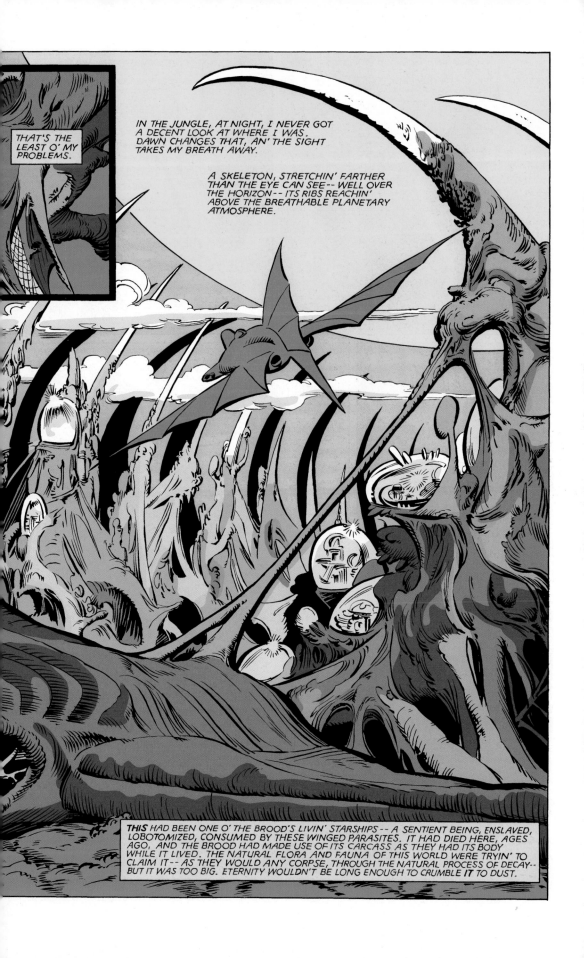

THAT'S THE LEAST O' MY PROBLEMS.

IN THE JUNGLE, AT NIGHT, I NEVER GOT A DECENT LOOK AT WHERE I WAS. DAWN CHANGES THAT, AN' THE SIGHT TAKES MY BREATH AWAY.

A SKELETON, STRETCHIN' FARTHER THAN THE EYE CAN SEE-- WELL OVER THE HORIZON-- ITS RIBS REACHIN' ABOVE THE BREATHABLE PLANETARY ATMOSPHERE.

THIS HAD BEEN ONE O' THE BROOD'S LIVIN' STARSHIPS-- A SENTIENT BEING, ENSLAVED, LOBOTOMIZED, CONSUMED BY THESE WINGED PARASITES. IT HAD DIED HERE, AGES AGO, AND THE BROOD HAD MADE USE OF ITS CARCASS AS THEY HAD ITS BODY WHILE IT LIVED. THE NATURAL FLORA AND FAUNA OF THIS WORLD WERE TRYIN' TO CLAIM IT-- AS THEY WOULD ANY CORPSE, THROUGH THE NATURAL PROCESS OF DECAY-- BUT IT WAS TOO BIG. ETERNITY WOULDN'T BE LONG ENOUGH TO CRUMBLE IT TO DUST.

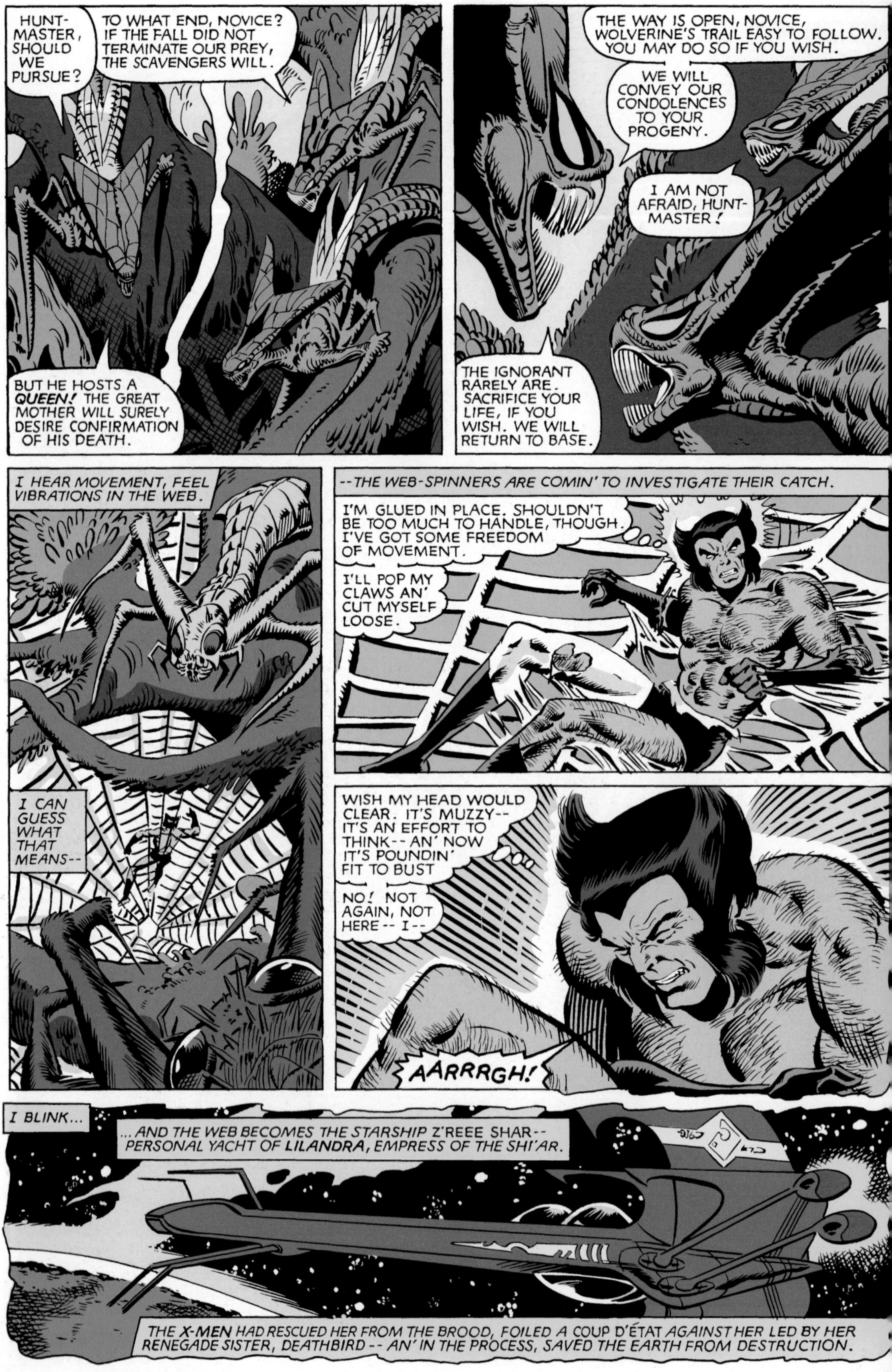
HUNT-MASTER, SHOULD WE PURSUE?
TO WHAT END, NOVICE? IF THE FALL DID NOT TERMINATE OUR PREY, THE SCAVENGERS WILL.
BUT HE HOSTS A QUEEN! THE GREAT MOTHER WILL SURELY DESIRE CONFIRMATION OF HIS DEATH.
THE WAY IS OPEN, NOVICE, WOLVERINE'S TRAIL EASY TO FOLLOW. YOU MAY DO SO IF YOU WISH.
WE WILL CONVEY OUR CONDOLENCES TO YOUR PROGENY.
I AM NOT AFRAID, HUNT-MASTER!
THE IGNORANT RARELY ARE. SACRIFICE YOUR LIFE, IF YOU WISH. WE WILL RETURN TO BASE.
I HEAR MOVEMENT, FEEL VIBRATIONS IN THE WEB.
I CAN GUESS WHAT THAT MEANS--
--THE WEB-SPINNERS ARE COMIN' TO INVESTIGATE THEIR CATCH.
I'M GLUED IN PLACE. SHOULDN'T BE TOO MUCH TO HANDLE, THOUGH. I'VE GOT SOME FREEDOM OF MOVEMENT.
I'LL POP MY CLAWS AN' CUT MYSELF LOOSE.
WISH MY HEAD WOULD CLEAR. IT'S MUZZY-- IT'S AN EFFORT TO THINK-- AN' NOW IT'S POUNDIN' FIT TO BUST
NO! NOT AGAIN, NOT HERE -- I--
AARRRGH!
I BLINK...
...AND THE WEB BECOMES THE STARSHIP Z'REEE SHAR-- PERSONAL YACHT OF LILANDRA, EMPRESS OF THE SHI'AR.
THE X-MEN HAD RESCUED HER FROM THE BROOD, FOILED A COUP D'ÉTAT AGAINST HER LED BY HER RENEGADE SISTER, DEATHBIRD -- AN' IN THE PROCESS, SAVED THE EARTH FROM DESTRUCTION.

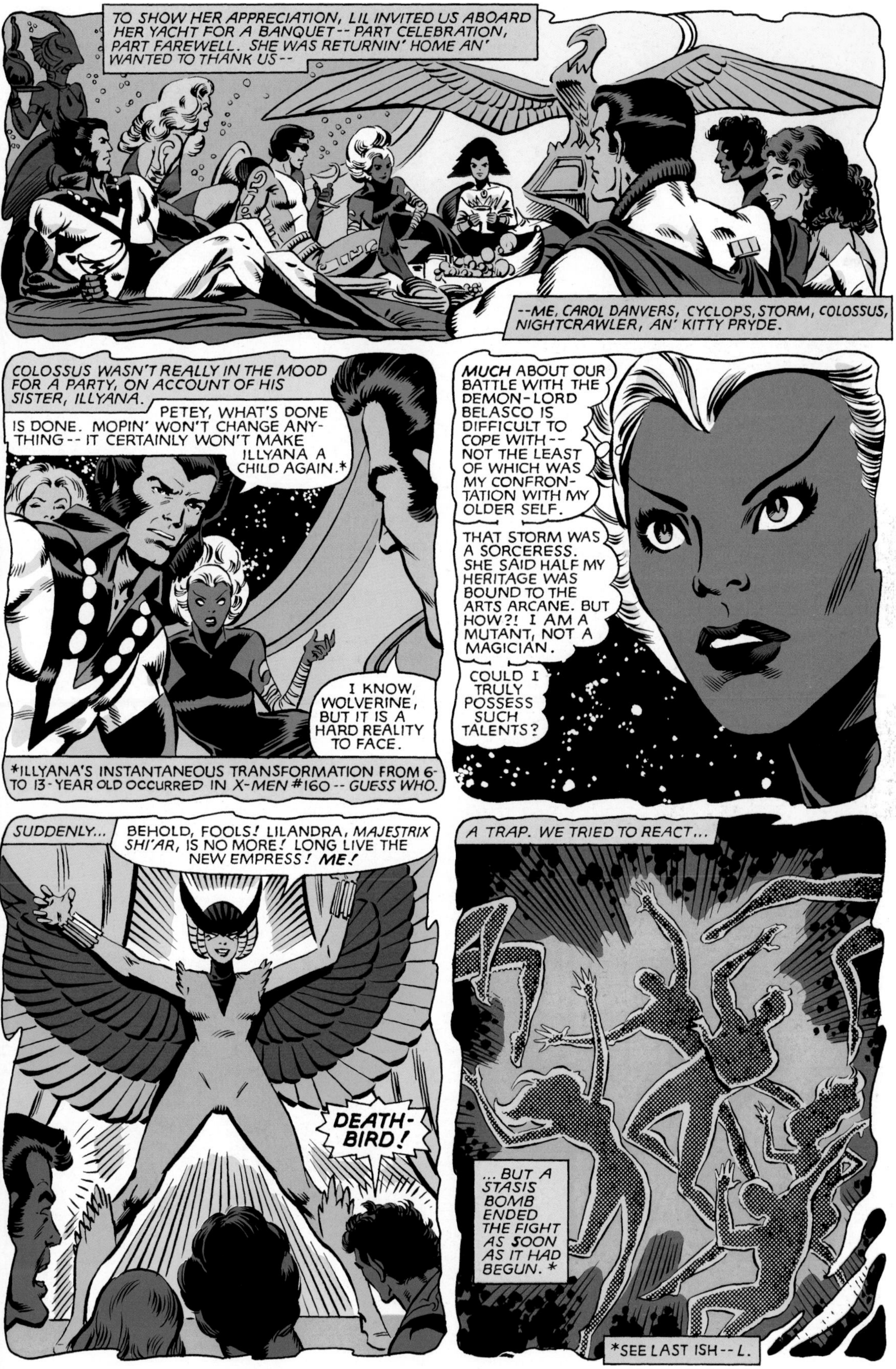
TO SHOW HER APPRECIATION, LIL INVITED US ABOARD HER YACHT FOR A BANQUET -- PART CELEBRATION, PART FAREWELL. SHE WAS RETURNIN' HOME AN' WANTED TO THANK US --
--ME, CAROL DANVERS, CYCLOPS, STORM, COLOSSUS, NIGHTCRAWLER, AN' KITTY PRYDE.
COLOSSUS WASN'T REALLY IN THE MOOD FOR A PARTY, ON ACCOUNT OF HIS SISTER, ILLYANA.
PETEY, WHAT'S DONE IS DONE. MOPIN' WON'T CHANGE ANY-THING -- IT CERTAINLY WON'T MAKE ILLYANA A CHILD AGAIN.*
I KNOW, WOLVERINE, BUT IT IS A HARD REALITY TO FACE.
*ILLYANA'S INSTANTANEOUS TRANSFORMATION FROM 6- TO 13-YEAR OLD OCCURRED IN X-MEN #160 -- GUESS WHO.
MUCH ABOUT OUR BATTLE WITH THE DEMON-LORD BELASCO IS DIFFICULT TO COPE WITH -- NOT THE LEAST OF WHICH WAS MY CONFRON-TATION WITH MY OLDER SELF.
THAT STORM WAS A SORCERESS. SHE SAID HALF MY HERITAGE WAS BOUND TO THE ARTS ARCANE. BUT HOW?! I AM A MUTANT, NOT A MAGICIAN.
COULD I TRULY POSSESS SUCH TALENTS?
SUDDENLY...
BEHOLD, FOOLS! LILANDRA, MAJESTRIX SHI'AR, IS NO MORE! LONG LIVE THE NEW EMPRESS! ME!
DEATH-BIRD!
A TRAP. WE TRIED TO REACT...
... BUT A STASIS BOMB ENDED THE FIGHT AS SOON AS IT HAD BEGUN.*
*SEE LAST ISH -- L.

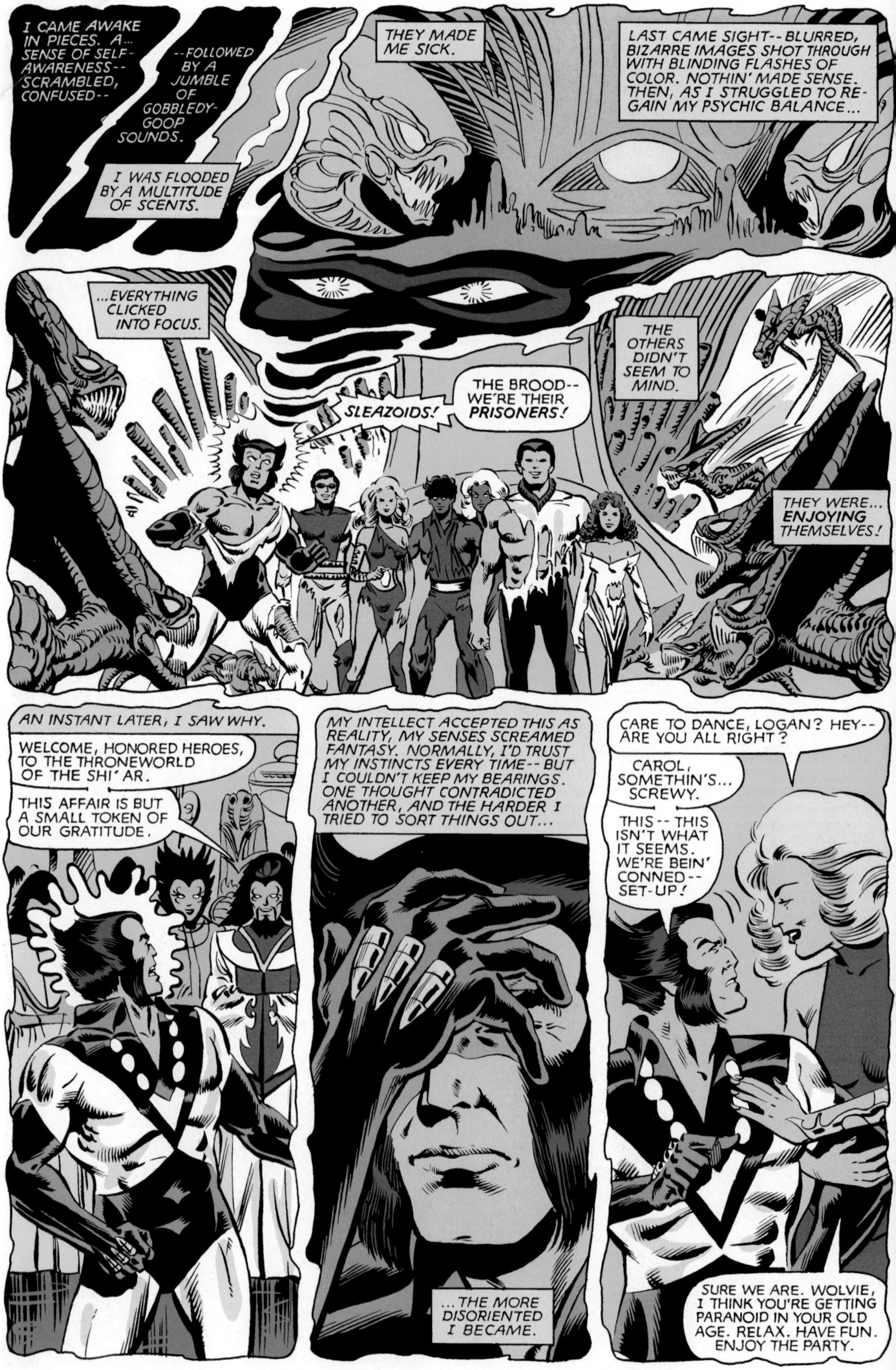
I CAME AWAKE IN PIECES. A... SENSE OF SELF-AWARENESS--SCRAMBLED, CONFUSED--
--FOLLOWED BY A JUMBLE OF GOBBLEDY-GOOP SOUNDS.
I WAS FLOODED BY A MULTITUDE OF SCENTS.
THEY MADE ME SICK.
LAST CAME SIGHT--BLURRED, BIZARRE IMAGES SHOT THROUGH WITH BLINDING FLASHES OF COLOR. NOTHIN' MADE SENSE. THEN, AS I STRUGGLED TO RE-GAIN MY PSYCHIC BALANCE...
...EVERYTHING CLICKED INTO FOCUS.
SLEAZOIDS!
THE BROOD--WE'RE THEIR PRISONERS!
THE OTHERS DIDN'T SEEM TO MIND.
THEY WERE... ENJOYING THEMSELVES!
AN INSTANT LATER, I SAW WHY.
WELCOME, HONORED HEROES, TO THE THRONEWORLD OF THE SHI'AR.
THIS AFFAIR IS BUT A SMALL TOKEN OF OUR GRATITUDE.
MY INTELLECT ACCEPTED THIS AS REALITY, MY SENSES SCREAMED FANTASY. NORMALLY, I'D TRUST MY INSTINCTS EVERY TIME--BUT I COULDN'T KEEP MY BEARINGS. ONE THOUGHT CONTRADICTED ANOTHER, AND THE HARDER I TRIED TO SORT THINGS OUT...
...THE MORE DISORIENTED I BECAME.
CARE TO DANCE, LOGAN? HEY--ARE YOU ALL RIGHT?
CAROL, SOMETHIN'S... SCREWY.
THIS--THIS ISN'T WHAT IT SEEMS. WE'RE BEIN' CONNED--SET-UP!
SURE WE ARE. WOLVIE, I THINK YOU'RE GETTING PARANOID IN YOUR OLD AGE. RELAX. HAVE FUN. ENJOY THE PARTY.

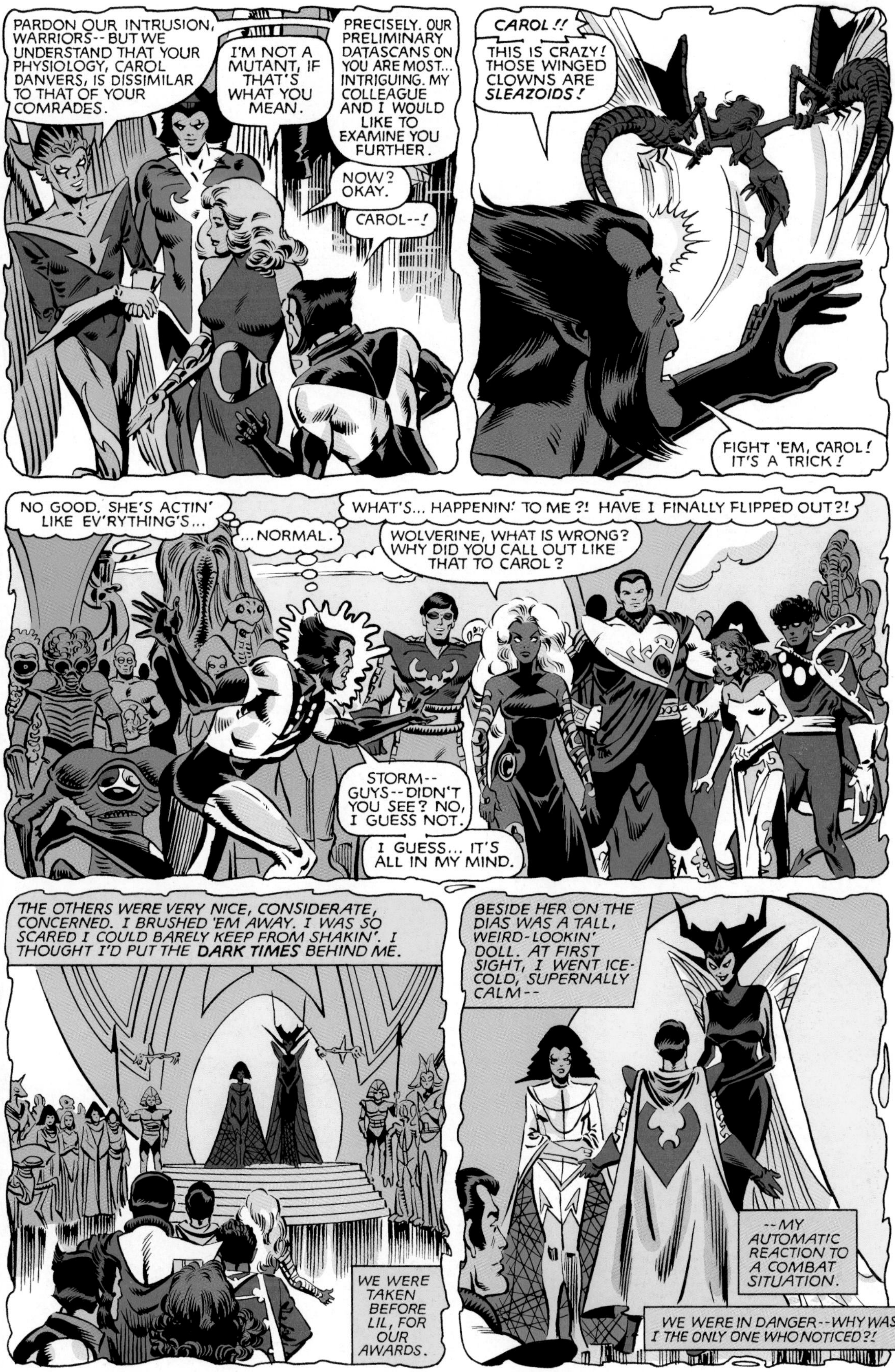
PARDON OUR INTRUSION, WARRIORS-- BUT WE UNDERSTAND THAT YOUR PHYSIOLOGY, CAROL DANVERS, IS DISSIMILAR TO THAT OF YOUR COMRADES.
I'M NOT A MUTANT, IF THAT'S WHAT YOU MEAN.
PRECISELY. OUR PRELIMINARY DATASCANS ON YOU ARE MOST... INTRIGUING. MY COLLEAGUE AND I WOULD LIKE TO EXAMINE YOU FURTHER.
NOW? OKAY.
CAROL--!
CAROL!!
THIS IS CRAZY! THOSE WINGED CLOWNS ARE SLEAZOIDS!
FIGHT 'EM, CAROL! IT'S A TRICK!
NO GOOD. SHE'S ACTIN' LIKE EV'RYTHING'S...
...NORMAL.
WHAT'S... HAPPENIN' TO ME?! HAVE I FINALLY FLIPPED OUT?!
WOLVERINE, WHAT IS WRONG? WHY DID YOU CALL OUT LIKE THAT TO CAROL?
STORM-- GUYS--DIDN'T YOU SEE? NO, I GUESS NOT.
I GUESS... IT'S ALL IN MY MIND.
THE OTHERS WERE VERY NICE, CONSIDERATE, CONCERNED. I BRUSHED 'EM AWAY. I WAS SO SCARED I COULD BARELY KEEP FROM SHAKIN'. I THOUGHT I'D PUT THE DARK TIMES BEHIND ME.
WE WERE TAKEN BEFORE LIL, FOR OUR AWARDS.
BESIDE HER ON THE DIAS WAS A TALL, WEIRD-LOOKIN' DOLL. AT FIRST SIGHT, I WENT ICE-COLD, SUPERNALLY CALM--
--MY AUTOMATIC REACTION TO A COMBAT SITUATION.
WE WERE IN DANGER--WHY WAS I THE ONLY ONE WHO NOTICED?!

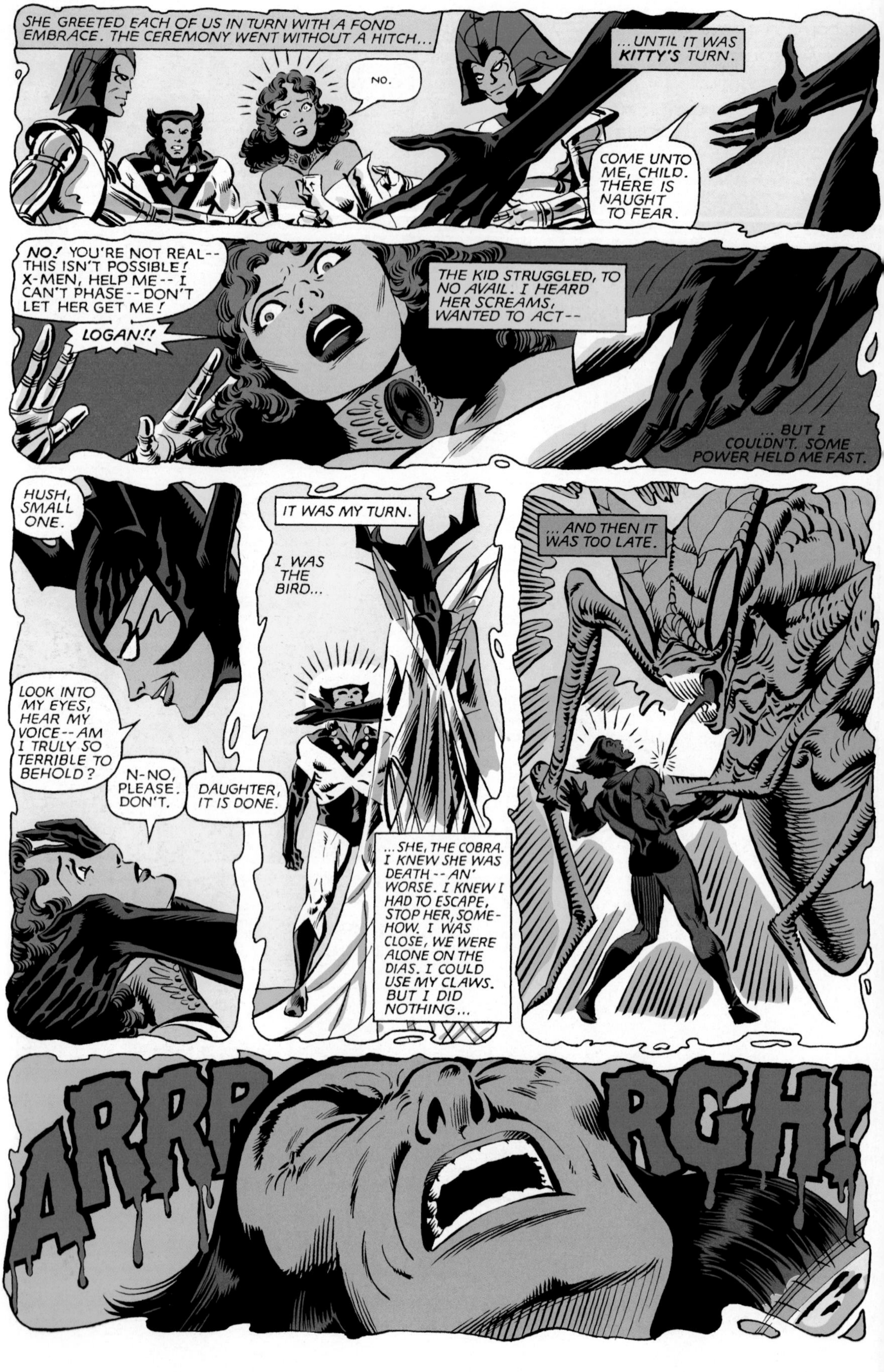
SHE GREETED EACH OF US IN TURN WITH A FOND EMBRACE. THE CEREMONY WENT WITHOUT A HITCH...
NO.
...UNTIL IT WAS KITTY'S TURN.
COME UNTO ME, CHILD. THERE IS NAUGHT TO FEAR.
NO! YOU'RE NOT REAL-- THIS ISN'T POSSIBLE! X-MEN, HELP ME-- I CAN'T PHASE-- DON'T LET HER GET ME!
LOGAN!!
THE KID STRUGGLED, TO NO AVAIL. I HEARD HER SCREAMS, WANTED TO ACT--
... BUT I COULDN'T. SOME POWER HELD ME FAST.
HUSH, SMALL ONE.
LOOK INTO MY EYES, HEAR MY VOICE-- AM I TRULY SO TERRIBLE TO BEHOLD?
N-NO, PLEASE. DON'T.
IT WAS MY TURN.
I WAS THE BIRD...
DAUGHTER, IT IS DONE.
...SHE, THE COBRA. I KNEW SHE WAS DEATH -- AN' WORSE. I KNEW I HAD TO ESCAPE, STOP HER, SOMEHOW. I WAS CLOSE, WE WERE ALONE ON THE DIAS. I COULD USE MY CLAWS. BUT I DID NOTHING...
...AND THEN IT WAS TOO LATE.
ARRRGH!

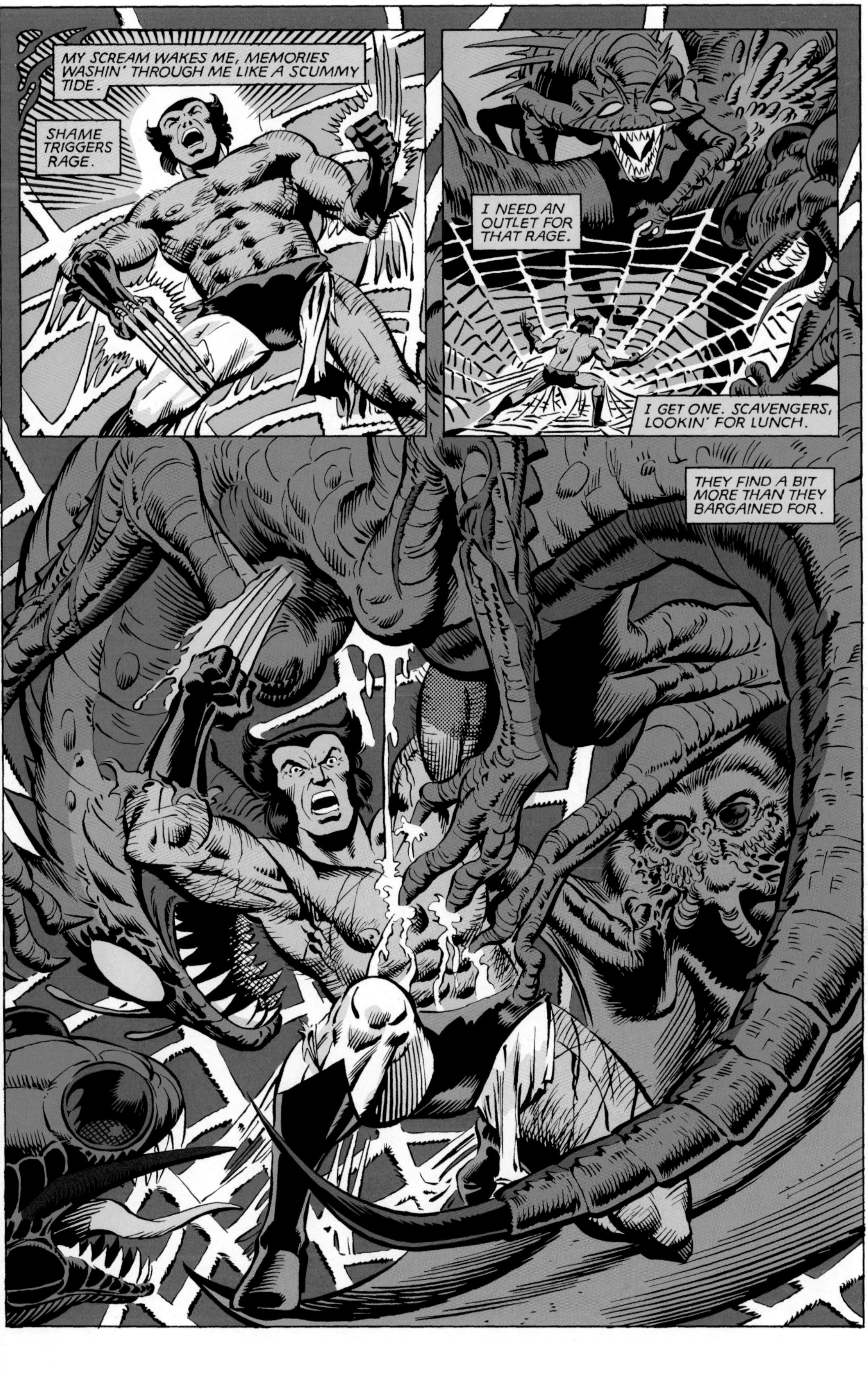
MY SCREAM WAKES ME, MEMORIES WASHIN' THROUGH ME LIKE A SCUMMY TIDE.
SHAME TRIGGERS RAGE.
I NEED AN OUTLET FOR THAT RAGE.
I GET ONE. SCAVENGERS, LOOKIN' FOR LUNCH.
THEY FIND A BIT MORE THAN THEY BARGAINED FOR.

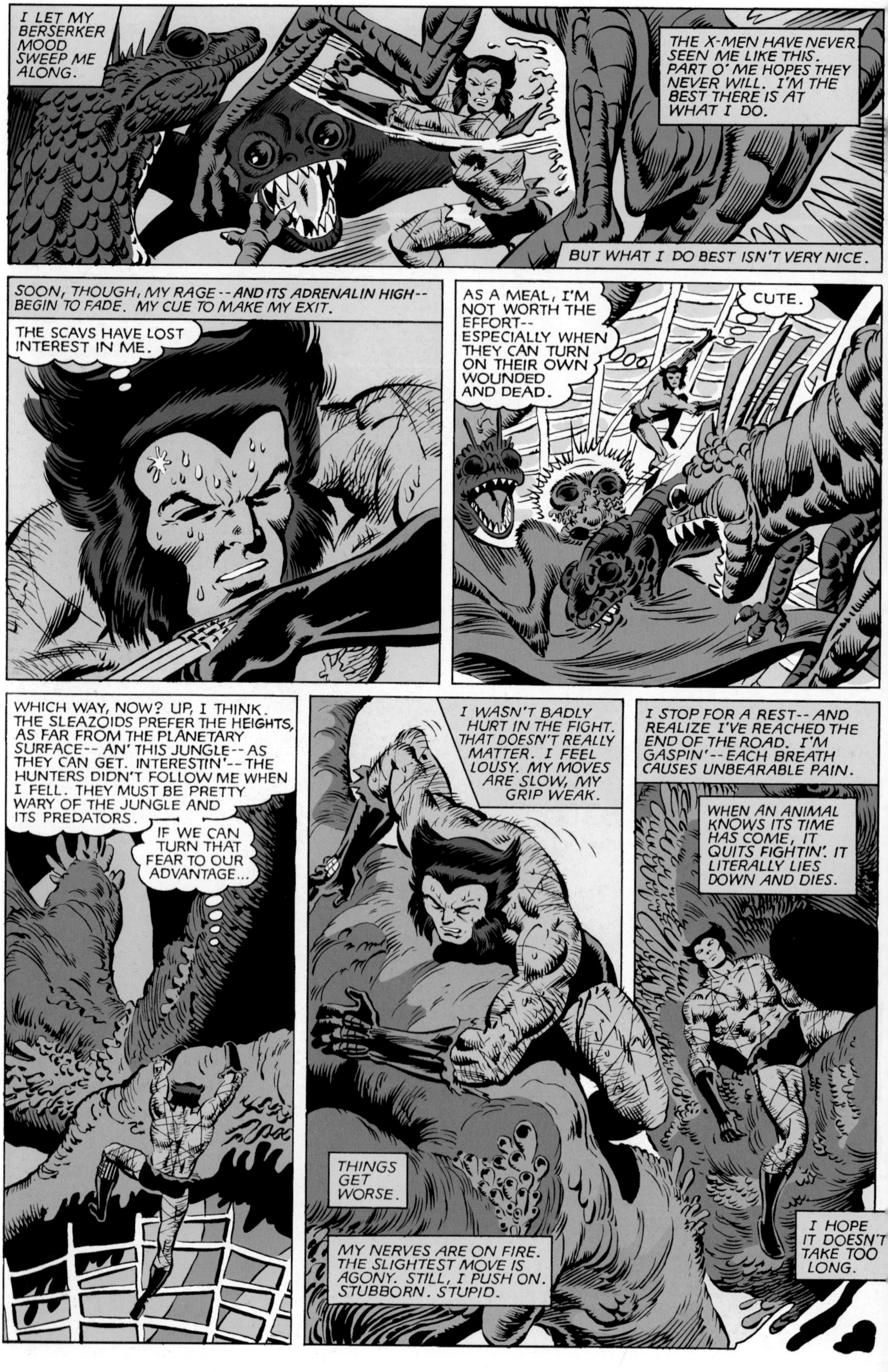
I LET MY BERSERKER MOOD SWEEP ME ALONG.
THE X-MEN HAVE NEVER SEEN ME LIKE THIS. PART O' ME HOPES THEY NEVER WILL. I'M THE BEST THERE IS AT WHAT I DO.
BUT WHAT I DO BEST ISN'T VERY NICE.
SOON, THOUGH, MY RAGE--AND ITS ADRENALIN HIGH--BEGIN TO FADE. MY CUE TO MAKE MY EXIT.
THE SCAVS HAVE LOST INTEREST IN ME.
AS A MEAL, I'M NOT WORTH THE EFFORT-- ESPECIALLY WHEN THEY CAN TURN ON THEIR OWN WOUNDED AND DEAD.
CUTE.
WHICH WAY, NOW? UP, I THINK. THE SLEAZOIDS PREFER THE HEIGHTS, AS FAR FROM THE PLANETARY SURFACE-- AN' THIS JUNGLE--AS THEY CAN GET. INTERESTIN'--THE HUNTERS DIDN'T FOLLOW ME WHEN I FELL. THEY MUST BE PRETTY WARY OF THE JUNGLE AND ITS PREDATORS.
IF WE CAN TURN THAT FEAR TO OUR ADVANTAGE...
I WASN'T BADLY HURT IN THE FIGHT. THAT DOESN'T REALLY MATTER. I FEEL LOUSY. MY MOVES ARE SLOW, MY GRIP WEAK.
THINGS GET WORSE.
MY NERVES ARE ON FIRE. THE SLIGHTEST MOVE IS AGONY. STILL, I PUSH ON. STUBBORN. STUPID.
I STOP FOR A REST--AND REALIZE I'VE REACHED THE END OF THE ROAD. I'M GASPIN'--EACH BREATH CAUSES UNBEARABLE PAIN.
WHEN AN ANIMAL KNOWS ITS TIME HAS COME, IT QUITS FIGHTIN'. IT LITERALLY LIES DOWN AND DIES.
I HOPE IT DOESN'T TAKE TOO LONG.

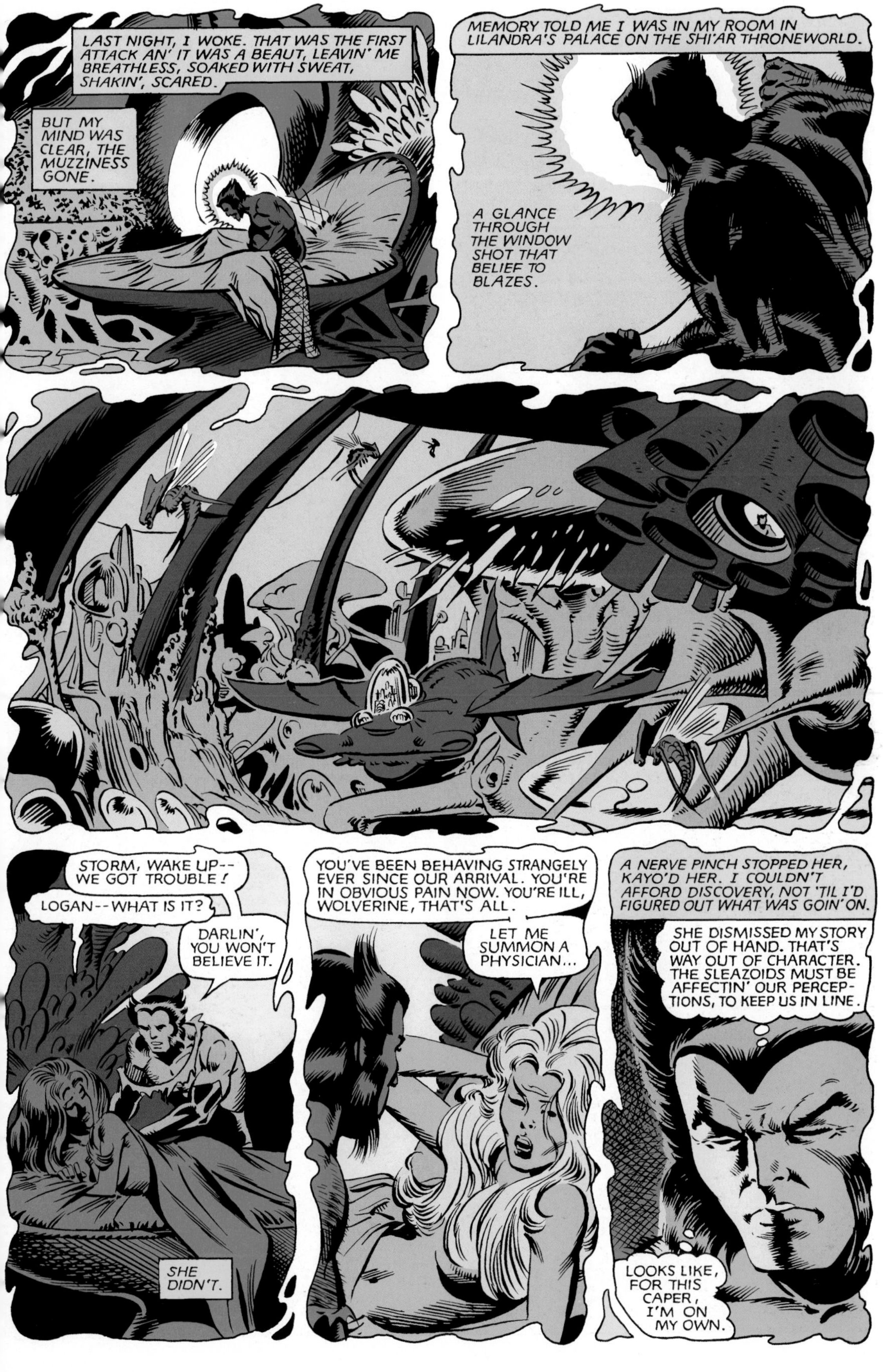
LAST NIGHT, I WOKE. THAT WAS THE FIRST ATTACK AN' IT WAS A BEAUT, LEAVIN' ME BREATHLESS, SOAKED WITH SWEAT, SHAKIN', SCARED.
BUT MY MIND WAS CLEAR, THE MUZZINESS GONE.
MEMORY TOLD ME I WAS IN MY ROOM IN LILANDRA'S PALACE ON THE SHI'AR THRONEWORLD.
A GLANCE THROUGH THE WINDOW SHOT THAT BELIEF TO BLAZES.
STORM, WAKE UP-- WE GOT TROUBLE!
LOGAN--WHAT IS IT?
DARLIN', YOU WON'T BELIEVE IT.
SHE DIDN'T.
YOU'VE BEEN BEHAVING STRANGELY EVER SINCE OUR ARRIVAL. YOU'RE IN OBVIOUS PAIN NOW. YOU'RE ILL, WOLVERINE, THAT'S ALL.
LET ME SUMMON A PHYSICIAN...
A NERVE PINCH STOPPED HER, KAYO'D HER. I COULDN'T AFFORD DISCOVERY, NOT 'TIL I'D FIGURED OUT WHAT WAS GOIN' ON.
SHE DISMISSED MY STORY OUT OF HAND. THAT'S WAY OUT OF CHARACTER. THE SLEAZOIDS MUST BE AFFECTIN' OUR PERCEPTIONS, TO KEEP US IN LINE.
LOOKS LIKE, FOR THIS CAPER, I'M ON MY OWN.

I MADE ONE STOP BEFORE I LEFT-- KITTY'S ROOM.

KID SHE MAY BE, BUT SHE'S PROVED -- TIME AN' AGAIN -- THAT SHE'S GOT MORE GUTS AN' SMARTS THAN MOST ADULTS. THAN MOST HEROES.

I REMEMBERED HER STRUGGLIN' IN THE THRONE ROOM-- AN' HOW ALL I DID WAS WATCH. WHAT HAD BEEN DONE TO US? WHY WAS I SO SICK, AN' NONE OF THE OTHERS?

I WANTED TO TAKE THE KID WITH ME. BUT I'D BE MOVIN' HARD AN' FAST-- AN' PLAYIN' ROUGH-- AN' I COULDN'T GUARANTEE HER SURVIVAL.

I'M SORRY, KIDDO.

BUT DON'T FRET. I'LL BE BACK. WE'LL GET OUT OF THIS MESS, AN' COME HOME SAFE AN' SOUND, YOU GOT MY WORD.

FOR NOW, SHE WAS BETTER OFF WHERE SHE WAS.

THE PROMISE SOUNDED HOLLOW.

SUDDENLY, AN IMAGE FLASHED THROUGH MY MIND-- KITTY CRADLED IN MY ARMS, MY RIGHT HAND LYIN' BELOW HER BREASTBONE, THE STACCATTO CLICK OF CLAWS EXTENDING, RETRACTING, THE LIGHT FADIN' FROM HER EYES...

WHAT HAD BEEN **DONE** TO US, TO MAKE ME THINK SUCH THINGS?!

ELSEWHERE IN THE PALACE, I FOUND THE ANSWER.

A CADRE OF SLEAZOIDS HAD GATHERED FOR A CEREMONY. THE OBJECT OF THEIR ATTENTION WAS AN OLD FOE OF THE X-MEN, A RENEGADE MEMBER OF LILANDRA'S IMPERIAL GUARD: **FANG.**

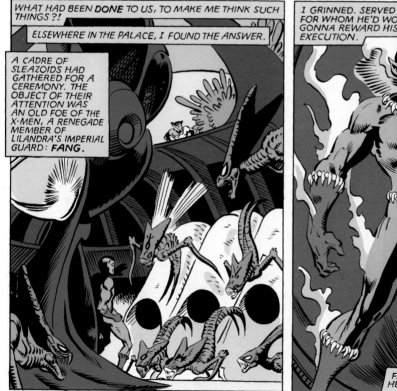

I GRINNED. SERVED THE SUCKER RIGHT IF THE BROOD-- FOR WHOM HE'D WORKED TO OVERTHROW LIL-- WERE GONNA REWARD HIS TREACHERY WITH TORTURE OR EXECUTION.

HE WAS PLEADIN'. THEY WERE LAUGHIN'. SURPRISINGLY, I UNDERSTOOD THEIR LANGUAGE.

FANG'S BODY BEGAN TO SMOKE. HE SHRIEKED. I STOPPED GRINNIN'.

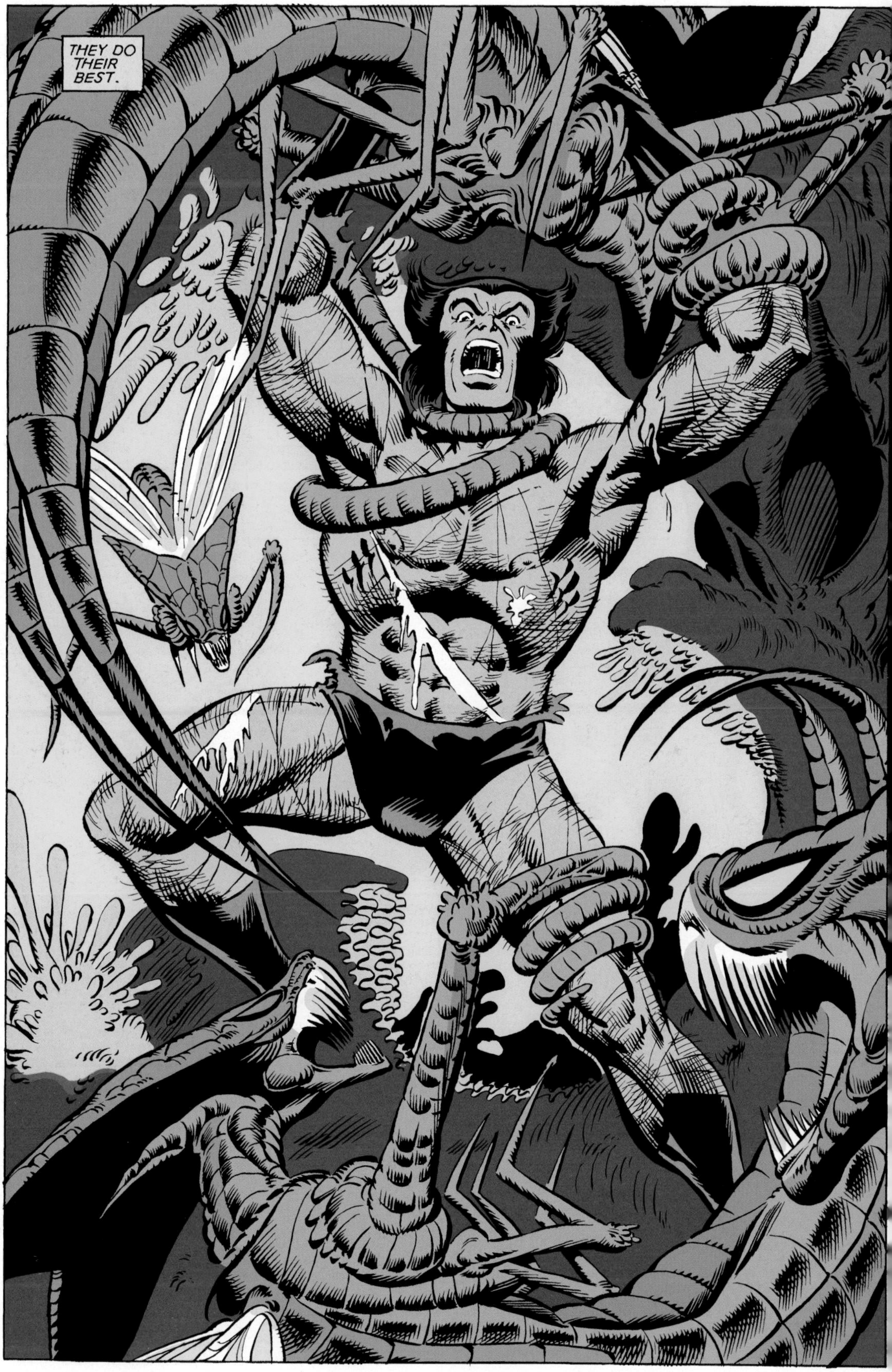
THEY DO THEIR BEST.

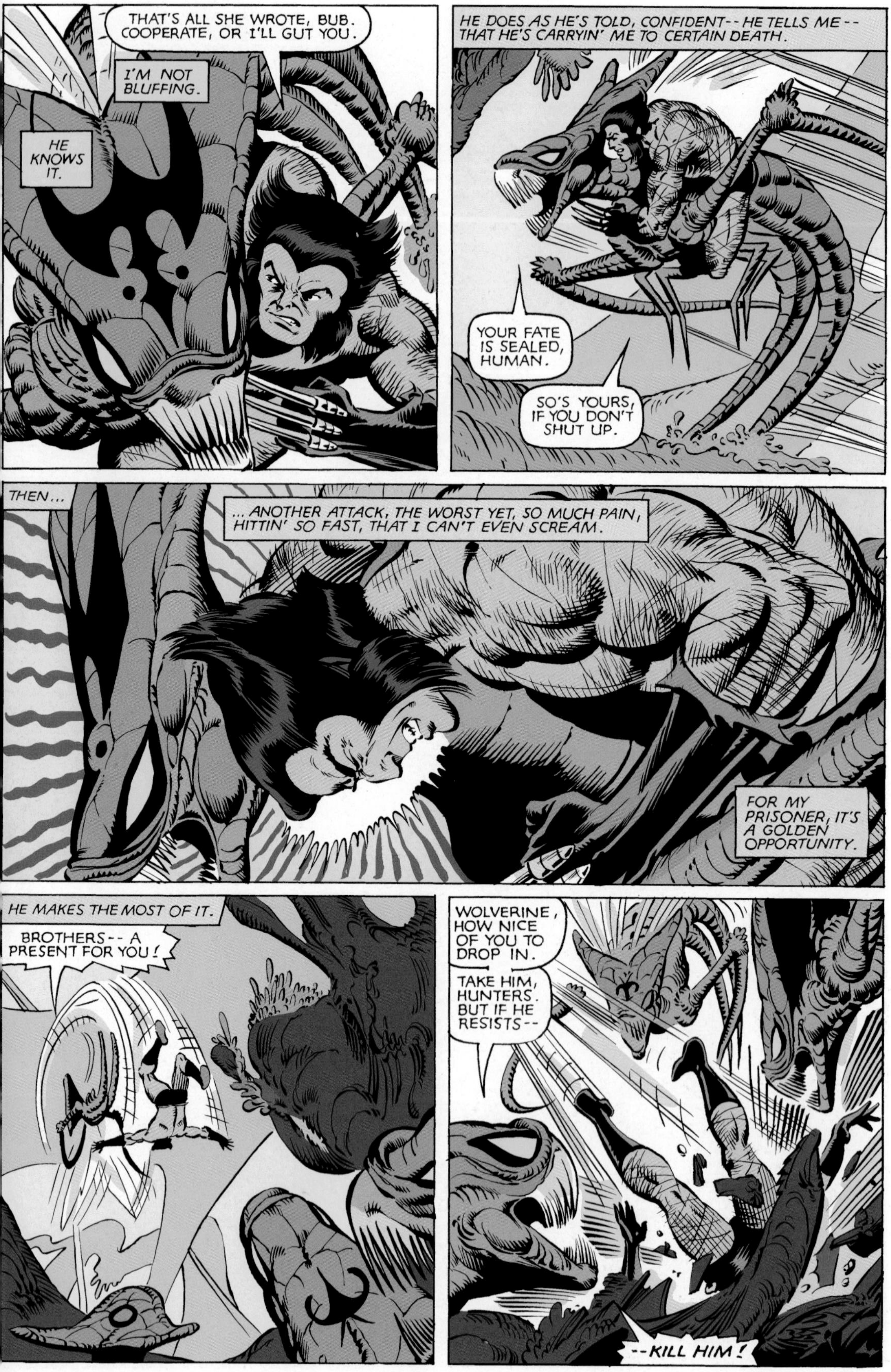
THAT'S ALL SHE WROTE, BUB. COOPERATE, OR I'LL GUT YOU.
I'M NOT BLUFFING.
HE KNOWS IT.
HE DOES AS HE'S TOLD, CONFIDENT-- HE TELLS ME-- THAT HE'S CARRYIN' ME TO CERTAIN DEATH.
YOUR FATE IS SEALED, HUMAN.
SO'S YOURS, IF YOU DON'T SHUT UP.
THEN...
...ANOTHER ATTACK, THE WORST YET, SO MUCH PAIN, HITTIN' SO FAST, THAT I CAN'T EVEN SCREAM.
FOR MY PRISONER, IT'S A GOLDEN OPPORTUNITY.
HE MAKES THE MOST OF IT.
BROTHERS-- A PRESENT FOR YOU!
WOLVERINE, HOW NICE OF YOU TO DROP IN.
TAKE HIM, HUNTERS. BUT IF HE RESISTS--
--KILL HIM!

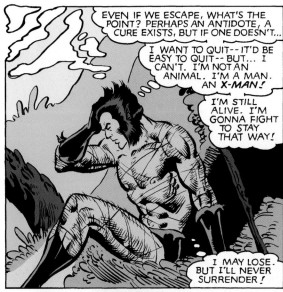

EVEN IF WE ESCAPE, WHAT'S THE POINT? PERHAPS AN ANTIDOTE, A CURE EXISTS, BUT IF ONE DOESN'T...

I WANT TO QUIT--IT'D BE EASY TO QUIT--BUT... I CAN'T. I'M NOT AN ANIMAL. I'M A MAN. AN *X-MAN!*

I'M STILL ALIVE. I'M GONNA FIGHT TO STAY THAT WAY!

I MAY LOSE. BUT I'LL NEVER SURRENDER!

THAT NOISE-- A SLEAZOID!

I RECOGNIZE THE MARKINGS-- IT'S THE WARRIOR FANG HOSTED. I LIKE THE IRONY.

HE'S MY TICKET BACK INTO THE PALACE. BY SKY-DIVING, I CAN REACH HIM.

IT'S RISKY-- IF HE HEARS ME AND DODGES, THERE'S NOTHIN' BUT MILES OF OPEN AIR BETWEEN ME AND THE GROUND.

MY KIND OF GAMBLE. I PLAY IT PERFECTLY.

THE SLEAZOID IS ON HIS FIRST FLIGHT, TESTING HIS WINGS.

INEXPERIENCED, A LITTLE OVERCONFIDENT AND CARELESS, HIS MIND ON OTHER THINGS...

...HE NEVER KNOWS WHAT HITS HIM.

SNIKT!

HE TRIES TO IMPALE ME ON HIS STINGERS. I MAKE SURE HE CAN'T.

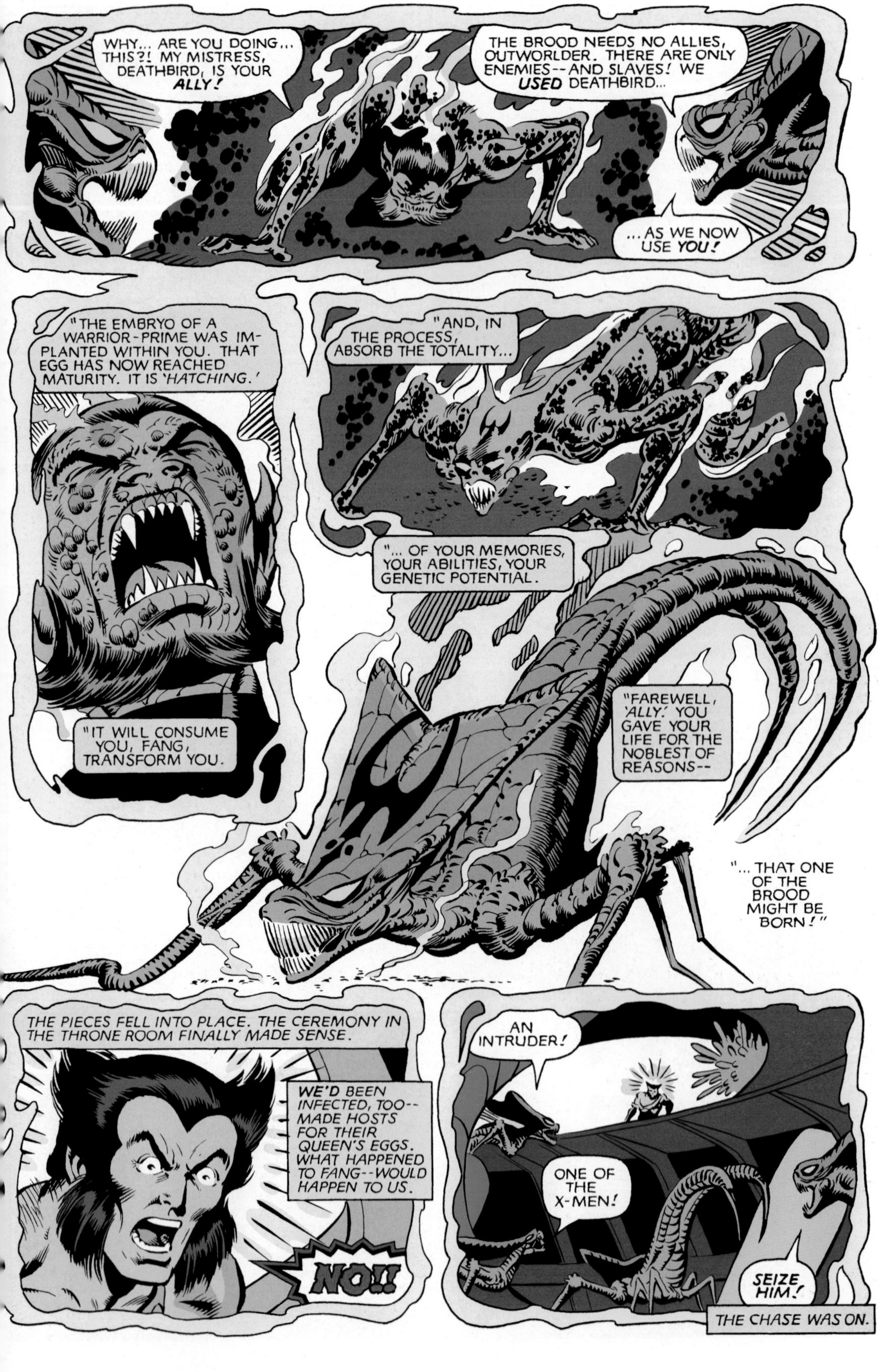

WHY... ARE YOU DOING... THIS?! MY MISTRESS, DEATHBIRD, IS YOUR ALLY!
THE BROOD NEEDS NO ALLIES, OUTWORLDER. THERE ARE ONLY ENEMIES--AND SLAVES! WE USED DEATHBIRD...
...AS WE NOW USE YOU!
"THE EMBRYO OF A WARRIOR-PRIME WAS IMPLANTED WITHIN YOU. THAT EGG HAS NOW REACHED MATURITY. IT IS 'HATCHING.'
"IT WILL CONSUME YOU, FANG, TRANSFORM YOU.
"AND, IN THE PROCESS, ABSORB THE TOTALITY...
"... OF YOUR MEMORIES, YOUR ABILITIES, YOUR GENETIC POTENTIAL.
"FAREWELL, 'ALLY.' YOU GAVE YOUR LIFE FOR THE NOBLEST OF REASONS--
"... THAT ONE OF THE BROOD MIGHT BE BORN!"
THE PIECES FELL INTO PLACE. THE CEREMONY IN THE THRONE ROOM FINALLY MADE SENSE.
WE'D BEEN INFECTED, TOO--MADE HOSTS FOR THEIR QUEEN'S EGGS. WHAT HAPPENED TO FANG--WOULD HAPPEN TO US.
NO!!
AN INTRUDER!
ONE OF THE X-MEN!
SEIZE HIM!
THE CHASE WAS ON.

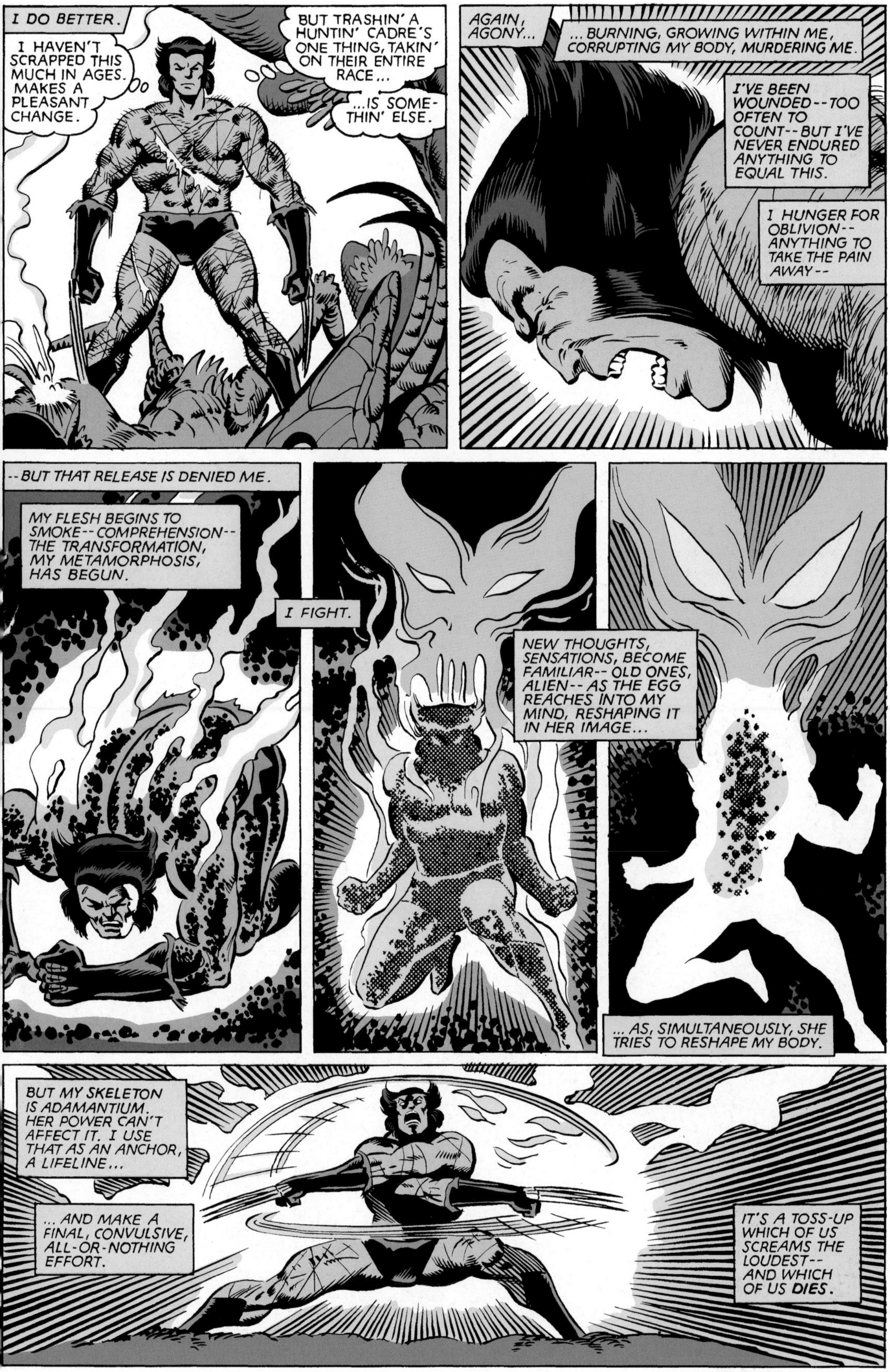
I DO BETTER.
I HAVEN'T SCRAPPED THIS MUCH IN AGES. MAKES A PLEASANT CHANGE.
BUT TRASHIN' A HUNTIN' CADRE'S ONE THING, TAKIN' ON THEIR ENTIRE RACE...
...IS SOMETHIN' ELSE.
AGAIN, AGONY...
...BURNING, GROWING WITHIN ME, CORRUPTING MY BODY, MURDERING ME.
I'VE BEEN WOUNDED--TOO OFTEN TO COUNT--BUT I'VE NEVER ENDURED ANYTHING TO EQUAL THIS.
I HUNGER FOR OBLIVION--ANYTHING TO TAKE THE PAIN AWAY--
--BUT THAT RELEASE IS DENIED ME.
MY FLESH BEGINS TO SMOKE--COMPREHENSION--THE TRANSFORMATION, MY METAMORPHOSIS, HAS BEGUN.
I FIGHT.
NEW THOUGHTS, SENSATIONS, BECOME FAMILIAR--OLD ONES, ALIEN--AS THE EGG REACHES INTO MY MIND, RESHAPING IT IN HER IMAGE...
...AS, SIMULTANEOUSLY, SHE TRIES TO RESHAPE MY BODY.
BUT MY SKELETON IS ADAMANTIUM. HER POWER CAN'T AFFECT IT. I USE THAT AS AN ANCHOR, A LIFELINE...
...AND MAKE A FINAL, CONVULSIVE, ALL-OR-NOTHING EFFORT.
IT'S A TOSS-UP WHICH OF US SCREAMS THE LOUDEST--AND WHICH OF US DIES.

SUNRISE.

ANOTHER NIGHT HAS PASSED.

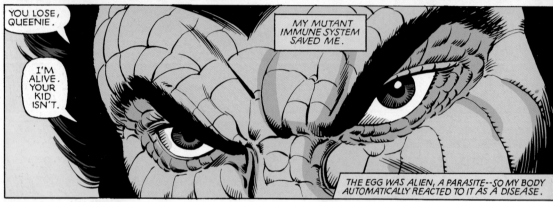

YOU LOSE, QUEENIE.

I'M ALIVE. YOUR KID ISN'T.

MY MUTANT IMMUNE SYSTEM SAVED ME.

THE EGG WAS ALIEN, A PARASITE--SO MY BODY AUTOMATICALLY REACTED TO IT AS A DISEASE.

THAT WAS WHY I WAS SO SICK...SIDE-EFFECTS OF MY BODY'S STRUGGLE TO EXPUNGE THE INVADER, AND ITS TO SURVIVE. BUT ALTHOUGH IT NEVER GAINED MORE THAN A TOEHOLD, THE EGG STILL PUT UP A HELLUVA FIGHT.

I ALMOST LOST. AN' THE STRAIN FLAMIN' NEAR KILLED ME.

I CAN SEE THE PALACE, IMAGINE THE X-MEN HYPNOTISED-'N'-HAPPY WITHIN.

THEY'RE INFECTED, TOO. ONLY I CAN'T SAVE 'EM THE WAY I DID MYSELF. FOR ALL I KNOW, I MAY ALREADY BE TOO LATE. THEIR METAMOR-PHOSES MAY ALREADY HAVE TAKEN PLACE.

I REMEMBER MY HALLUCINATION ABOUT KILLING KITTY. IF I HAVE TO -- IF SHE CAN'T BE CURED -- I'LL DO IT.

I'LL... KILL THEM ALL. MY FRIENDS.

THEN, IT'LL BE THE SLEAZOIDS' TURN.

NEXT> RESCUE MISSION!